Child Social Work
Policy & Practice

Child Social Work
Policy & Practice

LEARNING RESOURCES
CENTRE
Havering College
of Further and Higher Education

Derek Kirton

Los Angeles • London • New Delhi • Singapore • Washington DC

First published 2009

SAGE Publications Ltd
1 Oliver's Yard
55 City Road
London EC1Y 1SP

SAGE Publications Inc.
2455 Teller Road
Thousand Oaks, California 91320

SAGE Publications India Pvt Ltd
B 1/I 1 Mohan Cooperative Industrial Area
Mathura Road
New Delhi 110 044

SAGE Publications Asia-Pacific Pte Ltd
33 Pekin Street #02-01
Far East Square
Singapore 048763

Library of Congress Control Number: 2008925839

British Library Cataloguing in Publication data

A catalogue record for this book is available from the British Library

ISBN 978-1-4129-2054-4
ISBN 978-1-4129-2055-1 (pbk)

Typeset by C&M Digitals (P) Ltd, Chennai, India
Printed in Great Britain by The Cromwell Press Ltd, Trowbridge, Wiltshire
Printed on paper from sustainable resources

To Linda and Anna and the memory of Betty, Tom and Lyn

CONTENTS

LIST OF FIGURES, BOXES AND TABLES

FIGURES

BOXES

TABLES

TIMELINE

Child Social Work in the United Kingdom (1984–2008) – A Timeline

Year	Key Legislation	Major Policy Initiatives, Inquiries and Reports
1984		*Short Report* (House of Commons, 1984)
1985		*Social Work Decisions in Child Care* (DHSS) *A Child in Trust* (Beckford Report) (London Borough of Brent)
1986		Establishment of Childline
1987	Adoption (Northern Ireland) Order	
1988		*Cleveland Report* (Lord Justice Butler-Sloss) *Working Together: A Guide to Inter-Agency Co-operation for the Protection of Children from Abuse* (DHSS)
1989	Children Act (England and Wales)	
1991		Ratification of the United Nations Convention on the Rights of the Child *Looking After Children: Assessing Outcomes in Child Care* (Parker et al.) *Pindown Report* (Levy and Kahan)
1992		*Memorandum of Good Practice on Video Recorded Interviews with Child Witnesses for Criminal Proceedings* (Home Office)
1995	Children (Scotland) Act Children (Northern Ireland) Order Disability Discrimination Act	*Child Protection: Messages from Research* (DH)
1997		*People Like Us: The Review of the Safeguards for Children Living Away from Home* (Utting Report) *Children's Safeguards Review* (Kent Report)
1998	Human Rights Act	Quality Protects Initiative (England) Children First (Wales)
1999	Protection of Children Act	
2000	Children (Leaving Care) Act Carers and Disabled Children Act Care Standards Act	*Framework for the Assessment of Children in Need and their families* (DH et al.) *Lost in Care* (Waterhouse Report into Abuse in North Wales Children's Homes)

2001		*For Scotland's Children: Better Integrated Children's Services* (Scottish Executive)
2002	Adoption and Children Act Children (Leaving Care) Act (Northern Ireland)	*It's Everyone's Job to Make Sure I'm Alright* (Scottish Executive)
2003	Protection of Children Act (Scotland)	*Every Child Matters* (Chief Secretary to the Treasury) *Getting It Right for Every Child: A Review of the Children's Hearings System* (Scottish Executive) *The Victoria Climbié Inquiry* (Lord Laming)
2004	Children Act (England and Wales)	*Children and Young People: Rights to Action* (Welsh Assembly Government) *Supporting Young People Leaving Care in Scotland* (Scottish Executive) *National Service Framework for Children, Young People and Maternity Services* (DH)
2006	Safeguarding Vulnerable Groups Act (England and Wales)	*Care Matters: Transforming the Lives of Children and Young People in Care* (DfES) *Our Children and Young People – Our Pledge* (OFMDPM, Northern Ireland)
2007	Adoption and Children (Scotland) Act Protection of Vulnerable Groups (Scotland) Act Safeguarding Vulnerable Groups (Northern Ireland) Order	*The Children's Plan: Building Brighter Futures* (DCSF) *Aiming High For Disabled Children: Better Support For Families* (HM Treasury)

PREFACE

This book seeks to provide an overview of contemporary child care policy and practice in the United Kingdom (UK). In broad terms, the issues examined relate to the domains of 'social work with children and families', or the more broadly defined 'child social care'. As will be seen, services for the care and protection of children encompass a wide range of situations, from families under stress or in conflict, to intervention in cases of suspected maltreatment, to life in the care system and beyond. The book is written primarily for two groups of readers, namely, those working with children and families (or training to do so) and other students or lay readers with an interest in childhood studies. No single volume can cover every relevant topic in depth and therefore a major aim is to serve as a guide and sourcebook for further investigation. This will entail providing pointers to relevant social science debates, while also highlighting practice issues and guidance for practitioners.

Although there will be occasional references made to earlier eras, the historical focus of the book rests with the period from the passing of the Children Act 1989 to the present day, and especially since the election in 1997 of a New Labour government. (For longer historical perspectives, readers should consult Frost and Stein (1989) or Stevenson (1999).) There will also be an attempt to reflect the commonalities and diversity to be found in the four countries of the United Kingdom, a task given added impetus by recent developments in devolved government. Thus, while recognising the dominant influence of England in areas such as legislation, research and practice guidance, the distinctive nature of policy and practice in Wales. Scotland and Northern Ireland will be highlighted where appropriate.

ACKNOWLEDGEMENTS

A number of people have helpfully contributed to the writing of this book. I would like to thank especially Linda Prince, Rosalind Hargreaves and Cliff Thomas for reading and commenting on draft versions. I would also like to thank one of my anonymous reviewers for some very detailed commentary, posing some interesting challenges that I hope I have at least partially met. Finally, I would like to express my appreciation to various staff at Sage, notably Susannah Trefgarne and Anne Birtchnell and their predecessors working on the book, and also Zoe Elliott-Fawcett and Anna Luker, for their help and patience.

ABBREVIATIONS

ACPC	Area Child Protection Committee
ARC	area review committees
ASD	autistic spectrum disorder
BAAF	British Association for Adoption and Fostering
BME	black and minority ethnic
CAF	Common Assessment Framework
CAFCASS	Children and Family Court Advisory and Support Service
CAMHS	Child and Adolescent Mental Health Services
CEOP	Child Exploitation and Online Protection Centre
CRAE	Children's Rights Alliance for England
CSCI	Commission for Social Care Inspection
CYPP	Children and Young People's Plans
DCLG	Department of Communities and Local Government
DCSF	Department for Children, Schools and Families
DfEE	Department for Education and Employment
DfES	Department for Education and Skills
DH	Department of Health
DHSS	Department of Health and Social Security
DHSSPS	Department of Health, Social Services and Public Safety (Northern Ireland)
ECM	Every Child Matters
EPO	emergency protection order
FFAC	family and friends as carers
FGC	family group conference
FII	fabricated or induced illness
FRG	Family Rights Group
FTT	failure to thrive
JAR	Joint Area Review
LAC	Looked After Children project
LSCB	Local Safeguarding Children Boards
NLCAS	National Leaving Care Advisory Service
PC	political correctness
PMSU	Prime Minister's Strategy Unit

PSM	parental substance misuse
RCCL	Review of Child Care Law
SCIE	Social Care Institute for Excellence
SCR	serious case review
SCRA	Scottish Children's Reporter Administration
TPS	Teenage Pregnancy Strategy
UASC	unaccompanied asylum-seeking children
UNCRC	United Nations Convention on the Rights of the Child
VCS	voluntary and community sector

OUTLINE OF THE BOOK

The opening chapter will seek to locate contemporary child social work policy in a wider context, by examining changes in childhood(s) and family life, the growing emphasis on children's rights, and wider government policies relating to children and families. Thereafter, the book is loosely organised around a model that moves from initial involvement with child welfare services, to longer-term possibilities such as entry into public care and subsequently the latter's 'exit' routes through adoption or reaching young adulthood.

Chapter 2 examines the process of assessment, whether for 'children in need' or in cases of child protection, which marks the starting point for children and families in their involvement with child care services. This leads on to a chapter setting out debates on 'prevention' and family support for 'children in need' under the Children Act 1989 and similar legislation in Scotland and Northern Ireland. Chapter 4 examines recent historical developments in child protection in three main areas: the changing social construction of maltreatment; the evolution of the child protection system; and the experiences of children and families within it. The following chapter outlines the contemporary knowledge base for those working with child maltreatment, analysing theoretical perspectives and research evidence relating to the four main official categories of maltreatment – physical abuse, neglect, sexual abuse and emotional abuse.

The next two chapters (6 and 7) focus on looked after children. The first explores the multifaceted role of the state as 'corporate parent', and examines policy initiatives to improve children's life chances, while the second addresses the major forms of provision within public care – adoption, foster care and residential care. Chapter 8 continues the theme of life chances by looking at the challenges facing care leavers and the support they receive.

Chapter 9 considers the intersection of childhood disability with key areas of provision covered elsewhere in the book, while the final chapter looks at contemporary child care policy trends and possible future directions.

1

CHILD SOCIAL WORK POLICY & PRACTICE
An Introduction

CHILD SOCIAL WORK, STATE AND FAMILY

In principle, the UK's framework for child welfare is fairly straightforward. The dominant assumption is that the upbringing of children is largely a matter for parents or guardians. In turn, the state's role is threefold. First, it sets the legal parameters for parental rights and responsibilities. Second, it offers support to families in areas such as health care, education, housing or cash benefits, either 'universally' to all families or more 'selectively', based on criteria of deprivation or 'special needs'. Third, the state has evolved powers and duties to 'intervene' in families when there are concerns regarding child welfare, and it is broadly with this role that our focus rests.

This framework, however, hides great complexity. In the political and ideological arena, there are struggles over the nature and level of service provision to families and frequently over whether the state should have greater or lesser powers of intervention in its protective role. Arguably the central tension is between philosophies of 'child rescue' and 'family support'. In the former, greater emphasis is placed on the individuality of the child, their vulnerability to abuse and the appropriateness of removal from the family in such circumstances. In the latter, the unity and caring qualities of families are emphasised, with child welfare to be secured primarily through better support to parents. It is also important to recognise that the 'state' comprises a complex apparatus – with a separation between government and judiciary, divisions of responsibility between government departments (including devolved institutions within the UK) and the delivery of services through local authorities, private and voluntary organisations. Unsurprisingly, this complexity, allied to frequent reorganisations, gives rise to inconsistencies and contradictions in policy and practice, and an ongoing quest for effective co-ordination. Meanwhile, on the front line, individual workers are faced with difficult and far-reaching decisions regarding the adequacy of parenting and how to address perceived risks to children's safety and development.

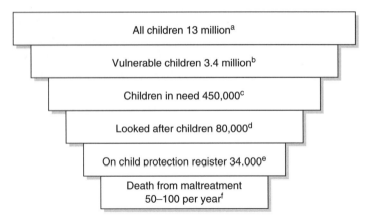

Figure 1.1   Children's involvement with social care services – a statistical overview

Source:
[a]Office for National Statistics (2005) *Key Population and Vital Statistics Local and Health Authority Areas*. London: ONS;
[b]Palmer, G., MacInnes, T. and Kenway, P. (2006) *Monitoring Poverty and Social Exclusion 2006*. York: Joseph Rowntree Foundation;
[c]Extrapolated for UK from English data (DfES 2006a);
[d]Figures accessed from www.haaf.org.uk/info/stats/index.shtml;
[e]Figures collated from www.nspcc.org.uk/Inform/statitics;
[f]Extrapolated from Creighton, S. and Tissier, G. (2003) *Child Killings in England and Wales*. London: NSPCC.

In subsequent chapters, more detailed statistics will be reported on a range of issues, but at this point, a few headline figures may serve to convey an initial sense of the scale and scope of child social care. Figure 1.1 presents these statistics in the context of broader child populations and thus introduces the notion of 'filters' prior to, and following contact with, social care services.

The category of vulnerable children is based on child poverty using the widely accepted benchmark of living in a household below 60 per cent median income. The Children Act 1989 section (hereafter s) 17 defines a child as 'in need' if any of the following conditions apply, namely:

(a) he is unlikely to achieve or maintain, or to have the opportunity of achieving or maintaining, a reasonable standard of health or development without the provision for him of services by a local authority;
(b) his health or development is likely to be significantly impaired, or further impaired, without the provision for him of such services; or
(c) he is disabled.

Being deemed a child in need represents the gateway to receiving 'family support' services, which will be analysed in Chapter 3. As can be seen from Figure 1.1, the number of children in need represents approximately one in eight vulnerable children. Most, though not all, children in need come from families living below the poverty line, and the relationship between poverty and child welfare concerns will be discussed later in the book. The term 'looked after' was also introduced in the Children Act, replacing the term 'in care'. It encompasses all those being looked after by local authorities, whether on a voluntary basis or following a court order (or a supervision requirement in Scotland). Figure 1.1 shows that the number of 'looked after' children at any one time is roughly one-sixth of the children-in-need population and under 1 per cent of all children. Children, a minority of whom may be looked after children, are placed on the child protection register when they are regarded as at risk of significant harm (see Chapter 4).

These statistics are open to different interpretations. On the one hand, they show that only a minority of children are likely to have direct contact with child social care services, although more will do so during their lifetimes than these snapshot figures suggest. On the other, in raw terms, these numbers are substantial while their links with poverty and deprivation raise important issues of social justice. In addition, state child welfare services cast a long shadow in terms of public perception and fears.

In 2006–2007, expenditure on children's services accounted for £5 billion, 25 per cent of the social care budget and approximately 0.4 per cent of Gross Domestic Product (Information Centre, 2008). The children's social care workforce in England has been estimated at 127,000 (including foster carers), with roughly four-fifths working for local authorities and the remainder in the private and voluntary sectors (Department for Education and Skills (DfES), 2005a).

CHILD SOCIAL WORK AND SOCIAL CHANGE

Changing childhood(s)

Clearly, child social work policy and practice do not operate in a vacuum, but in particular social and historical contexts. In this section, we offer a review of recent developments and debates in thinking about childhood. Over the past two decades or so, sociological analysis has been increasingly influential in promoting awareness of the ways in which childhood is 'socially constructed' (Jenks, 1996). This viewpoint is critical of perspectives that construe childhood simply in terms of physical maturation, 'stages' of psychological development or passive socialisation. James et al. (1998) emphasise the need to see children as 'beings' (the fully fledged social actors they are in the present) rather than as 'becomings' (the adults they may be in the future).

Following Aries's pioneering (1962) work, the most powerful evidence for the social constructionist view stems from wide historical and cross-cultural variations found in ideas and practice relating to childhood, which refute notions that it represents a 'natural state' (Kehily, 2004). Writers such as Lee (2001) and Hendrick (2003) have mapped the rise in western societies of childhood as a progressively extended period of preparation for adulthood built around compulsory schooling and removal from the world of work. From the early nineteenth century onwards, the state took an increasing role in managing its populations, with children particular targets for intervention. Ideas of childhood 'innocence' were central to this endeavour, whether this was seen as the natural state of children ('little angels') or the product of hard-fought battle against their innate sinfulness ('little devils') (Jenks, 1996).

In recent times, there has been significant debate on the state of childhood – variously described as 'disappearing' (Postman, 1982), in 'crisis' (Scraton, 1997) or 'toxic' (Palmer, 2006). Ideas of lost innocence are central to these debates. This may be in relation to the perceived loss of a more carefree life for children due to parental fears and a risk avoidant culture, or the way in which protective confinement in homes saturated by the electronic media has brought about greater exposure to the 'adult' world, its secrets and painful issues. For critics, the loss of innocence has inexorably led to increases in both troubling (e.g. crime, drug abuse, sexual activity) and troubled (e.g. self-harm, eating disorders) behaviour among children and young people. While claims of the 'death of childhood' are somewhat exaggerated (Buckingham, 2000), there is widespread acceptance that today's children 'grow up more quickly' in many respects than previous generations, although some commentators welcome what they see as children's more 'savvy' approach to consumption, the media or social issues (Kenway and Bullen, 2001).

Although these debates may seem somewhat 'academic', they are relevant to child care policy and practice in a number of ways. First, judgements regarding children's developmental needs, whether they are suffering harm as a result of maltreatment, and what represents their 'best interests', are inextricably bound up with normative views of childhood. Social constructionist perspectives alert us both to the changing and contested nature of such norms and their complex relationship to variables such as social class, gender, ethnicity, disability and sexuality. Second, constructions of childhood are equally salient for looked after children and the care to be provided by the state. Third, awareness of social construction can also encourage a questioning approach to the seeming 'hard evidence' gleaned from developmental measurement, psychological testing and tendencies to medicalise behaviours deemed to be problematic. However, as Fawcett et al. (2004) argue, it is important not to be dismissive of the biological and psychological domains and to avoid the relativistic view of phenomena as '*only* constructions'. Finally, the social constructionist emphasis on children's agency is supportive of promoting their 'voice' and participation within social care services.

Changing families, changing parenting

As noted earlier, the seemingly straightforward framework for relationships between the state and the family hides great complexity. At the level of government policy, this reflects both political ideology and changing economic and social conditions. The New Labour government has identified the family as 'at the heart of our society' due to its provision of love, support, education and moral guidance, a means of promoting economic prosperity while ameliorating a range of social problems linked to social exclusion and deviant behaviour (Home Office, 1998). However, in a period of rapid social change, the family has been increasingly cast as vulnerable due to economic pressures, breakdown through divorce and for many, the effects of poverty, crime and drug misuse.

The context for such concerns developed in the closing decades of the twentieth century, which witnessed significant changes among families in the UK, prompting debates that mirror in many respects those relating to the changes in childhood described above (Barrett, 2004). The broad contours of change are well known and concisely captured in *Social Trends 2007* (Self and Zealey, 2007). Marriages declined from 480,300 in 1972 to 283,700 in 2005, while divorces rose from around 50,0000 in the late 1960s to 155,00 in 2005. Lone-parent families have risen from 7 per cent of those with dependent children in 1972, to 24 per cent in 2006. Rising cohabitation meant that the percentage of children born outside of marriage increased from 12 to 43 per cent between 1980 and 2005. Self and Zealey (2007) also report significantly later marriage and first-time childbirth since the 1970s.

Crucially, these changes coincided with greater female participation in the labour market. Employment rates among women of working age rose from 56 per cent in 1971 to 70 per cent in 2005 (Self and Zealey, 2007) This included significant rises in both full- and part-time work, although the one-and-a-half-earner household is closer to the norm in two-parent families (Lister, 2006). It must be noted, of course, that these broad trends in family structure, formation and employment mask significant differences based on socio-economic status, ethnicity and religion (Berthoud, 2007).

Such family changes have been the subject of fierce controversy and ideological conflict. For conservative traditionalists, these and other developments (such as recognition of same-sex partnerships) signify the demise of the family as a stabilising social force. Significant blame for this is attached to feminism and a wider 'rights culture' for encouraging women to forsake the homemaker role, with family relationships and parenthood reduced to a 'lifestyle choice' (Davies, 1993). Many of these themes coalesce in conservative analysis of the 'underclass', where lone mothers stand accused of welfare dependency, rearing their children without appropriate (male) role models and fuelling crime and anti-social behaviour (Murray, 1990).

For the centre-left, such changes have evoked a more mixed response, with recognition of the damaging effects of family instability on children but support for changes in gender roles and greater opportunities for women. Recent family changes are broadly interpreted as promoting adult relationships based on intimacy and self-fulfilment and more 'democratic' relationships between parents and children (Giddens, 1992; Beck, 1997). Critical perspectives on the family are also seen as promoting awareness of problems such as domestic violence and intra-familial child maltreatment. Overall, the centre-left tends to embrace a more pluralistic view of family forms.

Drawing on Etzioni's (1993) concept of 'parenting deficit' as a major contributing factor to social problems, the New Labour government has considerably increased intervention in relation to parenting, with an uneasy amalgam of the supportive and punitive (Henricson, 2003). Thus, more generous tax credits and child-related benefits have been introduced, along with measures to promote 'family-friendly' employment. Other supportive measures include dedicated helplines – such as Parentline Plus – for those facing difficulties and the establishment of a National Family and Parenting Institute. Yet parents are also increasingly held responsible for their children's misdemeanours – truancy, anti-social behaviour and offending – and may be ordered to undertake parenting education as part of court orders. Critics argue that by ignoring the impact of social deprivation, such policies effectively 'blame the victim', while the gender-neutral term 'parent' masks an overwhelming focus on mothers (Gillies, 2005).

There are sharply divergent views on the benefits of interventionism. Supporters tend to emphasise parenting as an increasingly demanding 'job' requiring regulation, professional guidance and even a parents' code setting out rights and responsibilities (Henricson, 2003). Opponents, however, argue that intense scrutiny of parents has served to undermine their confidence and authority, which, allied to heightened concerns about children's safety, has generated 'paranoid parenting' (Furedi, 2001).

Debates on the nature of family and parenting are important for child welfare services in various ways. First, the assessment of 'parenting capacity' (see Chapter 2) is influenced not only by wider social norms but also by understandings of the impact of parenting on outcomes for children (Golombok, 2000). Second, competing value systems generate different paradigms for relationships between the family and the state (see below). Third, legislation and policy construct 'family' in important ways, for example, the importance attached to siblings or extended family in children's lives or the role of fathers in families (Featherstone, 2004). Fourth, normative views of family are crucial to the 'corporate parenting' provided for those in, and leaving, public care. Finally, it is important to recognise that the experiences of children, living in whatever setting, will be significantly influenced by the wider norms of family life.

PERSPECTIVES IN CHILD CARE POLICY

In her classic (1997) work, Fox Harding sets out four ideal typical perspectives on the tripartite relationships between family, state and children, which can be summarised briefly as follows.

Fox Harding's first perspective, which she terms *laissez faire and the patriarchal family*, contends that leaving parents to bring up children as they see fit offers the best way of serving the latter's interests. State intervention should be limited to cases of serious maltreatment and should generally involve the child being removed and placed for adoption (Goldstein et al., 1979). Below this threshold, state intervention is regarded as 'interference', as undermining family autonomy and frequently proving ineffective or damaging. The laissez-faire perspective advocacy of a 'minimal state' has a natural affinity with the political right but may also chime with civil liberties' concerns from the left.

A second perspective, *state paternalism and child protection*, gives much greater weight to the vulnerability of children within the family and supports a significantly higher level of state intervention to protect them. Families must be held accountable while the state has a legitimate and important role in scrutinising the care of their children (Dingwall et al., 1983). Fox Harding rightly notes that this stance tends to ignore the pressures faced by many parents and the potential for state intervention to be oppressive of poor and marginalised families.

These issues are taken up in the third perspective, *the modern defence of the birth family and parents' rights*. Like the laissez-faire perspective, the 'modern defence' is supportive of families and parental rights and opposed to what is regarded as oppressive state intervention but there are key differences between the two. First, whereas laissez-faire writers such as Goldstein et al. (1979) see parenting in psychological terms, the 'modern defence' emphasises the enduring importance of biological relationships or 'blood ties'. This view underpins support for policies that keep families together, reunite them, and sustain contact even when the children are living permanently in another family. A second difference is that the 'modern defence' is politically left-leaning, seeing child welfare problems as rooted in material deprivation and regarding state support for families as beneficial (Holman, 1988). However, Fox Harding argues that this perspective oversimplifies complex relationships between parents and children and is perhaps too sanguine on the potential for welfare provision to prevent maltreatment and family breakdown.

Fox Harding's final perspective, *children's rights and child liberation*, is radically different from the first three, all of which tend to enshrine paternalistic views that emphasise protection rather than children's voice or participation. Paternalism, whether that of family or state, fits well with what Archard (2004) refers to as the *caretaker* view of children's rights. This view emphasises the need for a guardian figure who will make decisions in children's interests until they are competent to do so on their own behalf as adults. This view can be criticised both for the assumptions it makes about the abilities of children and the motives of (some) caretakers, and for its denial to children of fundamental rights. By contrast, the *liberationist* view of children's rights takes as its starting point the idea of children as an oppressed group, lacking power and discriminated against, with paternalism merely a mask for exclusion and control (Holt, 1975). In its strongest form, liberationist advocacy for children having the same rights as adults has predictably received little support, but in a more moderate guise, has been influential in promoting children's participation in planning and decision making.

CHILDREN'S RIGHTS AND HUMAN RIGHTS

The influence of children's rights and human rights over contemporary child care policy and practice in the UK is open to different interpretations. On the one hand, it can be argued that they have exerted a steadily growing influence, both in law and debates over policy, supported by organisations such as the Children's Legal Centre and umbrella bodies such as the Children's Rights Alliance (for details see end of chapter). Conversely, their impact may be seen as limited, due in part to inherent limitations and to significant opposition to their workings.

Children's rights

A full discussion of the historical evolution and dynamics of children's rights is beyond our scope here, and interested readers are referred to Franklin (2002) and Archard (2004) for further information. The contemporary framework for children's rights is set out by the UN Convention on the Rights of the Child (UNCRC). The UNCRC's 54 articles address a wide range of issues, and are often placed within the following three categories (adapted from www.unicef.org/crc/index_30177.html):

1   *Provision (survival and development) rights*
    family support (preservation); health, social security, education; leisure and play; special care and protection e.g. disabled children, refugees; identity, nationality, freedom of religion.
2   *Protection rights*
    from violence and abuse; kidnap and trafficking; child labour; sexual exploitation; war and armed conflict; drug abuse; inhumane treatment for young offenders.
3   *Participation rights*
    respect for views; freedom of association and expression; access to information privacy.

In broad terms the UNCRC can be seen to represent a compromise between the caretaker and (moderate) liberationist views. Although ratified by almost all countries in the world, the impact of the UNCRC is limited for several reasons. These include differences of interpretation and implementation between countries, their capacity to 'opt out' of certain areas of the UNCRC, the lack of resources in poorer countries (e.g. to deal with poverty or AIDS) and the lack of effective sanctions in response to countries' non-compliance with the Convention. Arguably the UNCRC's principal value is symbolic, providing a benchmark against which governments can be evaluated and possibly 'shamed' into improving compliance by international and domestic pressure.

Since ratifying the UNCRC in 1991, successive British governments have been at odds with the UN Committee on the Rights of the Child over issues such as child poverty, asylum and immigration, treatment of young offenders and the use of corporal punishment (CRAE, 2007). Hendrick (2003) has argued that the issue of children's rights is 'an uncomfortable concept' for New Labour. Thus, while participation for children and young people has increased significantly, critics argue that this is underpinned by an agenda of conformity, and does little to question or challenge children's relative lack of power or the constraints of childhood (Wyness et al., 2004). Nevertheless, the past decade has seen the creation of Children's Commissioners for the countries of the UK, a Children's Rights Director to safeguard the rights of children living away from home, ministerial posts with responsibility for children and networks of children's rights officers and advocates.

Human rights law

While again space does not permit a full discussion of how human rights law relates to children and families (see Kilkelly, 1999), a brief mention may be helpful here. Unlike the UNCRC, human rights law carries legal weight in the UK because of the European Convention on Human Rights (ECHR) and the Human Rights Act 1998. Consequently, Lyon (2007) argues that the ECHR is worthy of greater attention, outlining its impact to date in areas such as the use of corporal punishment; the failure of a local authority to prevent abuse of children; refusal of access to care records; and the trial of children in adult court.

SERVICES FOR CHILDREN AND FAMILIES UNDER THE CHILDREN ACT – A BRIEF OVERVIEW

In this section, we attempt to outline the major developments in child care law and policy since the passing of the Children Act 1989 in England and

Wales, a starting point chosen due to its (continuing) importance in governing child care policy and practice. A more detailed discussion of the Act will appear in later chapters, and here our purpose is to chart its broad contours and key principles.

The Children Act 1989 – background

The road to the Children Act can be mapped in two different though linked ways, first as a process of legal reform and second as a struggle between competing principles and perspectives in child care. The legal pathway is usually traced to a Select Committee Report on Child Care (known as the Short Report) (House of Commons, 1984). Broadly supportive of Fox Harding's 'modern defence of the birth family', the report advocated greater effort and resources be put into keeping children with their families or reuniting them once admitted to public care. This stance was bolstered by research showing that social work practice was often neglectful or even obstructive of contact between children in care and their families, while the care system frequently failed to provide stability for children or prepare them to leave care (Department of Health and Social Security (DHSS), 1985a). Thus, concern about the injustices experienced by many families coalesced with a growing scepticism regarding the efficacy of state intervention. These themes were taken up in the government's Review of Child Care Law (RCCL) (DHSS, 1985b), which laid many of the foundations for the Children Act 1989, including the promotion of 'partnership' between parents and child care services.

Legislative reform also had to address the thorny area of child maltreatment, where debate had become increasingly intense and fractious during the mid-1980s (see Chapter 4). Growing recognition of (especially sexual) abuse and highly publicised child deaths, such as those of Jasmine Beckford, Tyra Henry and Kimberley Carlile, generated pressures for further protective state intervention. Yet the perception of an over-intrusive state also became more prominent, especially following the events in Cleveland in 1987, when large numbers of children were taken into care on the basis of controversial medical diagnoses and 'heavy handed' intervention (Parton, 1991).

The Children Act 1989 – principles and perspectives

The Children Act was widely seen as one of the most extensive reforms to child care law and represented a major reconfiguration of relationships between children, their families and the state (see Allen (2005) for an informative commentary on the Act and its workings). The guiding principles of the legislation are set out in Box 1.1.

Key features of the Children Act 1989

- more active involvement of courts in decision making about children;
- welfare of the child to be paramount;
- use of a welfare checklist for decision making;
- avoidance of delay;
- no order to be made unless better than not to do so;
- ascertaining and taking into account child's wishes;
- specific orders to deal with residence and contact;
- parental responsibility to be maximised, even when the child is in care;
- bringing together public (local authority, police powers, etc.) and private (divorce etc.) law;
- due consideration to be given to child's religious persuasion, racial origin, cultural and linguistic background.

The Children Act has been described as an 'uneasy synthesis' (Fox Harding, 1997), based on its appeal to disparate ideological strands within child care policy. Building on the RCCL's tenet that 'a child is not the child of the state', the influence of the 'modern defence' and even elements of 'laissez faire' are readily apparent in various measures designed to strengthen the position of parents. First, the Act introduced the concept of 'parental responsibility' (s3), which, while emphasising parents' duties towards their children, gave them increased 'rights' in order to carry these out. These included powers to challenge the removal of their children on an emergency basis (s45) (see Chapter 4) and ensured that compulsory removal into public care would require a court hearing (s31), abolishing the previous administrative powers. Second, even after compulsory removal, parental responsibility was, in principle, still to be shared between parents and local authorities, while the Act also mandated that children be returned to their families unless it was against their interests to do so (s23), and promoted contact with them while looked after (s34). Third, the 'no order' principle (s1) (see Box 1.1) signalled that state intervention could only be justified if it would improve upon family care. Fourth, family preservation was to be promoted by a range of support services, discussed further in Chapter 3. Finally, the Act's emphasis on the role of the courts in decision making for children could be seen as important in protecting families and making local authorities more accountable for their actions.

While the broad thrust of the Children Act was away from 'state paternalism', duties to protect children were also emphasised (s47) and in certain respects extended as in the introduction of the Child Assessment Order (s43) (see Chapter 4).

The Children Act 1989 can be seen as promoting children's rights in various ways. The emphasis on services for 'children in need', the welfare checklist (factors to be taken into account in decision making) and the minimising of delay (s1) can all be seen as examples of provision and protection rights. The Act also contains certain participatory rights, relating to separate legal representation, making complaints, refusing medical assessment, applying for section 8 orders (see below) and initiating legal proceedings (see Roche, 2002, for details). However, these rights, like the requirement to take the child's feelings and wishes into account, are all subject to the child's age and perceived level of understanding, and Roche argues persuasively that judicial interpretation has tended to roll back rather than extend them.

Implicit recognition was given in the Children Act to inequalities among children in two areas. First, following increasing controversy in the 1980s in relation to the treatment of black and minority ethnic (BME) children and families by child care services (Ahmed et al., 1986), the Act introduced duties demanding that due consideration be accorded to religious persuasion, racial origin, cultural and linguistic background and recruitment of carers who reflected the ethnic diversity of local children in need (s22 and Schedule 2,11). Second, the Act sought to improve provision for disabled children by including disability within the definition of children in need and by requiring local authorities to be more proactive in discovering levels of need among their population.

Another important feature of the Children Act was an attempt to promote effective co-ordination between different local authority departments (e.g. social services, education and housing) and with other agencies such as the health service and the police, across a range of services from child protection to looked after children and young people leaving care (s27,47)

Finally, it should be noted that the Act represented an important rationalising piece of legislation, bringing significant harmonisation between what is termed public law (i.e. state intervention in child welfare cases) and private law relating to families, notably in cases of divorce. This is perhaps most evident in section 8, under which the following four orders are applicable in either sphere:

- **residence order (stating who the child should live with);**
- **contact order (usually for contact with non-resident relatives);**
- **specific issues order (requiring certain actions);**
- **prohibited steps order (forbidding certain actions).**

Child Care law in the UK

The Children Act applied to England and Wales, but many of its features have been replicated elsewhere in the UK. The Children (Scotland) Act 1995 translated the Children Act into Scottish law, albeit with certain modifications, but it is important to recognise that the legal framework for child care in Scotland is significantly different from that in England and Wales – for an instructive guide see Plumtree (2005) and for a broader coverage of child and family social work in Scotland see Hothersall (2006). Arguably the principal difference is the role of the hearings system. This comprises panels of lay volunteers with a reporter to provide legal advice. The reporter also acts as an initial assessor, deciding whether further action is necessary and whether the matter should be referred to the local authority for assistance or to the hearings for possible compulsory supervision. Such supervision may be based on any of a wide range of conditions – from suffering impaired development or significant harm, to non-attendance at school, being beyond control, in moral danger, substance abuse or offending – that reflect the origins of the modern hearings system in the Kilbrandon Report (1964) and its 'welfarist' approach to deviant behaviour. Long since abandoned in England and Wales, this approach has persisted in Scotland, though coming under increasing strain in recent years (Tisdall, 2006).

In terms of its content, the Children (Northern Ireland) Order 1995 is very similar to the Children Act 1989 (see O'Halloran, 2003, for a detailed commentary), but the context for implementation is very different. Since the imposition of direct rule in 1972, child care services in Northern Ireland have been delivered through combined Health and Social Services Boards (now Trusts). As Kelly and Pinkerton (1996) argue, there has been less political commitment to the welfare state and relatively greater reliance on the family and religious institutions. Crucially, given the history of sectarian division and conflict, child care in Northern Ireland is also shaped by 'the contested legitimacy of the state' (Pinkerton, 2003).

Implementing the Children Act 1989

The Children Act was atypical in terms of Margaret Thatcher's third term of Conservative government. By contrast with adult social care, the Act did not signal any wholesale shift from state to private and voluntary sector services. Moreover, the notion of family support appeared to endorse welfare provision to largely poor families in ways that were at odds with the government's broader social policies. Crucially, however, local authorities were given no additional funding to implement the Act, while rising poverty and welfare cutbacks meant a growing population of potential 'children in need' (Tunstill, 1997). The Conservatives also attempted to bolster the 'traditional family' by measures outlawing the 'promotion' of homosexual relationships as an alternative family form (Local Government Act 1988, s28), and responded to debate regarding an emerging 'underclass' (see above) with the increasing demonisation of lone parents as welfare scroungers. Parents were to be made more responsible for their children, whether financially through the Child Support Agency (1993) or in cases of truancy and criminal offences under the Criminal Justice Act 1991. The early 1990s also witnessed a punitive turn towards children and young people themselves as offenders. A series of moral panics in relation to joyriding, bail bandits and 'persistent young offenders' brought forth legislation to increase the use of custody (Muncie, 2004). Meanwhile, the murder of toddler James Bulger by two young boys was widely seen as heralding harsher attitudes towards childhood, not least among populist politicians (Jenks, 1996)

The refocusing debate

Within child social care, there was mixed evidence on the early effects of the Children Act. Statistically, the idea of a less 'interventionist' approach initially appeared to be borne out by a steady fall in the exercise of compulsory powers and declining numbers of looked after children and those placed on the child protection register (Colton et al., 2001). However, research studies painted a gloomier picture on the development of services for children in need (Aldgate and Tunstill, 1995). In what came to be known as the 'refocusing debate', it was suggested that the continued prioritisation of child protection work was stifling the Children Act's emphasis on family support and partnership.

Scarce resources reinforced the prioritisation of child protection work, and led to fears that focusing on children in need would simply raise false expectations (Colton et al., 1995). Nonetheless, this situation was regarded as skewing child care practice in damaging ways. Findings summarised in *Child Protection: Messages from Research* (Department of Health (DH), 1995) suggested that a relatively narrow concentration on investigating abuse allegations was failing to take fully into account children's wider development and well-being. In cases where abuse was not substantiated, families rarely received support services, even when the children's needs might warrant them, while (over-)prioritisation of child protection created a perverse incentive for workers to exaggerate the degree of risk in order to secure services (Packman and Hall, 1998; Thoburn et al., 2000a). The 'refocusing' advocated entailed taking a wider view of children's needs and shifting resources towards the provision of family support, thereby preventing problems becoming more acute. The outcome of the refocusing debate will be discussed in later chapters, including the way in which it has been subsumed within New Labour's broader strategy towards children's services.

Looked after children

As noted earlier, the perceived failings of the care system came under scrutiny during the 1980s and were reinforced by a further series of research studies (DH, 1991). In response to these concerns, a working party was established to examine how to improve the life chances of looked after children. The resulting report (Parker et al., 1991) (discussed more fully in Chapter 6) argued that there was a lack of clarity in the assessment of children's needs, as well as planning and monitoring progress and that these failures of 'corporate parenting' were reflected in poor educational achievements, employment prospects and life skills. Arguably the report's greatest impact arose from the working materials that it generated, including *Assessment and Action Records* and *Planning and Review Forms* based upon the following seven dimensions of development:

- health;
- education;
- identity;
- family and social relationships;
- social presentation;
- emotional and behavioural development;
- self-care skills.

Following further refinement (Ward, 1995), these instruments were progressively adopted across the UK and in many other countries. This development has been widely seen as beneficial in terms of promoting rigour in assessment and planning for children and facilitating participation as looked after children and carers are able to record their views. However, the length and 'bureaucratic' quality of the forms have contributed to variable completion, and are regarded by some critics as 'alienating'. It has also been argued that the looked after children (LAC) forms overemphasise conformity and 'white middle class norms' (Garrett, 2003).

New Labour, children and the social investment state

An extended discussion of the New Labour government's social policy since 1997 is beyond our scope here (see for example Powell, 2002, for a fuller account). However, it is helpful to highlight certain key features in order to set its child care policies in context.

While its precise meaning is open to interpretation, the Third Way policies endorsed by New Labour essentially revolve around navigating between the free market policies of Thatcherite conservatism and 'Old Labour's' faith in state intervention. Ideology, for example in a preference for public or private provision, is said to give way to the pragmatic pursuit of 'what works'. The challenges of globalisation demand that social justice must work with the grain of economic competitiveness, and thus equality focuses increasingly on the opportunity to compete effectively in the labour market. In turn, social policy, including measures to combat poverty and social exclusion, must be justified more clearly as investment, for example, leading to a healthy, educated and hence productive workforce. The notion of welfare as investment (or social control) is far from new, but its intensity has prompted use of the term 'social investment state' to characterise New Labour's approach (Giddens, 1998). A key aspect of this intensification has been the development of 'managerialism' (discussed further in Chapter 10), with policy focused more tightly on value for money and a plethora of performance targets against which services are inspected and audited.

Representing 'the future' and relatively captive within childhood institutions, children are prime targets for social investment, within which they hold an 'iconic status' (Lister, 2006). What is beyond dispute is that the New Labour government has invested significantly in mainstream child welfare services and has launched a wide range of new initiatives, including *SureStart,* to provide integrated services for young children and their families (Belsky et al., 2007); the *Children's Fund* (and the *Changing Children's Services Fund* in Scotland) to promote voluntary initiatives to tackle disadvantage among 5 to 13 year-olds (Edwards et al., 2006); *Connexions,* an information and advice service for young people (Hoggarth and Smith, 2004); and the *National Child Care Strategy,* aimed at providing good quality, affordable child social work for children aged 0 to 14 in every neighbourhood (Penn and Randall, 2005).

The social investment approach can be seen to have a number of positive effects, including the symbolic value attached to children, a sense of collective responsibility for their well-being and a degree of redistribution towards poorer families and communities while avoiding a 'residual' welfare provision. However, it can be argued that the investment strategy comes at a price, with the emphasis on labour market participation adding to the pressures of the work–family balance, especially for women (Lister, 2006). For children, it is argued that the social investment approach tends to cast children in terms of their (future) productivity and conformity, as 'becomings' rather than 'beings', not least in the education system (Fawcett et al., 2004).

Governing children's services under New Labour

The relevance of the 'social investment state' for child social work policy and practice can be understood in different ways. On the one hand, many of the latter's traditional concerns, such as family support and child protection, have acquired a much wider reach. However, many children's initiatives have given at best a marginal role to social care services. Despite any such reservations, however, government investment in child social care has been significant. Initially, much of this was to be delivered through the *Quality Protects* programme (named *Children First* in Wales) (DH, 1998a) which ran from 1999 to 2004. Its objectives focused especially on improving the life chances of children in need and looked after children, supporting disabled children and their families, actively involving children and carers, training the workforce and making the best use of resources.

Alongside the wide-ranging concerns of the *Quality Protects* programme, the New Labour government also introduced more targeted policy initiatives, including legislation relating to care leavers and adoption. The continuing problems faced by care leavers and their perceived vulnerability to social exclusion (DH, 1999) led to the Children (Leaving Care) Act 2000. Its principal aims were to avoid early discharge from the care system and to improve the preparation for leaving care and subsequent ongoing support. The Act established the role of personal advisors and duties in respect of planning and maintaining contact with care leavers. (These provisions are discussed in Chapter 8.)

Adoption from public care provided another important focus for policy, especially in England and Wales. Prior to 1997, the Conservatives had become progressively enamoured of adoption, which was seen as a way of avoiding the failures of the care system, securing better outcomes for children and at less cost (Morgan, 1998). However, they failed to legislate while in office. Adoption also became a favoured cause of right-wing think-tanks and newspapers such as the *Daily Mail* and it was widely seen as a response to such campaigns when Tony Blair launched a review of adoption in 2000 (Garrett, 2003). This led to the Adoption and Children Act 2002, which aimed to promote adoption for looked after children, through a regime of target setting, tighter timescales for decision making, a national register to improve matching between families and children and improved support for adoptive parents. The Act also sought to increase the pool of adopters by allowing unmarried (including same-sex) couples to apply (see Chapter 7.)

The Victoria Climbié inquiry, *Every Child Matters* and the Children Act 2004

As was the case for the previous Children Act, the path to the Children Act 2004 reflected a blend of ongoing policy reforms and the impact of 'scandal'. The latter arose from the harrowing death of Victoria Climbié at the hands of her aunt and the latter's partner and the ensuing inquiry chaired by Lord Laming (2003). The central features of the case – failure to see the child alone, 'naivety' towards dangerous abusers, and lack of communication between professionals and agencies – were depressingly familiar from previous inquiries (Parton, 2006). Yet they were taking place in a new context, namely that of New Labour's commitment to reform and 'modernise' services for children. The government had already been considering organisational change, but the extreme nature of the failure in Victoria's case (with Laming identifying 12 'missed opportunities' for action that may have saved her life) appeared to demand radical action. While responding specifically to the child protection agenda and the Laming Report's recommendations (DfES et al., 2003), the government also launched a broader blueprint in a Green Paper entitled *Every Child Matters* (Chief Secretary to the Treasury, 2003). (Distinct but similar programmes have subsequently been introduced across the UK – see Welsh Assembly Government, 2004; Scottish

Executive, 2005a; Office of the First Minister and Deputy First Minister, 2006.) The Green Paper identified five outcomes for children and four broad areas for policy development. These are shown in Box 1.2.

BOX 1.2

Every Child Matters

Five outcomes for children and young people:

1. being healthy;
2. staying safe;
3. enjoying and achieving;
4. making a positive contribution;
5. economic well-being.

Four areas for policy development:

1. supporting parents and carers;
2. early intervention and protection;
3. accountability and integration;
4. workforce reform.

For the purposes of our overview, arguably the two most important themes within *Every Child Matters* (ECM) are those of early intervention and 'joined up' working. Both reflect deceptively simple logic. The case for early intervention has always rested on the proposition that, if problems can be 'nipped in the bud', there are benefits to service recipients and in broader social and economic terms (Scott et al., 2001) (see also Chapter 3). The Green Paper's 'preventive' approach was much wider than the traditional domains of child welfare, and linked child protection with the needs to 'improve children's lives as a whole' and 'maximise their potential'.

New Labour's emphasis on 'joined up' working between both professionals and organisations reflected a desire to tackle longstanding problems of poor co-ordination, manifest in duplication, service gaps, territorial and boundary disputes and a lack of common purpose. To do this required cutting across traditional boundaries and this was pursued in various ways, such as allowing 'pooled budgets' under the Health Act 1999 and, more radically, by creating multidisciplinary teams under a single organisational roof. Following the prototype of Youth Offending Teams, this model became more widely adopted within health and social care and formed the basis of the Children's Trust, a vehicle that comprises social care, education and (some) health services as they relate to children.

Concern for joined up working was also apparent in the development of children's centres to build on the SureStart initiative, in early years provision (Penn and Randall, 2005) and multilevel Local Strategic Partnerships to co-ordinate services for children and young people (Percy-Smith, 2006).

The Green Paper placed particular emphasis on information-sharing between agencies and promoted the use a common assessment framework among those working with children, a measure also designed to reduce duplication (see Chapter 2). More controversially, a single database – subsequently called Contact Point – was to be introduced with the details of all children and upon which professionals' concerns could be flagged. Portrayed as a means of improving communication in child protection and identifying educational or behavioural problems at an early stage, its critics argue that the database represents an unwelcome encroachment upon civil liberties and are sceptical regarding its effectiveness (Penna, 2005). More broadly, Fiona Williams (2004) has argued that *Every Child Matters* offers a 'dreary vision' of childhood based on a work ethic of academic achievement and social conformity.

The Children Act 2004 will be discussed more fully in subsequent chapters, but some of the main measures are summarised in Box 1.3. As can be seen, these measures focus particularly on organisational change and the themes of integration, accountability and advocacy.

BOX 1.3

Children Act 2004 – main provisions

- Local Safeguarding Children Boards
- Director of Children's Services
- Lead Member for Children's Services
- Children's Trusts
- Children's Commissioner for England

CONCLUSION

In this chapter, we have attempted to set the context for the book's subject matter by looking at both recent historical developments in child care policy and some of the ongoing debates surrounding it. The wider contexts include those of changes within childhood and family life and the changing priorities of government. Discussion of competing value positions or perspectives on child care highlights crucial tensions, notably between 'family support' and 'child rescue', which will be explored in later chapters.

GUIDE TO FURTHER READING

Useful reviews of contemporary childhood include Prout's *The Future of Childhood* (Routledge), which provides a theoretical account, and Madge's *Children These Days* (Policy Press), which draws on research with children and parents. Hendrick (2003) offers an excellent historical analysis of child-related social policy. Archard (2004) examines the conceptual basis of children's rights, while Franklin's edited (2002) collection also charts their implementation. Garrett (2003) presents a critical account of the early New Labour reform programme, while Parton (2006) brings this analysis more up to date. A comprehensive review of relevant legal issues can be found in Williams, *Child Law for Social Work* (Sage).

Reading and resources for practice

This being an introductory and largely contextual chapter, there are no specific practice-related references other than general texts, of which the most useful are probably Jowitt and O'Loughlin's *Social Work with Children and Families* (Learning Matters) and the near identically titled *Social Work with Children and Families: Getting into Practice* (Jessica Kingsley) by Butler and Roberts. McNeish et al. (eds) *What Works for Children: Effective Services for Children* (Open University Press) contains valuable summaries on a range of interventions. For information on children's rights see the websites of the Children's Legal Centre (www.childrens legalcentre.com/) and the Children's Rights Alliance (England) (www.crae.org.uk). A helpful practice guide to participation is provided by Wright et al's *Involving Children and Young People in Developing Social Care* (Social Care Institute for Excellence).

Discussion questions

Is the early twenty-first century a good time to be a child?

To what extent can the problems faced by children and young people be attributed to the decline of the 'traditional' family?

Do children have too many rights or too few?

Is the level of surveillance associated with early intervention and 'joined up working' a price worth paying to safeguard children?

Do the benefits of the social investment state for children's well-being outweigh any disadvantages?

2

ASSESSMENT OF CHILDREN AND FAMILIES

INTRODUCTION

The journeys undertaken by children and families in contact with statutory child care services are many and varied, but all will begin with some form of assessment. This may be relatively fleeting or extensive but will invariably play an important part in how the journey proceeds. At its simplest, the process of assessment refers to the gathering of information to provide the basis for decision making, planning and resource allocation. While 'assessment', both informal and formal, is an ongoing feature of all work with children and families, our primary focus rests with the early stages of such work.

Assessment has come to be seen as increasingly important in recent years as a cornerstone for effective work with children and families, but is challenging for a number of reasons. First, as discussed below, assessment may be seen as a 'top-down' technical exercise or an interactive process, which seeks to maximise the participation of children and their families. A second issue is what is to count as relevant information or 'evidence'. What types of information are to be gathered and from whom? Third, assessment inevitably takes place within a context of contested values. Many of these stem from the different perspectives identified by Fox Harding, for example, the importance given to 'blood ties' or interpretations of children's rights, but they may also arise in respect of gender roles within families, sexuality, religious beliefs or cultural traditions. Fourth, practitioners and agencies must manage the difficult relationship between an assessment of need and the provision of services, avoiding the twin pitfalls of making 'unrealistic demands' or tailoring assessment narrowly according to the resources available. Finally, it should be noted that these intrinsic challenges may increase where workers lack the requisite skills, training and crucially, the time for undertaking assessments.

HISTORICAL BACKGROUND

In the postwar years, formalised assessment was largely associated with choosing appropriate placements for children entering the care system based on needs and behaviour. During the 1980s, however, concern regarding the quality of child care practice prompted moves to improve assessment. In particular, the turmoil surrounding child protection led to the introduction of new guidance (subsequently known as 'the Orange Book'), which aimed to establish a more 'structured and systematic' framework for assessment (DH, 1988).

The guide comprised 167 questions, arranged under the following headings:

- cause for concern;
- the child (history, development);
- perceptions - child, parents and professionals;
- family composition;
- profile of parents/carers;
- couple relationship and family interactions;
- networks;
- finances;
- physical conditions.

Practitioners were also encouraged to employ genograms or family trees, ecomaps (which represent important relationships for the child), flow charts to catalogue changes in the child's life, and developmental charts to assess progress towards particular 'milestones'. However, despite warnings in the guide that it should not be deployed mechanistically, subsequent inspection and research evidence showed that workers frequently used the questions as a 'checklist' rather than a flexible tool to aid decision making (Horwath, 2001a). More importantly, as the refocusing debate (see Chapter 1) developed, pressure grew for a radical overhaul of assessment to facilitate a shift towards the required broader emphasis on children's development.

THE ASSESSMENT FRAMEWORK

In 2000, the New Labour government published the *Framework for the Assessment of Children in Need and Their Families* (DH et al., 2000) (hereafter the Assessment Framework) and its associated practice guidance (DH, 2000a) for England (and essentially replicated in Wales in 2001). The Framework was to be applied to all assessments under the Children Act 1989, whether for children in need (s17) or where 'significant harm' was suspected (s47), although in the latter case, there was additional guidance to follow (see Chapter 4). The aim was to encourage a broad approach to children's needs even when maltreatment was suspected by facilitating movement between s17 and s47 in the event of new information or changed circumstances. The Assessment Framework was also designed to identify different levels (as well as types) of need, particularly through the introduction of initial and core assessments (see below).

Contact with child social work services is ordinarily initiated through a process of referral: from parents or more rarely children themselves, other family members, neighbours, or professionals such as health visitors, doctors, teachers or police officers. In their analysis of referrals, Cleaver and Walker (2004) found that roughly 30 per cent came from non-professional sources. In England in 2006–2007, there were 545,000 child and family referrals to social services departments, 23 per cent of which were repeat referrals within the year (DfES, 2007a). Approximately 305,000 (or 56 per cent) received initial assessments, the remainder being dealt with by either information or advice, referral to other agencies, or requiring no further action. In Scotland in the same year, 56,199 children were referred (overwhelmingly by the police) to the Children's Reporter, 44,629 on non-offence (care and protection) grounds and 16,490 on offence grounds (4,920 children were referred on both types of grounds) (Scottish Children's Reporter Administration (SCRA), 2007)

A decision on whether to conduct an initial assessment should be taken within one working day and the assessment itself completed within seven days, although this target was met in only 68 per cent of cases. Information will typically be gathered from the child (who must be seen), family members and other agencies with relevant knowledge. The purpose of the initial assessment is to identify whether a child is 'in need' under the Children Act 1989 and if so, what services might be required to meet those needs. Where needs are more complex, including cases of (suspected) significant harm, a core assessment may be undertaken. Government statistics suggest that roughly 30 per cent of initial assessments led on to core assessments, or approximately 17 per cent of all referrals (DfES, 2007a). The prescribed timescale for the core assessment is 35 working days, a target that is met in 78 per cent of cases.

The Assessment Framework (DH et al., 2000: 10–16) sets out the following key principles, namely that assessments:

- are child-centred;
- are rooted in child development;
- are ecological in their approach;
- ensure equality of opportunity;
- involve working with children and families;
- build on strengths as well as identify difficulties;
- are inter-agency in their approach to assessment and the provision of services;
- are a continuing process, not a single event;
- are carried out in parallel with other action and providing services;
- are grounded in evidence-based knowledge.

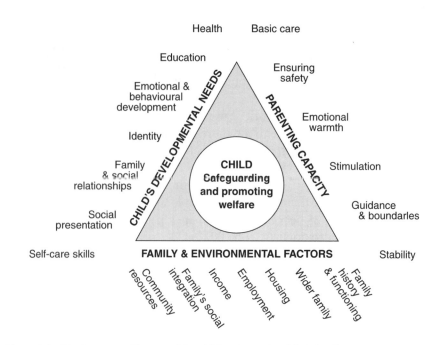

Health   Basic care

Education

Emotional &
behavioural
development   Ensuring
                                      safety

CHILD'S DEVELOPMENTAL NEEDS   PARENTING CAPACITY

Identity   Emotional
                                          warmth

Family
& social   CHILD   Stimulation
relationships   Safeguarding
                   and promoting
Social   welfare   Guidance
presentation   & boundaries

Self-care skills   **FAMILY & ENVIRONMENTAL FACTORS**   Stability

Community resources · Family's social integration · Income · Employment · Housing · Wider family · Family history & functioning

Figure 2.1   The Assessment Framework for children in need and their families

The Framework identifies three domains, relating to the child's developmental needs, parenting capacity and family and environmental factors, each with a number of dimensions as shown in Figure 2.1. (See Rose, 2001, for a discussion of the domains and dimensions.).

UNDERSTANDING ASSESSMENT

Before looking at the domains and their interrelationships in more depth, it is instructive to consider key aspects of the assessment process, of which Holland (2004) affords an excellent overview.

Holland rightly argues that approaches to assessment can be seen as mirroring positivist and interpretive perspectives within the social sciences. The former, with its belief that social behaviour is governed by 'laws', underpins a model of assessment that Holland describes as 'scientific observation'. Emphasis is placed on a relatively 'detached' process of gathering objective information through processes of questioning, observation and the use of scales or other tools (including those related to risk assessment, see Chapter 5) in order to reach a 'diagnosis' of a family's problems.

By contrast, a model that Holland terms 'reflective evaluation' can be aligned with the interpretive view that social behaviour should be understood in terms of interactions between social actors and the meanings that inform their actions. This model stresses dialogue and engagement between those involved in the assessment, an exchange of information, and an exploration of options with the family. Smale and Tuson (1993) have argued that this recognises the 'expertise' of those assessed and is thus well placed to build on their strengths. In interpreting information, workers should also reflect on their own values and assumptions.

Both 'scientific observation' and 'reflective evaluation' have their strengths and limitations. The former can be seen as more firmly based in (research) evidence and potentially more transparent in terms of information gathering and decision making. However, the latter may encourage engagement with families, be more empowering and able to promote change (Shemmings and Shemmings, 2001). Elements of the two approaches to assessment can of course be combined, although given their different assumptions, this must be done with care. As Holland (2004) argues, it is important that, irrespective of the approach taken, workers remain open to changing their assessment in the light of further evidence or dialogue.

Assessment as process

As Holland notes, the Assessment Framework is primarily focused on garnering qualitative information through interview (and for younger children, methods such as play or drawing), supplemented by observation and the construction of genograms and ecomaps. Quantitative data collection is encouraged through scales and questionnaires relating to children's and families' functioning (Cox and Bentovim, 2000), but these have been found to be rarely used (Cleaver and Walker, 2004).

Responding to some of the criticisms levelled at the Orange Book, the Assessment Framework afforded a higher profile than its predecessor to issues of process. It was recognised that assessment was in itself a form of intervention, with the potential to be therapeutic and lead to positive change, or conversely to have damaging effects (DH et al., 2000). For Millar and Corby (2006), therapeutic in this context means social workers promoting personal understanding and well-being for families by displaying warmth, empathy and reliability as well as listening skills in exploring problems. While some critics argue that the bureaucratic nature of the Assessment Framework tends to undermine such therapeutic endeavours, Millar and Corby argue that much depends on the skills of social workers and their willingness to apply the Framework creatively rather than seeing it simply in terms of constraint.

An emphasis on the therapeutic fits well with a broader aim to produce a cultural shift from a procedurally driven system to one based more on professional judgement (Horwath and Morrison, 2000). Arguably the most challenging aspect of this relates to the decision making itself, although as Holland (2004) observes, the Framework has relatively little to say on how to analyse the information once it has been gathered. Models or frameworks for decision making are beyond our scope here (see for example Adcock, 2001, for helpful discussion). Crucial elements, however, are likely to be those related to whether relevant thresholds (for significant harm or impaired development) have been reached, what changes are necessary, and how likely they are to occur and within what timescale, bearing in mind the child's developmental needs and the nature of difficulties within the family.

ASSESSMENT – AN ECOLOGICAL MODEL

A crucial element of the Framework was to emphasise the interconnectedness of the three domains identified in Figure 2.1, drawing on the ecological theory of Bronfenbrenner (1979). Bronfenbrenner's work is challenging, and readers may find the short overview in Colton et al. (2001:45–51) a good starting point. In essence, Bronfenbrenner construes the factors influencing the child's development as a series of four concentric circles, which he refers to as systems, ranging from the child's immediate environment to the broadest social context. The *microsystem* describes any setting where the child is an active participant, typically the family, school, peer group or immediate neighbourhood. The *mesosystem* comprises relationships between microsystems, for example between home and school. Bronfenbrenner deploys the term *exosystem* to describe those factors which are beyond the child's active participation but which stiu exert indirect influences on her or his development. These might include neighbourhood facilities and networks or parents' working environments. Finally, the *macrosystem* comprises the broader social environment in which children and families live, including cultural values, customs, economy and laws. Bronfenbrenner's model also emphasises the importance of time, whether in terms of children's physiological development and key social transitions or the impact of events such as divorce or bereavement at particular life stages.

CHILDREN'S DEVELOPMENT NEEDS

As noted, two key principles of the Assessment Framework are that it should be child-centred and rooted in understandings of child development but, as outlined in Chapter 1, that both terms are open to different interpretations. Meanwhile, the seeming objectivity of developmental psychology masks the extent to which needs are socially constructed and tends to underestimate the competence of children (Taylor, 2004). Nonetheless, discourses of need and development are central to assessment both as legal concepts within the Children Act 1989 and as ways of understanding child welfare. By utilising the dimensions of development originally developed in the LAC project (see Chapter 1), the Assessment Framework marked an important rationalising measure. Neither the Framework nor its associated guidance is particularly expansive on children's developmental needs, but excellent overviews can be found in Daniel et al. (1999) and Aldgate et al. (2005).

Contemporary thinking about children's needs has evolved over several decades and reflects a mixture of theoretical influences and evidence derived from research studies. Reviewing this evolutionary process, Taylor (2004) identifies the following needs:

- basic physical care;
- affection;
- security;
- stimulation;
- guidance;
- control and discipline;
- responsibility;
- independence.

As assessment has become increasingly rationalised, it has become more common to adopt a 'balance sheet' approach, often couched in terms of risk factors i.e. the increased probability of a particular (negative) outcome and protective factors that decrease its likelihood. Daniel et al. (1999) highlight two dimensions to this exercise, the first of which are sources of vulnerability and resilience for the child, which as Gilligan (2001) shows, can be identified within each of the Assessment Framework's domains (see Table 2.1).

The second dimension relates to environments that may be protective or adverse in their effects, either compensating for or exacerbating vulnerability. The 'balance sheet' approach can serve as an aid to the immediate assessment of thresholds in relation to (risk of) impaired development or significant harm but also to project into the future, for example, to consider what may happen in the absence of intervention, and which forms of intervention are most likely to be successful.

In relation to children's needs, resilience has been defined as normal development under difficult conditions (Fonagy et al., 1994) and interest in its workings reflects a desire to find ways of lessening the impact of adverse experiences. Gilligan (1999; 2001) has been the main exponent of applying the concept of resilience within child social care, arguing that it can be promoted in the following ways:

- encouraging purposeful contact with family members (including siblings) and significant others;
- positive school experience;
- friendships with peers;
- fostering interests and talents;
- working on problem-solving skills;
- promoting pro-social qualities.

Table 2.1   Sources of vulnerability and resilience

Child	
Sources of vulnerability	*Sources of resilience*
young age	high IQ
disability	good attachment
earlier history of abuse	good self-esteem
	good relationship with sibling

Parent/Carer	
Sources of vulnerability	*Sources of resilience*
domestic violence	social support
serious substance misuse	positive parental childhood
chronic serious psychiatric	good parental health
illness	education
	work role

Family and environment	
Sources of vulnerability	*Sources of resilience*
rundown neighbourhood	committed adult
poor relationship with school	good school experience
weak fabric of social support	strong community
poverty	good services/supports
isolation	

© NSPCC and the University of Sheffield, 2001. Horwath, J. (ed.), *The Child's World: Assessing Children in Need*. Reproduced by permission of Jessica Kingsley Publishers.

While widely recognised as important, resilience is challenging to study for a number of reasons (Little et al., 2004). First, it is often understood in terms of characteristics and traits or the temperament of the individual child, which are themselves difficult to explain. Second, although resilience may be associated with various factors such as educational achievement or the pursuit of interests, it is not easy to establish clear 'causal' relationships between them. A third challenge is gauging effects over time, given the dynamic nature of resilience, the importance of particular 'turning points' and whether these come from major changes or simply positive experiences of everyday life (Seden, 2002).

Attachment and assessment

Arguably the most influential theoretical framework within assessment and child social care more broadly is that based on attachment. Originally derived from the work of Bowlby (1953), attachment theory emphasises the importance of relationships between children and parental figures, especially mothers. Bowlby was particularly concerned with the negative consequences of lost or poor attachments which led to 'maternal deprivation'. Subsequently, his work attracted criticism for its gendered assumptions and ethnocentricity (see below), but having fallen out of fashion, attachment theory was 'redis-covered' during the 1990s (Thoburn, 1999) and its importance was made explicit in the Assessment Framework. Attachment theory is applicable to a wide range of issues within child care, including family support, child pro-tection and family placement and will be discussed further in later chapters. Howe et al. (1999) supply a good overview, while a more in-depth guide can be found in Prior and Glaser (2006).

Fahlberg (1994) has defined attachment as 'an affectionate bond between two individuals that endures through space and time and serves to join them emotionally'. She argues that the development of attachment occurs through a cycle of 'arousal and relaxation', wherein the child becomes aroused through needs such as food or comfort, but relaxes once these needs are met by the attachment figure. Repetition of the cycle develops trust and a sense of security for the child. Fahlberg also points to a positive interaction cycle, where play and humour make interaction enjoyable and mutually rewarding and attachment is strengthened. The longer-term importance of attachment is that it should provide children with a 'secure base' from which to explore the social world and give them an 'internal working model' for relationships based on trust. Although open to change through later experiences, these models exert a strong and often enduring influence over the lives of children and adults (Howe, 2001).

Needless to say, such processes do not always follow this path and, while a complete absence of attachment is rare, insecure attachment may affect up to half of the population (Howe, 2001). Building on Ainsworth et al's (1978) work, insecure attachments are customarily divided into three categories: anxious avoidant (detached), anxious resistant (ambivalent) and disorganised/controlling. Each is associated with specific attachment behaviours, such as the reaction to separation, and wider patterns of behaviour. These are summarised in Table 2.2.

Howe (2003) argues that attachment behaviours reflect how children 'make sense of adults' both emotionally and cognitively and are typically adaptive responses to their care environment. Within assessments, therefore, attachment behaviours can give important insights into children's well-being and development, while the theory may help to explain the factors that lie behind them and to gauge the potential for change. Understanding attachment is particularly pertinent when temporary or permanent removal of a child is being considered, both in terms of recognising the effects of removal and the importance of maintaining contact between children and birth family members including siblings (Sanders, 2004). Information on attachment can be gleaned from interviews, direct work with children, from other professionals and perhaps most importantly observation, but as Howe (2003) warns, assessing attachments is a complex task that requires experience and cautious handling.

Table 2.2   Types of attachment, responses to separation and patterns of behaviour

Type of attachment	Responses to separation	Wider patterns of behaviour
secure	explores actively, clings in presence of strangers	confident, curious, playful, mature, empathetic, competent
anxious avoidant	little distress at separation, avoids contact, ignores	child over-regulates emotions by downplaying, may prefer strangers to parents, isolated, distant
anxious resistant (ambivalent)	anxious – seeking and resisting contact	may be clingy and highly dependent but also resistant – hence ambivalent; impulsive, finds it difficult to follow through commitments
disorganised/controlling	contradictory behaviour patterns	occurs where a carer is dangerous and unpredictable – mixture of fear and need for reassurance. Controlling refers to coping with the overlay strategy e.g. compulsive compliance or care giving

Children's empowerment and participation

The Assessment Framework emphasises the importance of communication with children and that this should be as flexible as is necessary to ascertain their views, combining methods such as play, drawing and joint activities with more conventional forms of data-gathering such as interviews, observation and scales. Apart from the intrinsic importance of the child's 'voice' and priorities, this process can also help to avoid assumptions regarding the impact of particular events and environments. Bannister (2001) highlights the therapeutic aspects of this process, such as the need to build a rapport, creating a safe space for the child to explore issues, offering reassurance and working at the child's own pace. In this respect the relatively tight timescales for assessment may work as a barrier to relationship-building.

Considerable work has been done in recent years by children's organisations, researchers and practitioners to promote the participation of children in assessment and decision making, including the development of practical toolkits for the involvement of young children (Lancaster and Broadbent, 2003; Clark and Statham, 2005). Despite such efforts, however, research evidence paints a picture of the relatively limited involvement of children in assessments (Cleaver and Walker, 2004). Holland (2004) found that children were usually 'minor characters' within assessment narratives and that their opinions were frequently treated with 'ambivalence' or even 'dismissed'.

ASSESSING PARENTING CAPACITY

The dimensions set out in the second domain of the Assessment Framework can be viewed as a shorthand for the tasks and associated qualities expected of parents, and reflect earlier work in this area (Campion, 1995; Lloyd, 1999). As Jones (2001) argues, the assessment of parenting is 'firmly yoked to child outcomes', reflecting the sharpening focus on parenting in recent years. Yet, Golombok (2000) rightly observes that, while the idea of parental influence is widely accepted, knowledge is much more limited on precisely how, and to what degree, they influence children's lives. A key consideration in all discussions of parenting is how far this neutral term masks gendered assumptions regarding the roles of mothers and fathers. While the difficulties in engaging some fathers should not be underestimated, others may be valuable sources of help, while an exclusive focus on the role of mothers *risks* at best overemphasising their responsibilities and at worst results in a blaming culture (Featherstone, 2004; Daniel and Taylor, 2006).

The term *capacity* signals a need to assess potential as well as past and current performance. Capacity must also be assessed in relation to particular family relationships (for example a fraught relationship between a teenager and parent(s)), and wider environments as sources of stress and support. Information on parenting capacity is likely to be gathered by interview and observation, while several of the recommended questionnaires relate to parental stresses and functioning (Cox and Bentovim, 2000). Attachment theory represents one framework for understanding parenting, including how early attachment experiences may influence those (especially to partners) in adult life, and in turn parenting behaviour (Main and Goldwyn, 1984). Research evidence shows a mixed pattern, with elements of continuity between generations for some but also significant change for others (Golombok, 2000; Adam et al., 2004).

Baumrind's (1991) work has also been widely utilised to identify different styles of parenting. She utilises two axes, based on responsiveness or warmth and demandingness or control respectively. Different positions on these two axes combine to produce four broad types of parenting (see Baumrind, 1991, for further subdivisions). *Authoritative* parents are high on both warmth and control, setting clear boundaries and monitoring behaviour but exercising reasoning and non-punitive discipline to encourage autonomy. This style of parenting is generally regarded as producing the best outcomes for children. *Permissive or indulgent* parents combine warmth with low control, being responsive to their children's needs but relatively non-directive in relation to behaviour and lenient in terms of discipline. Low warmth and high control are characteristic of *authoritarian* parents who tend to be highly directive and expect unquestioning obedience. The fourth style, *uninvolved* or *indifferent*, scores low on both warmth and control. It may tend towards rejection or neglect of the children. Baumrind's typology was developed to categorise 'ordinary' parenting rather than specifically to address maltreatment, but it is clear that in more extreme forms all except authoritative parenting have the potential to produce these effects. While there has also been debate about the applicability of the typology across cultures, it is generally seen as a helpful aid to assessing parenting (Sorkhabi, 2005).

Concise overviews of the social work assessment of parenting capacity are provided by Jones (2001) and Hackett (2003), but insights can also be gleaned from research into the process of assessment. From a small qualitative study, Woodcock (2003) argues that social workers' constructions of parenting revolved around knowledge and the ability to meet developmental needs, routines of physical care, emotional availability and above all, the prevention of harm. She notes that, while social workers often identified psychological problems, there was little attempt to address these beyond exhorting them to change. Woodcock contends that parents' perceived level of resistance or co-operation was often the crucial element in deciding the course of an assessment, echoing Holland's (2004) observation that commitment to the assessment is frequently taken as a proxy for commitment to the child(ren). The power dynamics between professionals and families require sensitive handling, not least in a context where parents may be fearful and feel under intense scrutiny. While the Assessment Framework emphasises working in partnership, building on strengths and so forth, the spectre of child protection concerns will frequently produce a 'cat-and-mouse' quality with regard to the disclosure of information (Holland, 2004). However, research evidence suggests that these barriers can often be overcome by the skills and personal qualities of social workers (Millar and Corby, 2006). In their (2004) study, Cleaver and Walker found some evidence that the Assessment Framework had served to increase participation for families, but there remained weaknesses in terms of formally recording their views in core assessments or supplying them with copies of documents.

Parenting under pressure – parents with additional support needs

An important factor behind the increasing interest in parenting has been a focus on the impact of mental health problems, substance misuse and domestic violence on parents and, in turn, children. Research in the 1990s suggested that these played an important role in many child welfare cases, especially when present in combination, but that they were neither well understood nor addressed in practice (Cleaver et al., 1999). There has also been growing debate regarding the capacities and support needs of parents with learning disabilities.

These issues will be discussed further in later chapters (including the debates surrounding 'young carers' - see Chapter 3). At this point, however, they are considered in relation to assessment, where they are relevant in two main ways. First, background knowledge of their impact is an important factor in decision making and second, there may be particular implications for the process of assessment and how it is managed. While each of these areas has distinctive characteristics, there are also common threads. One is that assessment demands a careful balancing act to avoid over- or under-reaction. Thus, despite heightened risks to children's welfare, it is important to recognise that those suffering from mental health and other problems do not necessarily make poor parents, and that the majority of their children grow up without major ill-effects (Cleaver, 2002). Another common theme is the need for effective co-ordination between those working with children and families and those with adult health and social care expertise relevant to mental health or substance misuse. Research, however, has shown that such co-ordination is far from the norm and that different foci often lead to tensions and even conflict (Stanley et al., 2003). Some commentators believe that these difficulties may be exacerbated by the recent organisational separation between adult and children's social care services (Morris and Wates, 2006). A final common theme is the need to assess parenting in the wider contexts of poverty and social exclusion that those with additional support needs typically face (Tarleton et al., 2006).

Parents with mental health problems

Estimates of the number of children in the UK whose parents have mental health problems vary widely, from around 700,000 to 2.5 million (Morris and Wates, 2006). There is a considerable body of research examining the links between parental mental health and children's welfare, including any increased risks for the latter's mental health. Helpful reviews of the evidence on genetic vulnerability, the effects of parental beliefs and behaviour (delusion, lack of physical or emotional responsiveness, aggression) and separation due to hospitalisation are offered by Golombok (2000) and Weir (2003). Although the link is by no means uncontested (see Chapter 5), these factors are widely seen as increasing children's risks of maltreatment (Famularo et al., 1992). However, as Reder and Duncan (1999) argue, the effects of mental health problems on parenting behaviour and in turn upon children cannot be simply 'read off' from a diagnostic label, but must be carefully assessed in each individual case. This should include a consideration of children's resilience and the presence of protective factors such as other supportive adults. While the difficulties surrounding co-ordination in relation to parental mental health and child welfare are well documented (Stanley et al., 2003), there are also positive examples of schemes designed to overcome barriers and promote effective inter-agency practice (Falkov, 2002; Weir, 2003).

Assessment and parental substance misuse

It is estimated that there are 250,000–350,000 dependent children living with parental drug misuse and up to 1.3 million living with alcohol misuse in

England (Bancroft et al., 2004; Prime Minister's Strategy Unit (PMSU), 2004). The issues involved share many parallels with those described above in relation to mental health problems, including their heterogeneous nature, secrecy and stigma (Taylor and Kroll, 2004). Hogan (1998) provides a valuable, if now slightly dated review of research into parental substance misuse (PSM) and its effects on children, including their development and their own subsequent drug use. There is little doubt that PSM represents a risk factor in relation to parenting and child welfare (Bancroft et al. 2004). Cleaver (2002) identifies three broad areas of risk: erratic emotional and behavioural responses; deteriorating material and social circumstances; and a reduced capacity to attend to children's needs, ranging from preoccupation and a lack of awareness through to incapacity. Calder and Peake (2003) and Murphy and Harbin (2003) deliver informative short overviews on assessment in relation to alcohol and drug misuse respectively, with the latter offering their own addendum to the Assessment Framework.

Assessment, parenting and learning disabilities

A recent survey of adults with learning disabilities found that 1 in 15 were parents, indicating a steady rise during the past 20 years (Emerson et al., 2005). However, the survey also showed that roughly half of these children were no longer living with their parents, mirroring a wider international pattern (McConnell and Llewellyn, 2002). An unknown number of the children will have been looked after or adopted and opposition to this has become a significant campaigning issue for learning disability organisations (www.change people.co.uk). There is widespread consensus that parents with learning disabilities require additional support and this was recognised in the government's White Paper, *Valuing People* (Department of Health, 2001a). However, three contentious areas remain. The first relates to the level of support given and what might be considered 'reasonable', while a second is how support should be delivered and how the work of child care and learning disability professionals can be co-ordinated. The third factor is whether, even with support, children's needs can be adequately met. All three issues raise important questions for assessment.

The context for assessing the parenting capacity of adults with learning disabilities is a difficult one, reflecting high degrees of professional concern over possible neglect and suspicion on the part of parents that they will not be supported and may well have their children removed. Those supportive of improved treatment for parents (see for example Booth et al., 2006; Tarleton et al., 2006) highlight the following factors, namely that :

- they should not be expected to be 'perfect parents';
- parenting support should begin as early as possible, preferably during pregnancy;

- communication, especially of concerns, should be clear, and delivered in a form that is easy to understand;
- demonstration may be needed alongside verbal communication;
- additional time should be given for assessment if necessary;
- advocacy should be available in formal proceedings to represent parents' views and provide translation and mediation when necessary.

Instructive guidance on the assessment of parents with learning disabilities is given by McGaw and Newman (2005). If researchers such as Tarleton et al. (2006) are very sanguine about the prospects for children's needs being met given adequate support for parents, others are more 'sceptical', emphasising the longer-term difficulties, whether in terms of meeting the needs of older children or of sustaining levels of support (Cotson et al., 2001). Research evidence on outcomes for this group of children is mixed, with both positive aspects and problem areas (Booth and Booth, 1997).

ASSESSING FAMILY AND ENVIRONMENTAL FACTORS

The third domain of the Assessment Framework covers a diverse range of factors, although the unifying element is the need to view children's development and parenting capacity in wider contexts. These, in turn, may be seen as casting light on current circumstances and in particular identifying sources of stress and (potential) support. Within this domain, there are essentially three sub-groupings. The first is extended family, which also includes family history. It is widely documented that most parents will look first to other family members for support and problem solving (Edwards and Gillies, 2004; Leigh and Miller, 2004). For some, however, wider family involvement may be unavailable or (perceived as) intrusive or harmful. Gauging the positive and negative influences of wider family input is therefore an important part of the assessment. A second sub-grouping relates to community and social integration. These will be discussed more fully in the following chapter, but in relation to assessment may be viewed as sources of vulnerability or resilience for children and families. Jack (2000) argues that informal support within communities tends to be more effective than formal service provision. Tracy's social network map offers a way of charting relationships – via work or school, clubs, friendship, or neighbourhood in addition to family – and gauging their significance, level of contact and communication and value for support (Tracy and Whittaker, 1990). Meanwhile, Gilligan (1999) delivers an excellent overview of working with social networks, including the need to recognise that children's networks may be different to varying extents from those of their parents and siblings. The third sub-grouping, which includes income, housing and employment, relates largely though not exclusively to material circumstances. Inclusion of these dimensions can be seen as granting some recognition to the part played by material deprivation in child welfare problems. However, as Garrett (2003) observes, the general thrust of the Assessment Framework is uncritical of existing social and economic relations and is focused largely on the personal behaviour of parents. Debate over whether the Framework enshrines 'white, middle-class values' has arguably generated more heat than light. Ward (2001) refutes such claims, arguing that it is based on shared values but verbal responses can give a misleading air of consensus, which masks significant practical differences regarding, for example, forms of discipline or the importance given to education. To the extent that values may differ, the thorny question remains as to how far they should be 'respected' or whether the social work task is to 'raise aspirations'.

ASSESSMENT, 'RACE' AND ETHNICITY

The practice guidance accompanying the Assessment Framework includes additional commentary in relation to two groups, namely, black children and disabled children (see Chapter 9). In each case, this reflects an awareness of both the wider impact of discrimination on the lives of children and families and the danger of further discriminatory treatment from child care professionals and agencies.

Dutt and Phillips (2000) supply a helpful account of the ways in which issues of 'race' and ethnicity are relevant to all three of the Framework's domains. In the case of children, for example, this might entail sensitisation to the place of 'race' and ethnicity in relation to identity, an awareness of health risks linked to ethnicity and disadvantage, or the positions of different minority ethnic groups within the education system (Robinson, 2007). Assessing parenting capacity might require an acknowledgement that qualities such as emotional warmth may be demonstrated in different ways and that there may be (subtle) differences in approaches to feeding, sleeping, contact and so forth. In relation to family and environment, different understandings of family may be relevant in assessing attachments, while the environmental might include the ethnic composition of their locality and affinities rooted in diaspora communities (Barn et al., 2006).

An important element in all domains is the impact of racism (including racialised bullying or harassment), whether on children and families, their integration into wider communities, or their access to formal or informal support (Thoburn et al., 2004). In respect of cultural factors (or religion), it is important to appreciate their salience in families' lives without making assumptions that 'culture' either determines or explains their behaviour (Banks, 2001). A careful path must be negotiated between an ethnocentric adoption of 'white British' norms against which BME families may be judged as deviant and a cultural relativism that is unwilling to challenge harmful practices on the (often mistaken) grounds that they are part of a particular minority culture. Similarly, alongside the obvious problems of negative stereotyping, there are dangers of well-intentioned but naive 'positive stereotypes' – for example, of extended family support in South Asian communities or the capacities of lone African Caribbean mothers to meet competing demands in work and family life – that may work to the detriment of children. Research evidence suggests that practitioners often lack confidence in addressing issues of 'race' and ethnicity and that the quality of assessments in this regard remains highly variable (de Waal and Shergill, 2004; Wade et al., 2005).

Finally, it is important to recognise the complexities of ethnicity and discrimination. A longstanding criticism of much of the literature has been its neglect of certain minority groups such as those from Irish, Jewish, Chinese or traveller communities (Cemlyn, 1998; Garrett, 2003; Thoburn et al., 2004) and this charge can also been levelled at the Assessment Framework. The rise of asylum as a social and political issue has also produced important challenges for the assessment of unaccompanied asylum-seeking children (UASC). These may include language barriers and the lack of alternative sources of information, psychosocial problems arising from separation and possible trauma, difficulties in disclosure and the handling of information in the context of asylum claims and welfare entitlements (Mitchell, 2003a; Kohli, 2007).

ASSESSMENT IN CONTEXT – SUPPORT, MONITORING AND SURVEILLANCE

Beyond its practice implications, the Assessment Framework must be seen as part of a broader drive under New Labour both to rationalise and extend intervention in families (Garrett, 2003). As noted earlier, the Framework adopted the dimensions of child development already in use under the LAC project, but importantly extended the scope of formalised assessment to encompass all children in need. Subsequently, further rationalisation and extension have taken place via the Integrated Children's System (ICS) and the Common Assessment Framework (CAF), both of which utilise the domains and dimensions of the Assessment Framework (as with some modifications does the Integrated Assessment Framework for Scotland's Children (Scottish Executive, 2005b). The ICS is an electronic information system designed both to collate material relating to individual children and families and furnish management data (see www.everychildmatters.gov.uk/socialcare/integratedchildrenssystem/ for details). The CAF is intended to harmonise basic assessments across children's services, especially early years settings, schools, health agencies, youth support and youth justice. The rationale is to avoid unnecessary duplication (with service users having to 'retell their stories') and to facilitate an exchange of information between agencies. The level of need envisaged as appropriate for the CAF is below that of assessment for children in need or significant harm, but information gathered under the CAF (e.g. by a children's centre or school) could be incorporated under the Assessment Framework. The CAF is aimed at early identification of need or lack of progress on the five *Every Child Matters* outcomes. However, it represents a further extension of state intervention and information-gathering and, while this may in one sense be seen as supportive through its link to service provision, it also fuels concerns regarding a 'surveillance society' as discussed in the previous chapter. (See Brandon et al., 2006, for a review of the early workings of the CAF.)

CONCLUSION

In this chapter, we have reviewed the framework within which the needs of children and families are assessed. What is immediately striking is the complexity of the task. The ecological model alerts us to the wide range of factors that shape the lives of children, while in each of the domains there are difficult balances to be struck, for example, between the needs of children and parents or in addressing the impact of wider social inequalities. It is also clear that assessment can be understood and approached in different ways and that the personal qualities of social workers (and interpersonal dynamics with family members) are vital ingredients in the assessment process. Predictably perhaps, in the face of this complexity and often pressures of time, research shows that practice frequently falls short of the ideals prescribed in official guidance, whether in terms of depth, the participation of children and families, or co-ordination between professionals.

As we shall see in subsequent chapters, while any weaknesses in initial assessment are by no means irretrievable, they nonetheless exert a crucial influence over the future course of events for children and families.

GUIDE TO FURTHER READING

Probably the most comprehensive exploration of assessment can be found in Holland (2004). This can be complemented, however, by edited volumes such as those by Horwath (2001b), Ward and Rose (2002) or Calder and Hackett (2003), although this latter text is fairly demanding in places and may be of most relevance to experienced practitioners and managers.

Reading and resources for practice

In addition to the above texts, helpful practice guidance can be found in the Department of Health and others (2000) setting out of the Assessment Framework and the associated practice guidance (DH, 2000). Parmar and Spatcher's *Getting to Know Children and Their Families: A Framework of Questions to Help Social Workers Gather Appropriate Information* (Russell House) is a very user-friendly guide to assessment while, in relation to maltreatment, Fowler's *A Practitioners' Tool for Child Protection and the Assessment of Parents* (Jessica Kingsley) represents a valuable resource.

Discussion questions

What are the main challenges in ensuring children's active participation in the assessment process?

In what ways, if any, should assessment of children in black and minority ethnic families differ from that for children in white British families?

Taking disabled children as an example, consider the importance of the 'wider environment' in assessing the needs of children and improving their well-being.

Outline the main advantages and disadvantages of a 'scientific' approach to assessment.

Is conflict between adult and children's services inevitable in the assessment of parents with additional support needs?

3

SERVICES FOR CHILDREN IN NEED
Prevention and Family Support

In this chapter, following a short historical introduction, we will explore the meanings of prevention and family support, the 'philosophies' that underpin them and their practical manifestations in services for children in need. This will be followed by more detailed discussion of four key areas – short breaks, family centres, family group conferences (FGCs) and provision for 'young carers'.

Mapping the respective terrains of 'prevention' and 'family support' is challenging but at their heart lie ideas of helping families in their childrearing and avoiding the need for more coercive measures such as the removal of children. In that sense, they have an obvious affinity with Fox Harding's 'modern defence' perspective outlined in Chapter 1. Within child social care, prevention and family support relate primarily to situations categorised as 'child concern' rather than 'child protection' (Thorpe and Bilson, 1998). The threshold between these categories is neither clear nor fixed (see below), but is nonetheless important both for the way an intervention is viewed by those involved and the legal and policy framework within which practice takes place. The *lower* threshold of 'child concern' is also significant in terms of the levels of need required to trigger intervention and service provision.

HISTORICAL BACKGROUND

While we tend to think of the Victorian era as one dominated by 'child rescue', it also witnessed efforts, not least by the NSPCC, to solve problems and help keep families together (Ferguson, 2004). In more modern times, however, preventive work is customarily traced to the 1950s, when, with less punitive attitudes to poverty and influenced by Bowlby's work on attachment, the newly established Children's Departments successfully sought to extend their work beyond the domain of public care (James, 1998). Subsequently, the Children and Young Persons Act 1963 created a duty to promote the welfare of children 'by diminishing the need to receive them into or keep them in care or to bring them before a juvenile court' (s1). In addition to casework, the Act allowed material help 'in kind or exceptionally in cash' to be provided, but no new resources were allocated to local authorities and the spectre of 'less eligibility' (see below) ensured that these powers were used sparingly (Hill and Laing, 1979).

During the 1970s, an increasing awareness of child maltreatment and an interest in substitute family care led to a shift of emphasis away from preventive work. However, as explained in Chapter 1, in the following decade the pendulum swung back towards a more sympathetic view of birth families and their treatment by the state. This was reflected in Part III of the Children Act 1989, which set out a duty for local authorities to reduce the need to bring care and other legal proceedings (Schedule 2(7)). Apart from reaffirming the possibility of material help (s17(6)), the Act also specified a range of services to support families, including: advice, guidance and counselling; occupational, social, cultural or recreational activities; home help; and the provision of holidays and family centres (Schedule 2(8,9)). It was envisaged that many of these services would be supplied by voluntary organisations, some of which had taken a key role in developing family support services (Holman, 1988; 1998).

In principle, the Children Act 1989 marked an extension beyond earlier ideas of prevention, by introducing the concept of 'children in need' and specifying services that might be offered to their families. Yet, as described in Chapter 1, implementation proved difficult, leading initially to the refocusing debate and subsequently to New Labour's broader agenda of early intervention. By comparison with earlier incarnations in the 1950s or even the 1980s, however, this preventive agenda is framed more by the 'tough love' of the Third Way, with a strong, even authoritarian emphasis on parental responsibilities.

UNDERSTANDING PREVENTION

The idea of prevention is deceptively simple, captured in popular sayings such as 'a stitch in time saves nine', its rationale being that tackling problems before they escalate not only avoids unnecessary suffering but is also cost-effective, avoiding more expensive measures at a later date (Glass, 1999). Prevention has been applied to a range of possible outcomes, from maltreatment to children becoming offenders, but perhaps most commonly to preventing the need for entry into care (Holman, 1988). The idea of prevention also has an enduring appeal and is currently being emphasised throughout the UK (Scottish Executive, 2006a; Social Services Inspectorate of Wales, 2006; Department of Health, Social Services and Public Safety (DHSSPS), 2007a; HM Treasury/DfES, 2007a). Behind this appeal, however, lie complex questions and challenges, such as how to identify likely problems and subsequently how to intervene effectively.

Freeman (1999) puts forward an interesting theoretical account of prevention, arguing that it represents a form of social engineering rooted in modernist notions of science, prediction, government intervention, and faith in the power of experts. He suggests that, while support for prevention is deeply embedded in 'common sense', this often dissipates if specific measures are seen as intrusive, costly, or authoritarian. Freeman also points to the paradox whereby 'failure' of prevention often produces calls for further preventive measures – including those from welfare agencies bargaining with governments.

Levels of prevention

Originating in the field of public health, the concept of different levels has dominated understandings of policy in relation to prevention (Hardiker et al., 1991; Little and Mount, 1999). While the details of different models may vary, they find common ground in the idea that prevention starts with relatively 'universal' services for general populations, becoming increasingly targeted and specialised as the needs of children and families become greater. It is worth noting that prevention has historically been related both to issues of child welfare and (deviant) behaviour, although the emphasis has varied in different eras (Holman, 1998). An early model depicting three levels of prevention is set out in Box 3.1.

BOX 3.1

Levels of prevention

- Primary prevention – services providing general support to families and helping to reduce pressures arising from poverty, housing problems or ill health;
- Secondary prevention – offering specialised help when children have been identified as 'at risk' or vulnerable;
- Tertiary prevention – avoiding the negative consequences of children spending long periods in substitute care.

From: Parker (1980)

In addition to educational campaigns, Parker's primary level of prevention could comprise both 'universal' services such as health, education or child benefit and more targeted provision such as means-tested benefits or tax credits, social housing, or area-based programmes such as SureStart. At this level, although there is no 'child concern', there is recognition that deprivation represents a 'risk factor'. Parker's secondary prevention again covers a wide range, and Hardiker et al. (1991), for example, divide this category into two, depending on whether the risk is perceived as low or high (i.e. entry to public care). It is this secondary level of prevention that constitutes our focus in this chapter. Tertiary prevention applies following entry to public care and usually relates to finding children a permanent home, whether with their birth or extended family, or through foster care or adoption.

The concept of levels of prevention is helpful in two main ways. First, it provides a way of understanding 'progressive difficulty' for children and families and invites consideration of how this can be halted by strengthening provision at each level. Second, it facilitates a broader understanding of service provision within a particular type of welfare regime (Hardiker et al., 1991). Attitudes to prevention can be broadly linked to different political perspectives. For instance, strong primary prevention tends to be favoured by the centre-left, on the grounds that universal services (such as the NHS) promote collective solidarity and avoid stigma for those using them. By contrast, those on the political right tend to favour targeted services at the higher levels, arguing that universal services are wasteful and should be offered on a private or voluntary basis rather than by the state. Those on the more radical left may also oppose extensive state provision, regarding this as controlling and oppressive of less powerful groups.

PRINCIPLES OF FAMILY SUPPORT

Most writers on family support acknowledge that it is an elusive concept, in part because the term serves to describe both an approach to child welfare and a set of services (Tilbury, 2005). Frost (2003) identifies four key principles in family support:

1 support for all families;
2 no stigma attached;
3 support across the board (wide-ranging and joined up);
4 accessible.

Desire to avoid 'stigmatising' families is reflected in the idea that parenting is challenging and may require additional help, and a preference for universal provision and voluntary sector involvement in service delivery. Crucially, there is an emphasis on building relationships and working in partnership with parents, distinguishing the family support ethos from wider views of prevention (Quinton, 2004). Yet, as Broadhurst (2003) observes, knowing precisely what makes seeking help stigmatising is extremely difficult and it is important to recognise that the social origins of stigma are likely to run deep, whether in terms of parental failure or the already stigmatised identities of marginalised groups.

Considering the meaning of 'family' is particularly important in relation to family support because of the dangers of subsuming the interests of individual members under this umbrella term, not only in relation to gender and parenting but, for example, when the interests of children and parents diverge or in the treatment of siblings (Frost, 2003). It is also important to consider the role of the extended family, whether through formal mechanisms such as the FGC (see below) or more routinely.

Support, too, is a complex term, not least due to its subjective aspects on the part of recipients. In addition to its connotations of helping people cope with difficulties, support may also be linked to agendas of change. In relation to the content of support, Quinton (2004) identifies five key elements:

1 emotional support and comfort;
2 advice;
3 practical help;
4 resources;
5 specialist services.

Both the philosophy of family support and resource pressures would dictate that, where possible, support should come from informal (family, friends and neighbours), or semi-formal (local voluntary projects or groups) sources, with involvement from formal, especially statutory, services only when strictly necessary.

SOCIAL NETWORKS AND SOCIAL CAPITAL

A key aspect of the ecological approach to child welfare is to recognise wider social networks as (potential) sources of both support and stress for families (Jack, 2000). Some of these may be fairly specific to particular families, for example, relationships with extended family, friends and neighbours, whether heavenly or hellish, while others can relate to broader area characteristics, such as facilities, local services, transport links, and 'appearance'.

In recent years, there has been growing interest in 'social capital' as a resource. Amid its varied and contested meanings, the core elements relate to social cohesion and community involvement or spirit (Halpern, 2004). These, in turn, rest on the quality of social relations based on trust, reciprocity, and co-operation, reflected in a thriving local organisation. In a context where it is widely perceived to have declined, policy makers have seen the restoration of social capital as a desirable goal (Putnam, 2000). While there is a danger that this focus may divert attention away from structural inequalities, there are clearly advantages to be gained from vibrant communities, something long recognised by advocates of prevention (Holman, 1988; Jack and Jordan, 1999). Moreover, as Jack (2005) argues, social capital can be outward-looking and challenging as well as strengthening internal bonds and networks. Despite their potential advantages, however, strategies based around the building of social capital remain largely unproven, with the effects of community projects both difficult to evaluate and replicate (Smith, 1999). (An interesting analysis of the relationships between children, families and communities can be found in J. Barnes et al., 2006.)

FAMILY SUPPORT SERVICES

Although our main focus rests with the family support offered by child social care agencies, it is important to remember the wide range of provision from other organisations, whether voluntary, private or statutory. This would include the work of health visitors and agencies working with parents in the fields of mental health and substance misuse. Such services are important in their own right, but also as referral routes and for assessment and planning. Little and Mount (1999) argue that there has been a steady rise in family support since the 1950s, a trend arguably boosted by the increasing focus on parenting.

Many services are targeted primarily at (new) parents with young children, typically involving experienced parents acting as volunteers in visiting new and/or vulnerable parents, offering a mixture of practical help, advice and emotional support (Armstrong and Hill, 2001). More structured parenting programmes are also seen as a good means of delivering family support (Moran and Ghate, 2005). The day care sector – comprising nursery education, nurseries, play groups and childminders – also provides important resources, with children in need often 'placed and paid for' to address developmental needs, assist with monitoring and sometimes to give 'respite' for parents (Dillon and Statham, 1998; Steele, 2000). This mixed economy of care poses challenges for volunteers and those in direct caring roles, not least in being prepared to pass on information or concerns to social workers without being seen as 'spies' for statutory services. While most services are aimed at young children, it is also important to remember that *early* intervention may relate to the onset of problems rather than age and is thus highly relevant to preventive services for adolescents (Cleaver, 1996; Biehal, 2005).

DELIVERING FAMILY SUPPORT

The provision of family support in the UK has largely been framed by the struggle to square the circle between the potentially wide definition of 'children in need' and comparatively limited resources. Two major research studies by Aldgate and Tunstill (1995) and Colton et al. (1995) catalogued the difficulties of implementing family support provision in England and Wales respectively, while later research revealed similar difficulties in Northern Ireland and Scotland (Higgins, 2000; McGhee and Waterhouse, 2002).

The Children Act 1989 enshrined a proactive approach to children in need, requiring local authorities to publicise services, and to carry out needs assessments to inform service planning. Studies found, however, that many local authorities struggled with this task, in part due to poor information systems, but perhaps more importantly because of a widespread fear that being proactive would 'open the floodgates', stimulating a demand for services that could not be satisfied. While some agencies welcomed the broader definition of children in need and the discretion it afforded them, the more common response was to retreat to the 'core business' of child protection, with family support often regarded as 'optional and a luxury' (Aldgate and Tunstill, 1995).

Two groups of children in particular suffered from the prioritisation of child protection concerns, namely disabled children and those from poor families. The Children Act required local authorities to establish a register of disabled children but progress was extremely slow due to lack of co-ordination and common definition between health, education and social care agencies (see Chapter 9). Studies also found significant confusion regarding whether disability itself constituted a criterion for need or only in conjunction with other factors (Aldgate and Tunstill, 1995). Similar issues faced children from poor families, for while in principle material circumstances constituted a potential basis for need, in practice local authorities tended to give them the lowest priority unless the children were demonstrably 'at risk' (Colton et al., 1995).

An underlying problem in relation to provision of family support is the principle of 'less eligibility' – originally a Poor Law term meaning that those in receipt of state help should not be treated more favourably than those who are 'independent'. Any significant provision of help to poor parents runs the risk of contravening this principle by 'rewarding' those who are seen as failing, even abusive, parents (Featherstone, 2006). This is partly countered by pragmatic concerns, namely that denying support may prove more expensive in the long term, but nonetheless ensures that family support tends to be limited and comes 'with strings attached'.

IN THE SHADOW OF CHILD PROTECTION?

While originating primarily from a critique of child protection practice, the refocusing debate (see Chapter 1) exhorted social workers to become more 'support-minded' in two main ways. First, there should be a significant re-categorisation of 'borderline' referrals, with research suggesting that many cases dealt with under s47 could be more appropriately and effectively handled under s17 (Thorpe and Bilson, 1998; Brandon et al., 1999). Second, those still classed as child protection (under s47) should encompass a broader enquiry into children's needs rather than simply a 'forensic' investigation into allegations of abuse.

Questions remained, however, as to whether any changes would mark a fundamental shift in relationships between the state and families of children in need. Research reveals a mixed picture, with families appreciative of a less intrusive approach, but with decision making still, in practice, largely governed by assessments of risk, despite efforts to expunge the term from the official vocabulary (Platt, 2001). Spratt and Callan (2004) argue that at a deeper level, support and surveillance are ever present in the UK system, which is highly legalistic and where child protection and family support services are generally provided, or overseen, by the same agencies. Despite this, however, they also argue that significantly different emphases are possible, with a family support orientation tending to combine covert surveillance and high engagement as compared with the overt surveillance/low engagement often associated with child protection. Crucially, the authors contend that skilled practitioners can overcome the contradictions of their role and that families' experiences are highly dependent on the personality and performance of the social worker involved.

CHILDREN IN NEED – A PROFILE

Within the child care literature, children in need remain a somewhat shadowy group, both under-researched and the under-theorised by comparison with looked after children and the victims of maltreatment. Differences of legal responsibility and (perceived) accountability ensure that poor provision of family support is unlikely to be headline news or the subject of a major inquiry. Most research on children in need (see below) has entailed evaluation of particular projects or initiatives, with a limited, and mostly short-term, examination of the outcomes for children (Little and Mount, 1999).

Until the introduction of the 'Children in Need' survey in 2000, there was no systematic data collection on services for this group. This and subsequent surveys have helped to build a profile of children in need, but are severely limited by their focus on 'activity and expenditure' within the census week. For example, they contain no background data on families apart from their ethnicity (which is not always recorded) and afford only broad-brush categorisation of the reasons for assessment as children in need. The most recent snapshot survey, undertaken in 2005 (DfES, 2006a), shows that there were approximately 386,000 children in England receiving services (though not all in the census week), a figure that has varied little since the first census. Of these, roughly 313,000 were being supported independently or in their families (the remainder being looked after children – see Chapter 6). Accounting for 30 per cent of cases, the most frequent reason given for receipt of services was abuse and neglect, the other main categories being family dysfunction (14 per cent), disability (12 per cent), family in acute distress (12 per cent) and socially unacceptable behaviour (7 per cent).

A telling statistic from the 2005 census for advocates of preventive work is that, while those supported independently or in their families comprise eight out of every ten children in need, they account for only a third of the total expenditure. However, the Holy Grail of shifting resources from child protection and looked after children to family support remains elusive.

THE EFFECTIVENESS OF FAMILY SUPPORT SERVICES

As Tilbury (2005) suggests, family support tends to be viewed as a self-evidently 'good thing', but there are significant challenges in demonstrating that it 'works'– either in general terms or in relation to specific services. Preventing entry into public care remains arguably the most popular measure, but it is always difficult to show that this would have occurred in the absence of service provision. Commentators, especially proponents of 'evidence-based practice' have frequently noted the paucity of high-quality research in relation to the effectiveness of family support (Little and Mount, 1999). They point to the dominance of 'case study' evaluations of individual projects or services that often lack one or more of the following factors: (randomised) control groups for comparison, the use of standardised measures and follow-up. However, even when such features are present, the tasks of demonstrating and, more so, explaining effectiveness remain daunting, given the range of variables even within projects and their complex interaction with wider social contexts. Similarly, while it is necessary to consider outcomes over time (short-lived benefits may be seen as limited in value), the methodological challenges of demonstrating and explaining effects also tend to increase through the life courses of children and families and changing economic and social climates.

Whatever its ultimate limitations, there is a now a considerable body of research evidence on family support services. In a wide-ranging meta-analysis of studies in the USA, Layzer et al. (2001: A5–42) offer 'some encouraging messages as well as some warnings'. On the one hand, they conclude that overall 'family support services produce small but significant effects across a range of outcomes for parents and children'. However, on the other hand they also point out that many projects produce no measurable gains and that there is no single model that is consistently effective. Layzer et al. also contend that some of the core premises of a family support philosophy – such as providing non-targeted services and working largely through parents – tend to be less successful.

The broad message that emerges from research in the UK is in many ways similar (Buchanan, 2002; Statham and Biehal, 2005). A fairly constant finding is that, while services are widely perceived as beneficial by parents and workers, evidence on measurable improvement for parents and children or cost-effectiveness is more equivocal (Little and Mount, 1999; Frost et al., 2000). Caution is also justified because sampling methods often exclude those parents who have ceased to attend or have never attended the services in question (Statham and Holtermann, 2004). Finally, researchers have frequently noted the limited impact of family support in a context of wider structural inqualities (Moran and Ghate, 2005). 'Effectiveness' can, of course, be viewed through a broader lens, as a means of promoting social cohesion and valuing marginalised groups, but this rests ultimately on moral and political judgements.

FAMILY SUPPORT FOR THOSE WITH ADDITIONAL SUPPORT NEEDS

Effective family support is particularly important where parents have additional needs (see Chapter 2), but these are also challenging for various reasons. Services for such families must strike a balance between 'normalisation' – recognising that difficulties may be similar to those faced by other families – and understanding the specific challenges arising from mental health problems and so forth. This in turn, raises questions about the capacity of mainstream family support services and the need for more specialised services. Wider recognition of these issues has given rise to a burgeoning literature and a small but growing network of dedicated resources. Morris and Wates (2006) furnish an excellent overview of legal and policy issues, research evidence and examples of good practice in respect of parents with additional support needs. Other relevant sources are given in Table 3.1.

FAMILY SUPPORT FOR THE 'HARD-TO-REACH'

Providing services for families deemed 'hard-to-reach', due to their lack of engagement with services, represents one of the thornier aspects of prevention and family support. The rationale for improving engagement can be seen as an uneasy amalgam of support and surveillance, of a desire to satisfy unmet needs and to ensure supervision of the 'dangerous classes'. This duality is reflected in the make-up of 'hard-to-reach' families, comprising both those who might wish

Table 3.1   Sources for parents with additional support needs

Additional parental support needs arising from:	Sources
mental health	Sheppard (2001); Bates and Coren (2006)
learning disabilities/difficulties	Booth and Booth (1999); Tarleton et al. (2006); Department of Health/DfES (2007)
physical disability	Wates (2002a); Olsen and Clarke (2003); Olsen and Tyers (2004)
alcohol misuse	B. Williams (2004); Turning Point (2006)
drug misuse	Kroll and Taylor (2003); Harbin and Murphy (2006); Advisory Council on Misuse of Drugs (2007)
HIV/AIDS	Knight and Aggleton (1999); Lewis (2001)

to engage but are prevented by various 'barriers' and those with a strong desire to avoid engagement (Gustafsson and Driver, 2005). The label hard-to-reach can arguably be applied to any group under-represented as service users: fathers, certain BME communities (including travellers), asylum-seekers, homeless families and parents with additional support needs as described above.

Research studies have cast some light on the perspectives of the 'hard-to-reach', although unsurprisingly perhaps, such families are also frequently hard-to-reach for researchers. Broadhurst (2003) highlights a number of factors, including differences of perspective on the nature of family problems, reportedly juxtaposing parental concerns over practical and material help with professionals' 'talk' focused on emotions and behaviour (though Tunstill and Aldgate, 2000, report a contrary view, namely that service users found talking and listening valuable). Other stated reasons included being 'too busy', lacking trust and resenting intrusion from someone perceived as living a comfortable life far removed from those of respondents. Resistance to social work involvement has been found to be particularly strong among teenage mothers, especially those (formerly) in the care system (Corlyon and McGuire, 1999). While persisting with support in such circumstances can be challenging, it remains important because those lacking formal support have frequently been found to also have lower levels of informal support (Quinton, 2004).

FAMILY SUPPORT, 'RACE' AND ETHNICITY

While the reasons are complex and defy simple labels of discrimination, research studies have frequently found that BME families have received less 'preventive' work (Barn, 1993) or less appropriate services than white families (Thoburn et al., 2000a). The quality of services for BME families must be seen in the wider context of racialised inequalities, and the challenge of alleviating rather than exacerbating the effects of material deprivation, racism and discrimination. The challenge includes publicising and raising awareness of services, not only through the use of appropriate languages, but via proactive contact with community groups. Availability of interpreters has been found to be limited outside of formal meetings such as child protection conferences (Humphreys et al., 1999). Similarly, concerns have been raised about the training given to interpreters, for instance, in whether they have an advocacy role beyond simple translation (Richards and Ince, 2000).

In providing services, many of the issues, such as understanding 'culture' in flexible ways and avoiding stereotypes, are similar to those described in Chapter 2 and need not be repeated here. Becher and Husain (2003) furnish an excellent review of the barriers that may be faced by South Asian families and examples of good practice in overcoming them. There are competing views, and no simple rules, on the value of ethnically dedicated provision and ethnic 'matching' of workers and service (Gray, 2003; Thoburn et al., 2004). Thus, there may be gains from shared culture and understanding, while conversely, some BME families may prefer not to work with someone from their own community (Brandon et al., 1999; Husain, 2006). There is also a danger that separate provision and/or the matching of workers by ethnicity will allow 'mainstream' services and majority workers to avoid the changes necessary to offer an ethnically sensitive service to all users.

Treatment of families seeking asylum has been particularly controversial. Reflecting an the overriding concern to deter immigration, the Asylum and Immigration (Treatment of Claimants etc.) Act 2002, s9, denies any support to failed asylum-seekers. Provision of help under s17 of the Children Act 1989 is forbidden under this legislation because it entails giving help to families as well as children. The only help available is for the children to become looked after (Cunningham and Tomlinson, 2005). While the intention is to exert crude pressure on families to leave the country, this measure is completely at odds with the Children Act principle of keeping families together (CRAE, 2007).

SHORT BREAKS – RELIEVING STRESSES?

Short breaks (the term respite care has largely been superseded due to its connotations that caring is a 'burden') for children are designed primarily to relieve stresses on families, and have been most widely employed for those with disabled children (see Chapter 9 and Fry, 2005, for a helpful historical overview). Such breaks may be achieved through day care, sitting services or, most commonly, placement away from home. More attention has been paid in recent times to ensuring that the experience is positive for children also, perhaps through offering them new activities or expanding their social networks, but separation is often difficult for children and families alike. Short breaks have also been seen as a way of obviating the need for entry into public care and as such are subject to 'gatekeeping' processes both in terms of resources and the 'necessity' of offering short breaks.

Under the Children Act 1989, short breaks were promoted as a valuable resource for family support and an attempt was made to distance them from the bureaucracy and perceived stigma associated with the care system. Importantly, regulations allowed for a series of placements to be treated as a single placement, provided no one episode lasted more than four weeks and the annual total did not exceed 90 days (subsequently extended to 120 days). Informality between parents, carers and workers is seen as a way of combating stigma, maximising parental feelings of control and helping to lessen feelings of separation (Howard, 2005) Similarly, it is argued that placements should be managed with a 'light touch' rather than the full regulations that apply to looked after children. Some authorities have started to offer short breaks under s17 as a means of avoiding these requirements, while others have operated with 'slimmed-down' regulations in respect of reviews, medicals and care plans (Fry, 2005). However, there are doubts about the legality of such measures and concerns that the light touch can have adverse consequences for the quality of provision and the planning and scrutiny of placements (Statham and Greenfield, 2005).

Research on short-term placements for children in need has painted a broadly positive picture with some caveats. Parents have been overwhelmingly positive about the value of short breaks, while studies have also found gains in their self-esteem and awareness as parents (Sheppard, 2004). Researchers have also been keen to emphasise that there is minimal 'abuse' (i.e. over-use) of short breaks on the part of parents (S. Smith, 2005). Aldgate and Bradley (1999) identify several factors for successful placements, namely, that they should be tailored to individual needs and provide continuity in terms of carers and clear understanding and communication between the parties involved, including through written agreements. Their study reported the views of children as more ambivalent, although tending to become more positive over time.

Alongside widespread appreciation, studies have identified a number of problems associated with short breaks, perhaps above all, their limited availability (Steele, 2000; McConkey et al., 2004). Studies have also found weaknesses in provision for BME families, including in the recruitment of carers to meet the cultural, religious and language needs of children (Flynn, 2002). Aldgate and Bradley (1999) suggest that short breaks may be denied to some of the neediest families on the grounds that their 'chaotic' lifestyles would prevent arrangements from working smoothly. Finally, concerns have been expressed regarding inflexibility in short-break provision, whether in terms of the application of age limits or rules proscribing siblings accompanying children on placement (Dowling and Dolan, 2001). Some studies of short-break provision have highlighted their apparent success in preventing the entry of children into public care, but it remains difficult to demonstrate conclusively a causal link (Statham and Greenfield, 2005).

Roughly 15,000 children in the UK experienced short-term placements in 2006,[1] roughly three-quarters of whom were disabled. In England, most were aged over 10 and boys outnumbered girls by almost two to one. Family-based care is the majority form in Wales and Northern Ireland, but a minority in England and Scotland.

FAMILY CENTRES

The origins of family centres are generally traced to developments in the late 1970s and 1980s when day care, play group and nursery services began to widen their remit to include provision for parents, although in practice this has mainly involved mothers (see below). Other precursors include family advice centres. Amid their considerable diversity, it is still possible to identify a distinctive 'philosophy'. Two core elements in what some have referred to as the 'family centre *movement*' (Warren-Adamson, 2006) are first, location in areas of deprivation, and second, the offer of accessible, non-stigmatising services. Family centres became a focus for major voluntary organisations as they began to shift their efforts away from looked after children and towards preventive work. As noted earlier, centres were highlighted in the Children Act 1989 and regarded as a key site for the delivery of family support services.

Family centre models

Despite their common elements, family centres have always been extremely diverse, reflecting differences in evolutionary histories, their location in the voluntary or statutory sector and ethos. Warren-Adamson (2006) lists the following services that may be available at family centres:

- day care for the under-fives;
- mother and toddler groups;
- self-help groups for mothers and fathers;
- facilities for counselling, group work and family therapy;
- parenting and domestic skills;
- meeting places for community groups and voluntary organisations;
- centre for (supervised) contact;
- a focal point for those working with families.

---

[1]Department for Education and Skills (2007c) Children Looked After by Local Authorities, Year Ending 31 March 2006. Table R, London: DfES. Scottish Executive (2006) Looked After Children 2005–06: Tables 1.23, 1.24, Edinburgh: Scottish Executive. Local Government Data Unit, Wales (2006) Personal Social Services Statistics Wales 2006: Children, Cardiff: LGDU. Northern Ireland Statistics and Research Agency (2006) Children Order Statistical Bulletin 2006 Table 2.8. Belfast: Community Information Branch.

Services are often portrayed as a continuum that loosely approximates different levels of prevention, ranging from facilities for community groups to statutory child protection work. The spectrum includes a small number of residential family centres where, as the name suggests, families will live for a period of time, usually as part of an extended assessment of, and/or training in, parenting skills (Lindsay and Morgan, 2006). Most family centres offer a range of services, although some are more specialised and operate towards one end of the continuum only. Holman (1988) identified three distinct models of family centre. The *client-focused* model concentrates largely on work, such as assessment or therapy, undertaken by professional staff with families referred due to child protection concerns. By contrast, the *neighbourhood* model allows open access to local families and encourages volunteers to participate in activities. A third *community development* model extends this by encouraging community action and local 'ownership' of the centre through involvement in its management and decision making. Smith (1996) subsequently suggested a fourth model built on adult education. All these models are, of course, ideal typical and can be integrated to a greater or lesser degree.

The various models for family centres are underpinned by divergent understandings of the relationship between the state, family and community. 'Open access' is seen by its advocates as the best means of empowering families and avoiding the stigma associated with state child welfare services (Smith, 1996). During the 1990s, however, the open-access ethos came under increasing pressure as local authorities sought to target scarce resources towards families where child welfare concerns were already identified, while research cast doubt on the effectiveness of open-access centres in reaching those most in need or building community resources (Pithouse and Holland, 1999).

More radical attempts to create user-led services are always likely to raise concerns regarding their 'accountability', and it is perhaps unsurprising that in Jordan's (1997) case study on partnership, family centre provision lay at the heart of disputes over 'professional control'. Further issues arise in relation to the perceived accessibility of family centre provision for all families and family members. Butt and Box (1998) found that BME families were often under-represented as users and that this was more pronounced when there were few or no workers from similar backgrounds or services that recognised cultural differences.

Gender and family centres

Family centres have also been a focal point for debates on gender within child social care. Ghate et al. (2000) refer to these centres' 'overwhelming sense of feminisation' and the 'physical and conceptual' absence of fathers, noting that male attendance is low and largely confined to 'unusual men' such as lone parents or main carers. In principle, there are strong reasons for increasing fathers' participation, whether in terms of their potential value for children, on the basis of rights or promoting shared parenting. Yet, as Daniel and Taylor (2006) contend, men often represent risks as well as assets, in some instances directly to children, but also to their (ex) partners through domestic violence. Such concerns partly explain the development of family centres as 'spaces' or 'sanctuaries' for women, although clearly the challenge is to avoid a negative stereotyping that disadvantages all men.

A key element of family support is working with parents to meet their own needs, to boost skills and self-esteem on the assumption that this will have indirect benefits for children. In practice, given the highly gendered nature of parenting, the emphasis of work has customarily focused on encouraging women to develop other aspects of their lives while facilitating men to become more practically involved as parents. According to Ghate et al. (2000), centres face a dilemma in organising activities for a 'parent' between a gender neutrality that effectively pressures men to become 'pseudo-women' and gender differentiation which leads to reinforcing more traditional masculine roles.

The effectiveness of family centres

Beyond the lack of consensus as to their purpose, evaluating the effectiveness of family centres has faced the challenges described earlier in respect of prevention and family support more broadly. Studies show consistently high levels of user satisfaction but, as Smith (1996) notes, this may be based on views of services and facilities rather than the official goals of 'empowerment' or 'prevention' and a perception that family centre staff are more supportive and less 'threatening' than local authority social workers. Less attention has been given to child outcomes, although Pithouse et al. (2001) judged the work of a specialist centre broadly successful in preventing the re-abuse of children. They also highlighted an important feature of the family centre, namely the synergy that arises from having a range of activities taking place on the same site. Similarly, the potential for family centres to offer a therapeutic 'holding environment' has often been highlighted (Schofield and Brown, 1999; McMahon and Ward, 2001).

The emergence of children's centres (and extended schools) has raised questions regarding the future of family centres, with Tunstill et al. (2006) reporting that some have been or are in the process of being redesignated as children's centres, with others carrying on as family centres and some ceasing to operate.

FAMILY GROUP CONFERENCES

FGCs represent a fairly recent innovation in child welfare within the UK, being introduced in 1991. In its simplest terms, the FGC creates a forum in which a child's immediate network of family and significant others meets and attempts to formulate a plan that will address relevant concerns regarding the child. FGCs originated in New Zealand, where traditional Maori practices for family problem solving were adopted by the state in the late 1980s, and have since spread to at least 17 countries, where they function predominantly in two main areas, child welfare and youth justice (Nixon et al., 2005).

FGCs fit particularly well with Fox Harding's 'modern defence of the birth family' and have been strongly promoted by the Family Rights Group (FRG) and by Children First in Scotland. Conferences involve a shift in decision making power from the state and professionals to the family, although the extent and nature of 'empowerment' remain contentious (see below). In principle, the state's lower key role fits well with ideas of family support, working with 'strengths' rather than 'deficits', while FGCs can be seen as preventive if they obviate the need for (further) state intervention. The stages of the FGC are set out in Table 3.2.

Family group conferences as empowerment?

There has been considerable debate regarding the extent to which the FGC process (as practised in the UK) represents a genuine 'empowerment' of families. In the policy domain, it may be asked whether family 'self-reliance' is viewed as a means of reducing state expenditure, but Lupton (1998) found no evidence that family help or resources were being substituted for state provision. In relation to practice, the major issue is whether the FGC merely gives the appearance of family empowerment while control remains with the professionals who must agree any plan. Within these parameters, however, there may be significant variation in terms of the professionals' willingness to accept plans and in their exertion of influence over those plans. For example, Holland et al. (2005) found instances where workers tried to steer families in terms of options to consider, became involved in formulating plans, or changed the plan after the meeting.

In part, such difficulties stem from the 'marginal' position of FGCs within the UK child welfare system. From her survey (excluding Scotland), Brown (2003) concludes that FGCs remain heavily reliant on local initiatives and that availability is highly variable. In 2001, 38 per cent of local authorities were operating FGCs, with Brown estimating that their rapid growth during the 1990s had by then peaked. Crucially, while the government has often made encouraging pronouncements (DfES, 2006b), FGCs have no legal status in the UK and it has been made clear that they cannot replace child

Table 3.2 Family group conference – stages (Family Rights Group)

Stage	Key steps
1 Referral	• decision to hold conference • appointment of independent co-ordinator
2 Preparation	• identification of family members and significant others to participate • practical arrangements • decision on use of advocates or supporters
3 Meeting	
a) professionals provide information	• share concerns • explain duties • set out tasks of the FGC
b) private family time	• professionals and co-ordinator withdraw (though co-ordinator remains available) leaving family three basic tasks (i) to agree a plan (ii) to make a contingency plan (iii) to agree how to monitor and review the plan
c) agreeing the plan	• co-ordinator and professionals rejoin • agree plan(s) (unless there is risk of significant harm) • negotiate resources
4 Reviewing the plan	• monitoring to be provided by family and/or professionals • possible review conference

Reproduced by kind permission of the Family Rights Group.

protection conferences (HM Government, 2006a). Studies suggest that the main contribution of FGCs is in respect of low-risk or borderline child protection cases (Brown, 2003). Despite such limitations, research has painted a broadly favourable picture of FGCs (Marsh and Crow, 1998). They have been found to yield 'creative solutions', with extended family members and significant others either providing help or changing family dynamics in such a way as to help alleviate seemingly intractable situations. Holland et al. (2005) report that, while FGCs can be highly emotional, this often has therapeutic consequences as conflicts are resolved. In contrast to fears that certain family members would dominate proceedings, they also conclude that FGCs did have some potential to 'democratise' relationships through their focus on the child and by the introduction of ground rules relating to hearing everyone's point of view. Bell and Wilson (2006) found that children who participated in FGCs were generally, though by no means invariably, positive about the experience and the outcomes.

If FGCs have been a valuable innovation in child welfare, it is nonetheless important not to regard them as a panacea. Research in the UK has generally been small-scale and there is little evidence to date on outcomes in the medium or longer term. Similarly, while there may be advantages to incorporating FGCs into the mainstream of child welfare provision, experience from New Zealand shows that problems such as professional control and a lack of resources may persist (Connolly, 2006).

'YOUNG CARERS' AND THEIR FAMILIES

Debates surrounding 'young carers' highlight the importance of social construction in conceptualising children's needs. For while the practical tasks and emotional issues are far from new, the emergence of a distinctive discourse has brought increased recognition from researchers, charities, politicians and policy-makers. The contentious nature of the term young carer revolves around two main questions, first, what distinguishes them from other children and young people, and second, what does the term signify about their relationships with parents. Becker (2000: 378) offers the following definition.

> Young carers are children and young persons under 18 who provide, or intend to provide, care, assistance or support to another family member. They carry out, often on a regular basis, significant or substantial caring tasks and assume a level of responsibility, which would usually be associated with an adult.

Typically, family member(s) have needs arising from physical disability or illness, mental health problems or substance misuse. As Becker (2000) observes, individual situations depend on the extent and nature of young carers' tasks and responsibilities and the availability of supporting services. They are also mediated by factors such as gender, age, culture and families' material circumstances.

Needs and numbers

The identification of young carers as a group emerged in part from the wider recognition of carers during the 1980s and 1990s (Becker et al., 1998). The process of 'discovery' is readily apparent in the rapidly changing estimates of the number of young carers in the UK, which rose from around 10,000 in the mid-1990s to approximately 175,000 currently (Barnardo's, 2006). Accurate estimates are, of course, rendered extremely problematic due to the private nature of caring activities and the inherent difficulties in measuring their psychological components. Studies show that young carers are more likely to be girls and that at least half of their families are headed by a lone parent (Aldridge and Becker, 2003).

Research has found that young carers may be signficantly involved in domestic and practical tasks, personal care, looking after siblings and sometimes assisting with medical care e.g. medication. Figures from the 2001 census showed that the time commitment for 18,000 young carers reached 20 hours per week, with 9,000 exceeding 50 hours. Equally important, however, is the provision of emotional support and associated 'worry work' (Fawcett et al., 2004). The implications for young carers may include adverse effects on education, career aspirations and opportunities for play, leisure or friendships – for many, the essence of 'being a child'. Young carers commonly report a lack of understanding from peers and adults including teachers and social workers (Thomas et al., 2003). Cree (2003) found many young carers recounted problems in sleeping and eating, and especially among girls, a significant incidence of self-harm and suicidal thoughts. It is easy, however, to exaggerate the detrimental consequences of being a young carer, which may often be quite limited and significantly offset by the positive aspects of gaining responsibility and maturity while developing close family relationships. Thomas et al. (2003) argue tellingly that, while young carers may experience parenting deficits to varying degrees, they rarely wish to be 'rescued'. Aldridge and Becker (2003) also caution against simplistic ideas of 'role reversal' or young carers' 'parentification', pointing to the many ways in which parents may continue to fulfil aspects of their role.

Young carers and (family) support

Studies have consistently highlighted the lack of support received by young carers and their families. Reasons for this may include the 'hidden' nature of young carers' activities and concerns, a lack of awareness and proactivity on the part of agencies, stigma and a reluctance to seek help due to fears regarding state intervention. Research also shows that, when contact is made, young carers often find services either lacking or unhelpful (Thomas et al., 2003). Recurrent complaints relate to assumptions being made about young carers' ability to cope and a mismatch between 'adult' responsibilities and a lack of consultation (Morgan, 2006). For BME families, these problems have been found to be exacerbated by a lack of cultural awareness or sensitivity (Jones et al., 2002). Aldridge and Becker (2003) list the key requirements as follows:

- for young carers to articulate the nature and extent of caring responsibilities;
- for professionals to recognise the positives and strengths in the family;
- to reconcile support with fears about intervention;
- for young carers to have someone to talk to;
- to provide information relating to parental problems e.g. mental health, HIV.

Arguably the thorniest aspect of service provision has been the perceived lack of co-ordination between children's and adult services, whether in terms of legislation, policy or practice (see Aldridge and Becker 2003: 175–198). While carers' rights to assessment were strengthened under the Carers and Disabled Children Act 2000, this applies only to those aged 16 or over, thereby excluding the majority of young carers. Moreover, the right applies only to assessment of need rather than provision. Despite official guidance, it has proved difficult to ensure that adult care assessments take into account needs as parents (Wates, 2002a), while provision for 'children in need' under the Children Act 1989 tends to be set in the context of child development concerns and parental 'failure'.

These difficulties have attracted considerable fire from disability activists, who often dispute the term young carer on the basis that it arises only from a failure to adequately support disabled parents in their role (Morris, 2003; Olsen and Tyers, 2004). Over the past few years, there has been something of a rapprochement between this position and those advocating for young carers, coalescing around the need for a 'family' approach that recognises both the rights of parents to support and that children are still likely to have separate needs as young carers.

While statutory services have received relatively few plaudits from young carers, the approximately 230 support groups in the UK (www.youngcarer.com), mostly run by voluntary organisations, have been regarded more favourably, for their provision of 'space' away from home and opportunities for contact and mutual understanding (Aldridge and Becker, 2003).

CONCLUSION

In this chapter, we have explored the concepts of prevention and family support as they relate to services for children in need, both in general terms and by looking at four specific areas of provision. Ideas of prevention have become more prominent in recent years, albeit increasingly linked to the aims of the social investment state and the reduction of anti-social behaviour. Their strong 'common sense' appeal, allied to worries about the overemphasis on child protection, have also seen an international trend towards family support, especially in the USA and Australia (Tilbury, 2005). Yet there remain question marks about the long-term effectiveness of preventive programmes, which is extremely difficult to demonstrate. Moreover, a number of tensions can be identified within the preventive approach. First, there is always a danger that in supporting families insufficient attention may be given to children, whether in terms of safeguarding or 'voice' and participation. While supporting families may be the best route to promoting children's well-being, there is no necessary link between the two. Second, despite efforts to reduce stigma, support is likely to be experienced as double-edged by families, with beneficial services accompanied by intrusion and surveillance. Third, there are conflicting pressures in relation to the resources given to preventive work. For enthusiasts, such work has been thwarted by consistent under-resourcing, while for critics it may be seen as wasteful and likely to generate 'dependency'. The main challenge within both policy and practice, however, remains the complex and arguably at times, contradictory relationship between family support and child protection, an issue which will be explored further in the next chapter.

GUIDE TO FURTHER READING

Little and Mount (1999) afford a useful overview of preventive work in child welfare, while Quinton (2004) summarises and draws out key implications from recent research into parenting support. The edited collections by Frost et al. (2003) and those by Canavan et al., *Family Support: Direction from Diversity*, and Dolan et al., *Family Support as Reflective Practice* (both published by Jessica Kingsley), all provide a valuable combination of more theoretical approaches to family support and case studies. Finally, although focused on family centres, Tunstill et al. (2006) also offer a wider view of supportive services.

Reading and resources for practice

Kearney et al.'s *Alcohol, Drug and Mental Health Problems: Working with Families* (Social Care Institute for Excellence) offers helpful guidance for work with families experiencing such problems. Sutton's *Helping Families with Troubled Children: A Preventive Approach* (Wiley) is a good guide to assessment and practice in working with a variety of emotional and behavioural difficulties among children. In relation to the specific areas of provision looked at in the chapter, the following websites feature a range of useful information. For short breaks, the Shared Care Network's *All Kinds of Short Breaks* and Jones et al.'s *Stronger Links: A Guide to Good Practice for Children's Family-Based Respite Care* (Policy Press) are both valuable resources, as is the former's website www.sharedcarenetwork.org.uk. For family centres, the principal organisation is the Family and Children's Centre Network whose website can be reached via www.ncvcco.org.uk/ and then via 'Networks'. Further background on family group conferences can be found at www.frg.org.uk, while the Family Rights Group has also published *Family Group Conference Toolkit: A Practical Guide for Setting Up and Running an FGC Service* (Ashley et al.). For information and resources relating to young carers see www.youngcarer.com hosted by the Children's Society.

4

SAFEGUARDING CHILDREN
Contemporary Policy and Practice

In this, the first of two chapters on child maltreatment, our aim is to examine the way in which state interventions in the cause of 'child protection' have evolved since the passing of the Children Act 1989. This will entail consideration of both policy frameworks and processes of intervention and their wider social and political contexts, including the influence of the media and child maltreatment inquiries. A particular concern will be to explore the ways in which maltreatment is socially constructed and often highly contested in its meanings and parameters.

CHILD MALTREATMENT – A SOCIAL CONSTRUCTION?

It has become commonplace to acknowledge the socially constructed nature of child maltreatment. However, this is open to different interpretations. At its simplest, it may signify the intertwining of ideas of maltreatment with changing norms of child development, and sensitivities regarding appropriate discipline, supervision and (emotional) nurture. Yet social constructionist perspectives also invite deeper analysis of the meanings attached to maltreatment and the degree to which they enjoy consensus or are contested. At the macro-level, there may be efforts from pressure groups, media organisations and 'moral entrepreneurs' to influence legislation, policy direction or public opinion, while at the micro-level, professionals are involved in deciding what constitutes maltreatment and how it should be dealt with. Needless to say, their judgements may often be disputed and resisted by the families directly involved. At all levels, it can be seen that constructions of child maltreatment are profoundly influenced by power. This may be (inter)personal but also shaped by wider social divisions based on class, gender, ethnicity, sexuality or disability.

CHILD MALTREATMENT – A BRIEF MODERN HISTORY

Although our focus rests with the period since 1989, it is important to take a brief historical excursion to set this in context. (For readers interested in the (earlier) history of child maltreatment, Corby (2005: 22-50) provides an excellent overview of the period from 1870–1991, while more detailed accounts can be found in Ferguson (2004) and the relevant sections of Hendrick (2003).)

The modern history of child maltreatment is often traced to its 'rediscovery' (after around half a century during which its public profile was relatively low) in the 1960s, with US paediatrician Henry Kempe's term 'battered child syndrome' highlighting significant and often previously undetected physical abuse of children. This work was reflected in the UK in a heightened awareness of physical harm amongst the medical profession and campaigning from child welfare agencies, notably the NSPCC (Parton, 1985). Arguably a greater influence arose from the death of Maria Colwell in 1973 and public reaction to it. Seven-year-old Maria was returned to her mother and stepfather after being fostered for several years by her aunt, and subsequently suffered extreme neglect before being battered to death by her stepfather. An ensuing government inquiry was highly critical, especially of Maria's social worker, and media coverage saw the birth of the 'naive do-gooder' stereotype of the profession. Parton (1985) argues that reaction to Maria's death coincided with growing concerns about violence in society and a breakdown in law and order, permissiveness, and a perceived decline in the family.

Following its inquiry, the government introduced a number of measures that established a framework for dealing with cases of child maltreatment that has largely survived to the present day. These included the establishment of area review committees (ARCs) (the equivalent body in Scotland is the child protection committee) to co-ordinate policy and liaison between different agencies; a requirement for case conferences to bring all relevant professionals together to discuss individual children; tighter procedures for investigation; and the establishment of a register for children 'at risk' of abuse. The late 1970s witnessed a steady broadening of the scope of child maltreatment. The label of 'battered child' was initially replaced with 'non-accidental injury' before the first official use of the term child abuse in 1980. Four categories were identified for children 'at risk' – physical injury; physical neglect; 'failure to thrive' with emotional abuse; and living in the same household as someone who has committed serious offences against children.

During the 1980s, policy and practice in relation to child maltreatment were subject to increasing tensions. On the one hand, there appeared to be growing recognition of its scale, with the number of children placed on the child abuse register more than trebling between 1978 and 1988 (Corby, 2005). The most dramatic rise related to sexual abuse, where there was a sixfold rise in two years (1984-1986). This 'rediscovery' of child sexual abuse is widely attributed to feminist critique of the family as a site for patriarchal (sexual) control and violence and to the voice given to survivors of abuse (Frost and Stein, 1989). Mirroring research in the USA, a number of studies in the UK highlighted the fact that sexual abuse occurred on a much wider scale than previously thought (Baker and Duncan, 1985; Finkelhor et al., 1986). Further attention was drawn to the issue by the BBC programme *Childwatch* and the subsequent establishment of Childline – a free confidential telephone helpline for children experiencing maltreatment – in 1986. High-profile inquiries into child deaths also served to generate pressures towards increased intervention, especially in the case of Jasmine Beckford, where the inquiry emphasised the need to assess dangerousness in families and placed the *protection* of children centrally, a shift reflected in the redesignation of conferences, registers and area committees to include the term child protection (see Parton, 1991 for a fuller historical account).

Yet there were also countervailing forces. As noted in Chapter 1, in the early 1980s there was a growing sense that state intervention had become too heavy-handed, with children unnecessarily taken into, and remaining in care. While this trend was slowed sharply by the Beckford inquiry, it was to receive dramatic new impetus from events in Cleveland in 1987. When an unexpectedly large number of children were taken into care largely on the basis of a controversial medical diagnosis known as reflex anal dilatation, opinion was sharply divided between those who were inclined to see this as further uncovering of abuse and those, led by the local MP, Stuart Bell, who believed that certain doctors and social workers had 'gone mad' (Campbell, 1988). The ensuing inquiry (Butler-Sloss, 1988) was highly critical of many of the professionals involved, both for their 'kneejerk' reactions to medical diagnosis and for their flawed investigative techniques. The 'truth' of abuse in Cleveland remains hotly disputed but the public perception was one of 'over-zealous bungling' on the part of professionals (Kitzinger, 2004). Following Cleveland, child protection seemed to involve walking a tightrope between too little and too much intervention, between the ineffectual and the authoritarian. The Cleveland affair served to strengthen the legal position of parents in the Children Act 1989, while more broadly, the controversies of the 1980s prompted a shift towards a more legalistic approach to child maltreatment in which the courts would become more active overseers and when necessary arbiters between conflicting views.

Child maltreatment in the 1990s – changing parameters

In the early 1990s, the tightrope effect remained readily apparent, with further-high profile child deaths including that of Ricky Neave and cases of perceived over-zealous intrusion as in Rochdale and Orkney (Corby, 2005).

However, the character of child protection work underwent significant change, much of which can be interpreted as a shift of attention from maltreatment within the family towards dangers external to it. The 'refocusing debate' has been discussed in previous chapters, but it is helpful to refer briefly to its critique of incident-driven investigation and call for attention to the developmental needs of children experiencing low-level, but often chronic, maltreatment. Thus, one facet of the refocusing debate was to play down the 'dangerousness' of most families in the child protection system, emphasising instead their needs for support.

While the 'core business' of child protection in the UK has remained focused on dealing with abuse and neglect within families, the wider parameters of maltreatment have undergone significant change since the passing of the Children Act 1989. In particular, the Act's term 'safeguarding and promoting the welfare of children' has become more central but has also taken on a broader meaning. Alongside concerns with protection from maltreatment and impaired development, definitions of safeguarding now emphasise 'optimum life chances' and entering adulthood successfully (HM Government, 2006a). The broadening scope is apparent in the government's *Staying Safe* strategy, which constructs a tiered model of universal, targeted and responsive safeguarding, mirroring the 'levels of prevention' described in Chapter 3 (Department for Children, Schools and Families (DCSF), 2008). Change has been driven by two sets of factors (see Parton, 2006 for a comprehensive historical account). First, New Labour's 'social investment' approach to children (see Chapter 1) has emphasised early intervention and 'joined up working' to identify and address a range of obstacles to maximising children's potential. Second, the 1990s witnessed further discoveries (or sometimes rediscoveries) of 'sites' for child maltreatment, several of which were focused outside the family.

'Policing the paedophile'

Arguably the most important influence of the decade was the emerging figure of the 'paedophile'. Parton (2006:117–138) charts how, from concerns about child sex rings (where groups of abusers 'share' children) in the 1980s, paedophilia has become ever-more closely associated with (the threat of) murder in the public imagination, bolstered by high-profile cases such as those of Sarah Payne, Holly Wells and Jessica Chapman. In response to this perceived threat, a range of measures has been introduced. These include the establishment of a sex offenders register and multi-agency public protection panels, with various reporting requirements and, for high-risk offenders, additional forms of surveillance, including electronic tagging. Despite considerable public pressure, however, the government has to date resisted a UK version of 'Megan's Law' that would make the names and addresses of locally based sex offenders publicly available.

Abuse by those working with children

While much of the concern linked to paedophiles was directed towards strangers, there was also growing recognition in the 1990s of maltreatment by those working with children in a wide range of occupations, and evidence of perpetrators actively seeking such positions for this purpose. The question of institutional abuse within public care will be discussed in Chapter 6, but at this juncture, it should be noted that growing awareness of vulnerability prompted a significant extension of vetting and criminal records checks for all those, including volunteers, working with children (now governed by the Safeguarding Vulnerable Groups Act 2006 and equivalent legislation else-where in the UK). New units were also established within churches and sports bodies to promote a more proactive and rigorous approach to child protection within their domains.

Child maltreatment and cyber-space

New technologies such as the internet and third-generation mobile phones have brought new potentials for both bullying and forms of sexual abuse, including children's involvement in the viewing and production of pornog-raphy (with varying degrees of coercion) and the use of chatrooms for 'grooming' children (Gallagher et al., 2006). (For an excellent review of rele-vant research and safeguarding measures see Dombrowski et al., 2007.) Responding to campaigning led by children's charities such as National Children's Homes (NCH) (Carr, 2004), the government has introduced new legislation relating to grooming and child pornography and established a new body – the Child Exploitation and Online Protection Centre (www.ceop.gov.uk/) – to tackle abuse linked to the internet. Policing the internet, however, remains extremely challenging and some critics have sug-gested that there is a growing mismatch between ever-stronger legislation and the resources required for enforcement (K. Williams, 2004).

Children exploited through prostitution

Children's involvement in 'prostitution' re-emerged as a significant public issue in the 1980s and 1990s (for a longer history see Brown and Barrett, 2002) and was taken up strongly by some children's charities. Their aim to have the involvement of children in prostitution addressed in terms of mal-treatment and welfare rather than through the criminal justice system was largely realised under new guidance issued in 2000, although the option of criminal prosecution is retained as a last resort (DH, 2000b). While the change of approach has been widely welcomed, critics point to certain weaknesses, including the neglect of socio-economic factors, the possibility that victim status may make some young people more vulnerable and that child welfare services are poorly equipped to deliver the promised protection and support (Melrose and Barrett, 2004; Pearce, 2006). For an overview of relevant research on children's exploitation through prostitution, see Cusick (2002) and for the neglected area of research on male involvement, see Lillywhite and Skidmore (2006). Chase and Statham (2004) offer an informative wider view of the commercial sexual exploitation of children, especially through prostitution, pornography and trafficking.

Trafficking in children and modern slavery

As one aspect of increasing globalisation and migration, trafficking in children into, via or even from the UK has emerged as a significant issue, as documented in recent official and voluntary sector reports (Beddoe, 2007; CEOP, 2007). These reports suggest that the two main purposes behind trafficking in children are sexual exploitation and domestic servitude, followed by forced labour, forced marriages and criminal activities such as drug smuggling and benefit fraud. The focus for children's charities has been to ensure that victims of trafficking are treated within a framework of child protection. They have expressed particular concern about the lack of a proactive approach; the large number of children who go missing from the care system; and the government's perceived prioritisation of immigration control over child welfare (Beddoe, 2007).

Child runaways

Growing interest in the 1980s in the problems of children running away from home was reflected in research and campaigning to improve services for the children involved. Studies have suggested that around 100,000 children run away each year (Rees, 2001; Social Exclusion Unit (SEU), 2002). Particular issues relating to the care system are discussed in Chapter 6, but for the majority of children who are running from, or are forced to leave, their homes, the main reasons appear to be to escape relationship problems or (alleged) maltreatment within the family (Rees, 2001; Mitchell, 2003b). Services for children running away have relied almost entirely on voluntary sector initiatives and as a consequence have been limited in scope, patchy in geographical coverage and lacking secure funding. In response, campaigners have called for a national strategy, co-ordinated and financially supported by government. Relevant services would include emergency accommodation, conflict resolution, outreach and family support (Macaskill, 2006).

Ritual and faith-based maltreatment

In the early 1990s, a new frontier in the battle over child sexual abuse was opened with numerous claims from evangelical groups and some children's charities of hidden ritualistic or satanic abuse. Research commissioned by the government found negligible evidence of ritualistic abuse and the controversy largely faded from the public gaze, although survivors' groups claim that the problems have been suppressed (La Fontaine, 1994; Gallagher, 2001). A decade later, however, cases of maltreatment linked to beliefs in witchcraft and 'possession' by spirits emerged. Stobart (2006) describes how, typically, children are scapegoated on the basis of some 'difference' (often disability) or belief that they are 'evil' due to possession and subjected to various forms of (sometimes extreme) cruelty linked to attempts to 'exorcise' them. These exorcisms frequently involve faith-based groups although their role in the maltreatment may vary. (For further information see Africans Unite against Child Abuse, www.afruca.org)

Domestic violence and child maltreatment

One of the most important recent changes in conceptualising child maltreatment has been in its links with (adult) domestic violence, predominantly against women. Campaigners have attempted to address a situation where issues of domestic violence were often either avoided or dealt with in confrontational ways – with women pressured to leave their partners or risk having their children removed (Humphreys, 1999). One facet of this work has been to highlight the links between domestic violence and child maltreatment, with studies showing high correlations between the two (for a summary, see Humphreys, 2006), including situations where men may harm children as a means of attacking their partners. Equally influential, however, has been recognition of the indirect maltreatment suffered by children exposed to domestic violence (reflected in a revised definition of harm under the Adoption and Children Act 2002, s120). A second strand has been to have professionals take more fully into account the impact of domestic violence on mothers' parenting roles and capacities. Despite positive changes in policy and guidance, it is debatable as to how far they have permeated frontline practice (Holland, 2004; Cleaver et al., 2007) while there remain problems in relation to child contact arrangements with violent non-resident fathers (Wall, 2006).

There is now a substantial literature on domestic violence and child maltreatment (for reviews, see for example Hester et al. (2006) and Humphreys and Stanley (2006)). Mullender et al. (2002) provide an excellent account of children's perspectives (including their complex feelings towards parents) and of the particular challenges faced by families from BME communities.

SAFEGUARDING CHILDREN UNDER THE CHILDREN ACTS 1989 AND 2004

In the remainder of this chapter, our focus is on the policy and practice framework for child protection work as it has evolved since the Children Act 1989. More detailed accounts with helpful case study examples can be found in Beckett (2007) and May-Chahal and Coleman (2003). The analysis rests on three interlocking elements – namely assessment, the child protection 'process' and the relevant legal framework. Like other child welfare interventions, those relating to child protection are governed by the Assessment Framework. In particular, the core assessment is central to undertaking enquiries under s47 of the Children Act 1989. The Assessment Framework has been addressed at some length in Chapter 2, but there are certain aspects of the process specific to child protection interventions that can usefully be highlighted at this point.

Assessment in child protection – participation and engagement

For children, key issues include participation and the handling of information. While the principle of children's participation is thoroughly enshrined in legislation (most recently in the Children Act 2004, s53) and guidance (HM Government, 2006a), it often remains limited in practice. A recent study in Wales by Sanders and Mace (2006) described child protection processes as 'essentially child-unfriendly', suggesting that there is still significant resistance to the active involvement of children. For many children, there are also concerns about the use of information regarding (alleged) maltreatment. The contrast between children's extensive uptake of Childline's anonymous and confidential service and the very low level of self-referral to welfare agencies is striking and there are obvious tensions between the growing emphasis on information-sharing among professionals and a child's desire to retain some form of control over such flows. Dalrymple (2001) makes a powerful argument for a confidential advocacy service, possibly involving the 'professional secret' approach adopted in some European countries, while more generally, Parton (2006) argues for a protective system that gives much greater weight to children's views and wishes. Bell's (2002) study of children's experiences of investigations highlights the importance of social workers' skills in building relationships during the process.

In relation to parents or carers, assessment is crucially shaped by the tensions between 'child protection' and 'family support'. In contrast with much of continental Europe (and to some extent Scotland), 'Anglo-Saxon' countries have tended to separate child protection from family support and give it primacy within the child welfare system (Katz and Hetherington, 2006). These tensions have a long history, but it can be argued that they have been sharpened under the New Labour quest *both* to de-stigmatise support services *and* to strengthen the safeguarding of children through more pervasive surveillance (Parton, 2006).

A decade on from the refocusing debate of the 1990s, a study by the Commission for Social Care Inspection (CSCI) (2006) has again emphasised the lack of support given to parents involved in child protection interventions. However, it is important to locate such findings in the context of what is inevitably an emotionally charged situation. Parents may adopt a wide range of stances from collaboration to denial and (violent) opposition (Stanley and Goddard, 2002; Littlechild, 2005), fears of which have often led to failures to protect children (Brandon et al., 2008). More generally, much depends on the skills of social workers to overcome the various tensions within their role (Turnell and Essex, 2006). (May-Chahal and Coleman (2003:121–143) provide an insightful chapter on the challenges of working with parents in child protection.)

GOVERNING CHILD PROTECTION – WORKING TOGETHER TO SAFEGUARD CHILDREN

The 'process' of child protection work is set out in the *Working Together* guidance (HM Government, 2006a), which is to be followed in conjunction with the Assessment Framework and any local procedures and protocols. Under section 47 of the Children Act 1989, local authorities have a duty to make enquiries when there is reason to believe that a child is suffering, or is likely to suffer, significant harm (see below), including at or before birth where there are prior concerns e.g. from the treatment of siblings. Awareness of this possibility may arise from a new referral or in respect of a family already known to the authority. Referrals may come from other professionals (e.g. health, education, day care, police) and family members but rarely from children themselves (Cleaver and Walker, 2004).

The guidance requires that there is an acknowledgement and initial response to the referral within one day. Initial tasks include collating existing information on the child and family, deciding whether to take emergency protection measures (see below) and in the case of less serious allegations, whether these are to be dealt with under s47 or s17 as described in previous chapters. Where a s47 enquiry is being considered, a strategy meeting (or discussion) should be held immediately, involving social workers, police and any other relevant personnel such as a referring professional or when necessary those with medical or legal expertise. Apart from sharing information, the principal focus of the strategy meeting is on planning. This might include co-ordinating the enquiry with any criminal investigation, dealing with any immediate issues of safety, deciding what information may be shared with parents and whether any (further) medical examinations are required.

Child protection conferences

As noted above, the child protection conference has been pivotal to the system for dealing with maltreatment since the 1970s. Procedurally, a conference should be convened within 15 days of the strategy meeting if early enquiries indicate an ongoing risk of significant harm. Membership should minimally include social work/care representation from the local authority and two other professionals who have had direct contact with the child involved, but in practice may include a range of workers with the perceived relevant knowledge or expertise. Research studies have typically found an average of 8-10 professionals attending (Dale, 2004). Conferences should be chaired by someone who is independent of the line management for the case being discussed. The overarching purpose of a child protection conference is to assess the level of risk to a child and formulate a protective plan accordingly. A key decision is whether the child's name should be placed on the child protection register (note, the register will formally disappear in 2008 to be replaced by an indication that a child protection plan is in place). If this is deemed unnecessary, due to the relatively low level of risk or changed circumstances, options such as family support under s17 or recourse to an FGC may be appropriate. Where registration does take place, then a plan (see below) must be drawn up specifying the areas of concern and actions to be carried out to help secure the necessary changes. Research has highlighted a number of important features linked to child protection conferences, including the influence of 'groupthink' where decision making is adversely affected by a group desire for consensus and where 'defensible' decisions may be prioritised over correct ones (Munro, 2002).

Child protection plans and core groups

When a child's name is placed on the child protection register, the conference will appoint a lead professional (usually a local authority social worker) and a core group, comprising family members and relevant professionals who have the responsibility for developing and implementing the child protection plan. This plan will be reviewed at further conferences, initially within three months and six months thereafter. Depending on the degree of risk reduction, these subsequent meetings may decide to remove the child's name from the register. Research on core groups has identified challenges very similar to those facing conferences, especially in ensuring meaningful participation (Harlow and Shardlow, 2006).

From their study of 120 conferences, Farmer and Owen (1995) argued that the dominant focus was on assessing risk, with minimal time devoted to planning and little subsequent reappraisal. They expressed concern that plans often failed to offer therapeutic help to children or to address the needs of parents (including women subjected to domestic violence). More recent research has suggested that, although practical and therapeutic services are generally appreciated by parents, they are often not forthcoming (CSCI, 2006). In this respect, Scourfield and Welsh (2003) argue that child protection work is dominated by a neo-liberal emphasis on monitoring and exhorting parents to change or face losing their children. Despite these difficulties, and re-abuse rates of 25–30 per cent, studies in the 1990s found that in roughly two-thirds of cases, children's well-being improved while on the child protection register (DH, 1995).

DECISION MAKING IN CHILD PROTECTION

Although child protection intervention involves innumerable 'micro-decisions' in the course of practice, attention is customarily focused on those 'filtering' decisions linked to passage through the child protection process, for example whether to conduct an s47 enquiry, to convene a conference, to (de)register or institute care proceedings. In principle, decision making at each stage revolves around the concept of significant harm and its future projection. Gauging significant harm is notoriously complex, with legal definitions (s31) and official guidance offering only limited and often formulaic indicators (Ayre, 1998). To a large extent, this is inevitable given the myriad judgements that might be made in respect of child development and what constitutes 'good enough parenting'. These will reflect not only the views of the practitioners involved but also the wider contextual factors, such as (perceived) national priorities, local policies and workload pressures.

Once enquiries are undertaken, judgements are likely to be made on the basis of the severity of any incident(s) and/or wider patterns of treatment by parents (or carers). 'Signs' of maltreatment will be discussed more fully in the following chapter, but may include self-reporting, health, emotional, psychological or behavioural problems, physical appearance, sexually transmitted diseases or physical injury. Useful discussions on recognising and assessing harm can be found in May-Chahal and Coleman (2003: 45–59) and Beckett (2007: 63–77, 91–106) while the former also emphasise the need to gauge 'signs of safety'. Clearly there is no simple relationship between parenting and harm experienced but, as there is no legal requirement to show that significant harm has actually occurred, parental (usually maternal) behaviour and perceived potential for change are central to decision making. Over the past decade or so, there has been a subtle shift in child protection towards giving greater weight to abusive relationships rather than particular 'types' of maltreatment. While this development has much to commend it in terms of understanding maltreatment, it does add to the complexity of decision making and the gathering of evidence. Equally challenging is the task of setting parental behaviours in contexts such as those of material deprivation and 'cultural' factors in the case of BME families. Giving them appropriate weight requires a delicate balance between empathetic understanding and 'making excuses' for unacceptable standards of parenting.

Formal aids to decision making based on the identification of risk factors are discussed further in Chapter 5, but it is worth noting that such devices have been relatively little used by practitioners in the UK (Francis et al., 2006).

Inter-professional and inter-agency working

Failures of communication and co-ordination between professionals have been a recurring theme in child maltreatment 'scandals', but eliminating them has proved a daunting challenge.

One major concern has been to strike a balance between spreading responsibility for child protection as widely as possible while ensuring there are clear lines of accountability. For example, there have been moves to make child protection 'everyone's business' (Scottish Executive, 2002; HM Government, 2006b). In England and Wales, s11 of the Children Act 2004 and s175 of the Education Act 2002 created a general duty for a range of public bodies to safeguard and promote the welfare of children. *Working Together* (HM Government, 2006a: 39–73) sets out various requirements for organisations to nominate key professionals to co-ordinate child protection work at their particular level (see Murphy, 2004, for discussion), while the Children Act 2004, s12, creates a duty on professionals to notify any cause for concern to the information-sharing index. Training, especially on an inter-professional basis, has also been recognised as crucial to facilitating communication and co-ordination (Glennie, 2007).

Yet, despite the many positive developments in relation to co-ordination, the challenges remain significant (Murphy, 2004). Different professional roles and training generate particular 'ways of seeing' in respect of assessment and these are likely to be reinforced by agency cultures (Birchall and Hallett, 1995). In practice, this often means different thresholds for assessing significant harm and consequent tensions when these views are not shared by others (Stanley et al., 2003). Duties to co-operate have co-existed with increasing pressures on individual professionals and agencies and unsurprisingly, it has often proved difficult to engage those for whom child protection is not regarded as part of their 'core business' (Francis et al., 2006). Responsibilities have thus tended to remain with social workers, with some evidence that other professionals may seek to avoid involvement in child protection work (Harlow and Shardlow, 2006). Inter-professional relationships are also affected by issues of power and status and may be based on generalised or even stereotypical views of others.

In relation to communication, there are two related challenges to be faced. The first is that of confidentiality, which has both interpersonal and professional/organisational dimensions. Thus, individual practitioners must address issues of confidentiality in light of their relationship with service users, but professional cultures and agency rules will also shape what information must (not) be kept confidential. A second, broader challenge is to decide from the massive volume of information gleaned which items are to be exchanged, with whom, and in what form, something that ultimately relies on professional judgement but is also influenced by interpersonal processes (Reder and Duncan, 2003). Finally, it should be recognised that all the above challenges can be exacerbated by staff turnover and by agency reorganisations.

Local Safeguarding Children Boards

Since their introduction in the 1970s, arrangements for co-ordination between services involved in child protection have faced persistent difficulties. ARCs and later Area Child Protection Committees (ACPCs) lacked any clear statutory basis or funding – being essentially a 'voluntary' form of co-operation, unable to direct participating agencies to act or commit resources in particular ways. Furthermore, attendance was often poor or reliant on relatively junior staff. Far from its ideal of constituting a dynamic grouping of expertise, the ACPC was frequently found to be a 'slow cumbersome creature, lacking teeth and clear vision' (DH, 1995: 72).

Responding both to the Victoria Climbié inquiry and the wider safeguarding agenda, ACPCs were replaced in England and Wales by Local Safeguarding Children Boards (LSCBs) under the Children Act 2004. Section 13 of the Act specifies representation from bodies in the geographical area covered. These are listed in Box 4.1.

BOX 4.1

Statutory representation on Local Safeguarding Children Boards

- district councils;
- the chief police officer;
- the local probation board;
- the youth offending team;
- Strategic health authorities and primary care trusts;
- NHS trusts and NHS foundation trusts;
- the Connexions service;
- CAFCASS (Children and Family Courts Advisory and Support Service);
- the governor or director of any secure training centre or prison that ordinarily detains children.

In addition, there is a wide range of agencies that may be invited to send representatives: including adult social care services, the NSPCC, children's voluntary organisations, day care or schools (for a fuller list see HM Government, 2006a: 85–86). LSCBs have a wide co-ordinating brief in relation to safeguarding children, and may be involved in formulating local policy, procedure, training and the planning and commissioning of services. Their responsibilities in respect of serious case reviews are discussed below.

Yet LSCBs face significant challenges, inheriting a situation where some agencies have still been found to give insufficient priority to safeguarding children (CSCI et al., 2005). (For a review of child protection in Northern Ireland, see also DHSSPS, 2006). Despite their seemingly stronger foundations, LSCBs still lack clear funding arrangements or any operational role in relation to member agencies. Early research suggests that, despite some improvements, the problems associated with ACPCs have yet to be fully overcome (DfES, 2007b).

More radical reforms have been proposed to tackle the perceived failings of the child protection system, in particular, following the Cleveland Report and again more recently (Kendall and Harker, 2002) a national agency for child protection service to develop appropriate expertise and co-ordination. This has been strongly resisted within children's services on the grounds that it would create a false and unhelpful division between children in need and those at risk of maltreatment (Parton, 2006).

CHILD PROTECTION – THE LEGAL FRAMEWORK

The process of conducting child protection enquiries has been described in some detail above, but it is important to spell out aspects of the legal framework, which relate both to criminal and civil law (see Gray, 2004 for discussion). Most forms of maltreatment potentially constitute criminal offences, such as assault, indecency, neglect or cruelty (see Mesie et al., 2007: 163–167 for a comprehensive list of offences). Meanwhile, protective measures in respect of the child are governed by the civil law. As we shall see, the criminal and civil domains do not always sit easily alongside each other, not least because of their different burdens of proof – 'beyond reasonable doubt' and 'on the balance of probabilities' respectively.

Child protection and the criminal justice process

Since the Children Act 1989, there have been important developments in the treatment of children as (alleged) victims of maltreatment within the criminal justice system. An early step was the promotion of joint investigations by police and social workers. The rationale for this was to avoid 'therapeutic' interventions impeding criminal investigations by 'contaminating the evidence' but also situations where prosecutions were pursued to the detriment of the child's welfare. This initiative has generally been regarded as successful (Adams and Horrocks, 1999), although Garrett (2004) suggests that significant tensions remain.

Building on work by the Pigot Committee (1989), the possibility of children's evidence in chief being given by video was introduced under the Criminal Justice Act 1991, and subsequently extended to cross-examination via video link by the Youth Justice and Criminal Evidence Act 1999. A 'Memorandum of Good Practice' was introduced in 1992 to govern how evidence would be gathered from alleged victims, guidance that has since been updated (Home Office, 2002). Recourse to video evidence has been almost entirely confined to cases of alleged sexual abuse but has been criticised on various grounds. Responding to concerns over repeated and protracted 'disclosure interviews', the Memorandum sought to create a more structured process. However, Welbourne (2002) argues that the format of a single, time-limited interview has become too rigid. She summarises research showing that in practice video evidence is very rarely heard and that its availability has coincided with falling prosecutions and convictions. Sharland (1999) similarly suggests that, despite procedural changes to ease formality and shield children, criminal proceedings can often still be intimidating for them, whether in the experience of cross-examination or in the disclosure of information to defendants. She concludes that the crimino-legal process frequently does not serve the interests of children in terms of welfare or justice.

Emergency protection

In more serious cases of alleged maltreatment or imminent risk to the child, an emergency protection order (EPO) (Children Act 1989, s44) (or child protection order in Scotland) can be sought, allowing the child to be removed to, or retained in, a place of safety. The orders are granted by magistrates/ sheriffs but the applicant must produce evidence to show that the risk to the child necessitates emergency intervention. EPOs last for up to eight days and can be extended by a maximum of seven days. (Extension in Scotland is dealt with by warrants issued under the hearings system.) In most cases, they are followed by care proceedings (see below) under which the local authority gains parental responsibility for the child (Masson et al., 2007). Orders may make specific directions in relation to contact arrangements with family members and medical examination, while the courts may also make an exclusion order barring an alleged perpetrator from the home. Although parents were given greater legal powers to challenge EPOs under the Children Act 1989, applications are in practice rarely refused (Masson et al., 2007). In 2006, there

ere 1676 EPOs granted in England and Wales and 624 CPOs made in Scotland (Ministry of Justice, 2007; SCRA, 2007). It should be noted that there are also emergency powers (s46) for a child to be taken into police protection for up to three days. Masson et al. (2007) present a wide-ranging analysis of emergency powers, while for a valuable review of emergency protection in Scotland, see Francis et al., 2006.

Care and supervision orders

Under s31 of the Children Act, a local authority may apply to a court for a care order or supervision order, where there is (risk of) significant harm due to care falling short of that provided by a 'reasonable parent' or the child being beyond parental control. The legal effect of a care order is that the local authority acquires parental responsibility although this remains shared with the parent(s). The care order may last until the child is 18 unless discharged earlier. A supervision order does not involve any acquisition of parental responsibility but combines a role of advising and assisting parents with a monitoring brief in respect of the child's well-being. The order lasts for 12 months but can be extended to a maximum of three years.

While court proceedings are ongoing, interim care or supervision orders (s38) can be made for up to eight weeks and subsequently extended in four-week periods. Although interim orders often serve as a stage towards full orders, they may be deployed effectively as a time-limited intervention in order to seek necessary changes within the family. The longer-term implications of a care order are discussed in chapters 6 and 7 but here we focus on the application process or care proceedings. In Scotland, local authorities may acquire parental responsibilities under s86 of the Children (Scotland) Act 1995 (to be replaced by new and more flexible permanence orders under the Adoption and Children (Scotland) Act 2007), while hearings can make supervision requirements under s70 with options that include the child residing in foster or residential care.

Involving the potential or actual removal of children from families, care proceedings have an obvious capacity to evoke conflict, and it is sometimes argued that this is exacerbated by the adversarial nature of the UK's legal system. In her research review, Brophy (2006) suggests that care proceedings tend to be brought only in cases of serious maltreatment and where there is a lack of co-operation between parents and professionals. The profile of families involved in care proceedings is one of high levels of socio-economic deprivation and very significant incidences of domestic violence, substance misuse and mental health problems (Brophy, 2006). In England and Wales in 2006, there were 14,359 applications with over 90 per cent for care orders. The 7849 care orders and 3296 supervision orders granted show that the court is by no means a 'rubber stamp' for local authority decisions (Ministry of Justice, 2007).

Care proceedings and empowerment

In care proceedings, beyond demonstrating grounds under s31 (see above), local authorities must also present a care plan to the court (see Chapter 6). Crucially, this will address whether the child should (eventually) be returned to the family or be permanently placed for adoption or in public care. Social work with families in the course of care proceedings poses particular challenges. These include how to engage and be supportive with the spectre of (permanent) removal of a child, and how to encourage parents to discuss problems openly when such discussion may conceivably serve as evidence in court. Despite some improvements, research evidence has highlighted significant obstacles for parents involved in care proceedings: including lack of preparation, participation and follow-up, and difficulties gaining access to good legal representation and (alternative) expert witnesses (Freeman and Hunt, 1998). Discriminatory processes may add to the difficulties faced by some parents, such as those with learning disabilities (Booth et al., 2006) or those whose first language is not English (Chand, 2005).

In addition to any legal representation, a child involved in care proceedings is represented by a guardian appointed by the court. Guardians are employed by the Children and Family Court Advisory and Support Service (CAFCASS), which was established in 2001. A different system applies in Scottish courts and hearings, involving the two roles of curator and safeguarder (see Hill et al., 2003). The role of the guardian combines both welfare and rights elements, providing a voice for the child in proceedings but ultimately advising the court on a 'best interests' basis. This has led some critics to argue for greater use of advocacy to strengthen children's rights in proceedings (Bilson and White, 2005). Research studies have revealed mixed experiences among children, but also identified significant minorities who felt they had had insufficient say in proceedings (Masson and Winn Oakley, 1999; Ruegger, 2001). A key problem highlighted in care proceedings has been their length, which, despite the Children Act 1989's 'no-delay' principle and a target of 12 weeks, have become steadily more protracted, averaging almost a year and often longer (Beckett, 2001). Although delays may be 'purposeful' i.e. to allow for positive changes, they often reflect failings in the preparation of applications, problems in court timetabling, and difficulties in the allocation of guardians and in securing appropriate expert evidence (DfES/DCA, 2006).

SHAPING CHILD PROTECTION – MEDIA REPORTING AND OFFICIAL INQUIRIES

As Butler and Drakeford (2003) suggest, the construction of scandal emerges from a complex dynamic between the media, political reaction and the wider context rather than directly from the events themselves. We have seen how, in the modern era, a succession of scandals has shaped legislation and policy measures and prompted 'climates' supporting or opposing protective intervention in families. More generally, Ayre (2001) suggests that media reporting in the UK has contributed to a 'climate of fear, blame and mistrust' that has become endemic in child protection. In particular, it has helped to generate the templates of the ineffectual or over-zealous, but always bungling, social worker that have become part of 'folklore' (Kitzinger, 2004).

Inquiries and serious case reviews

The impact of major inquiries on child protection work has been powerful yet controversial. Their broad purpose has been to 'learn lessons', by establishing the facts of the case in question and making recommendations to improve practice, while it has also been suggested that they may have a certain memorial function, bringing closure for relatives and sometimes a wider social catharsis and reassurance (Cooper, 2005). Inquiries are often well resourced and thorough in their treatment of the issues. Above all, perhaps, their deliberations gain in gravity from the traumatic nature of the events that they address.

However, the influence of inquiries has also raised a number of concerns (see Corby, 2003, for discussion). First, they have been seen as focusing too heavily on individual error rather than context, taking little account of workload pressures, organisational factors or resource problems (Munro, 2005). A second related point is that the deliberations of inquiries can become too detached from routine child protection practices, with Parton (1997: 18) observing that inquiry conclusions and research findings 'seem to be in different worlds and speak different languages'. Third, especially in cases where a child has died, hindsight can create a misleading sense that events could have been foreseen and prevented. Fourth, recommendations have been overwhelmingly procedural, evoking criticism that this has undermined the importance of professional judgement and relationship-building with children and families, and has encouraged a defensive, bureaucratic approach to child protection (Ayre, 2001). Recent critiques of the Climbié inquiry argue that a failure to delve more deeply into the emotional complexities of child protection work makes progress less likely (Cooper, 2005).

Responding to such concerns, in 1991 there was an attempt to move away from public inquiries. Originally named as Part 8, but renamed in 1999, 'serious case reviews' (SCRs) (see Scottish Government, 2007a for the system in Scotland) were to be undertaken in cases of child death where maltreatment was known or suspected. SCRs take place away from the public gaze with an official rationale of speed in terms of reporting and learning lessons locally. Corby (2003) suggests that SCRs have been helpful in avoiding a 'blame culture' but argues that they could be more open in terms of scrutiny and publicising findings. Building on SCRs, the latest *Working Together* guidance requires LSCBs to produce overviews of child deaths in their areas in addition to the SCR system (HM Government, 2006a). Brandon et al. (2008) reviewed 161 SCRs over a two-year period, two-thirds of which involved a fatality. Their finding that only 12 per cent of cases involved those on the child protection register highlights the scale of 'hidden maltreatment'. The report also highlights the delicate balance to be struck in cases where there are previous histories of abuse between undue labelling of parents and over-optimistic efforts to 'start again' with a new child.

CONCLUSION

In this chapter, we have attempted to set out the main features of the system for safeguarding children as it has evolved in the UK. The past three to four decades have witnessed a significant expansion both of the concept of child maltreatment and measures to address it. Indeed, it might be argued that its compass has become too broad and risks losing meaning. Despite repeated efforts to focus on prevention and family support, successive 'scandals' have prompted the development and operation of an increasingly legalistic, procedurally-based approach to child protection work. The 'success' of these measures is difficult to judge for two main reasons. First, there is no way of knowing whether a different approach, for example, based more on support-ive services and/or professional judgement, would have yielded better results or not. Second, it is difficult to gauge the interaction between formal protec-tion systems and wider social changes impacting on parents' childrearing practices. While much attention is understandably devoted to the perfor-mance of child protection services, significant challenges remain in dealing with unreported maltreatment and achieving the right balance between pro-fessional autonomy and procedural frameworks.

GUIDE TO FURTHER READING

Numerous textbooks present good overviews of policy and practice in child protection. Particularly for social workers, Beckett (2007) strikes an excellent balance between wider discussion and practice relevance, while Munro's (2006) *Child Protection* (Sage) provides a very readable introductory text. A less recent text by May-Chahal and Coleman (2003) remains useful for its detailed discussion of key aspects of safeguarding work. For an account that places safeguarding in its wider social context, see Parton (2006).

Reading and resources for practice

There are also various 'handbooks' written for child protection, the most comprehensive of which is Wilson and James's *The Child Protection Handbook* (Bailliere Tindall). A shorter text written especially with health professionals in mind is Barker and Hodes's *The Child in Mind: A Child Protection Handbook* (Routledge). By far the most useful single online resource is the NSPCC's Inform (www.nspcc.org.uk/inform), which features statistical information, a reading list, directories and guidance to a wide range of practice issues. For work in relation to safeguarding children from abuse through prostitution, pornography and trafficking, see ECPAT UK's website www.ecpat.org.uk

Discussion questions

What part should family support services play in safeguarding children?

Is an expanding concept of child maltreatment to be welcomed? Or is it a sign of 'paranoia' on the part of parents and policy makers?

Is effective multi-agency working 'an impossible dream'?

How would you assess the impact of 'scandals' on the development of child protection in the UK?

Can child protection be made more 'child-friendly', and if so, how?

5

UNDERSTANDING CHILD MALTREATMENT: 'CAUSES' AND CONSEQUENCES

In this chapter, we examine what might be termed the 'knowledge base' for child maltreatment, which in broad terms has focused on four main areas: measurement; 'causes' of maltreatment; its consequences; and the effectiveness of intervention. All of these, however, are dependent upon issues of definition and it is with these that we start. Despite the expanding concept of maltreatment described in the previous chapter, the four main categories of physical abuse, neglect, sexual abuse and emotional abuse remain central.

PHYSICAL ABUSE

> Physical abuse may involve hitting, shaking, throwing, poisoning, burning or scalding, drowning, suffocating, or otherwise causing physical harm to a child. Physical harm may also be caused when a parent or carer fabricates the symptoms of, or deliberately induces, illness in a child. (HM Government, 2006a, para 1.30)

For those working with possible cases of physical abuse, the principal issues arising from this short but powerful definition are those of intent and in some instances thresholds. To merit treatment as abusive, such acts would generally have to be regarded as deliberate or reckless. While physical/medical evidence may often provide the starting point, investigations tend to focus on the credibility of parental accounts and judgements about their demeanour, apparent concern and co-operativeness (Cobley and Sanders, 2003). Professionals must often walk a fine line between a willingness to apply the 'rule of optimism' (essentially giving 'the benefit of the doubt' (Dingwall et al., 1983)) regarding parental care and being (seen as) naive if abuse is missed. Thresholds are also of great importance, especially perhaps in the controversial area of physical punishment, which may be seen as inherently abusive or a vital component of successful parenting, depending on one's viewpoint.

There has been a long-term trend away from the use of physical punishment, which is now largely restricted to parents or carers. However, successive governments have resisted calls from campaigners for the UK to follow at least 17 European countries in banning it, presumably regarding this a vote loser (Children Are Unbeatable! Alliance, 2006). Instead, the law has been tightened, most recently in England by s58 of the Children Act 2004, which prevents parents employing the defence of 'reasonable punishment' if the child suffers actual or grievous bodily harm.

Fabricated or induced illness (FII) has also been hugely controversial in recent years. Formerly known as Munchausen's Syndrome by Proxy, this relates to situations where a parent seeks attention from medical professionals by feigning or generating illness in their child. It can be extremely difficult to diagnose, due to the demeanour of a 'concerned parent' and frequently the involvement of many different professionals. Seeking evidence for FII has also been contentious, including debates on the ethics of covert video surveillance in hospitals (Thomas, 2003). (For an informative guide to assessment of FII see Precey, 2003). Campaigns for greater recognition of FII enjoyed some success in the 1990s, aided by a growing international body of research (Sheridan, 2003). However, this trend was called into question following the involvement of Sir Roy Meadow, a leading theorist of FII, in some high-profile miscarriages of justice.

NEGLECT

Neglect is the persistent failure to meet a child's basic physical and/or psychological needs, likely to result in the serious impairment of the child's health or development. Neglect may occur during pregnancy as a result of maternal substance abuse. Once a child is born, neglect may involve a parent or carer failing to:

- provide adequate food, clothing and shelter
- protect a child from physical and emotional harm or danger
- ensure adequate supervision (including the use of inadequate care-givers)
- ensure access to appropriate medical care or treatment.
- It may also include neglect of, or unresponsiveness to, a child's basic emotional needs. (HM Government, 2006a, para 1.33)

Other definitions have also made explicit references to children's needs for affection, stimulation and educational support (Horwath, 2007). Neglect has risen relentlessly over the past three decades as a category of child protection registration (see Table 5.1). The reasons for this are complex but include greater awareness of its harmful effects, higher expectations of parents in meeting children's needs, and perhaps a preference for using neglect over alternative categorisations (O'Hagan, 2006). Judgements on neglect inevitably involve threshold issues, e.g. what constitutes an inadequate diet, clothing or supervision, but also the necessary timescales for 'persistent failure' and whether some triggering event (e.g. 'home alone', serious accident) is necessary for intervention.

Another key challenge is to assess parenting capacity in relation to neglect. To what extent does the latter reflect a lack of knowledge or skill on the part of parents or simply a lack of concern? Some of the most difficult challenges arise when parents have additional support needs (see Chapter 2) that may lead to the neglect of children's needs on a temporary or more enduring basis. Similarly, assessing the part played by poverty in neglect poses acute dilemmas, not least those related to 'cultural relativism' in the assessment of parenting (Horwath, 2007).

One important change in the contours of neglect relates to the concept of 'failure to thrive' (FTT). This concept describes a situation where children fail to develop, especially in terms of height and weight, when there is no apparent physical cause. During the 1960s and 1970s, FTT came to be seen increasingly in terms of physical and emotional neglect. By the 1990s, however, these problems were significantly redefined as 'weight faltering' rooted in feeding difficulties and consequent malnutrition, with only a small minority of cases involving maltreatment (Wright et al., 2006; Batchelor, 2007). Dropped as a category of maltreatment in England, FTT is still currently retained in Scotland.

SEXUAL ABUSE

Sexual abuse involves forcing or enticing a child or young person to take part in sexual activities, including prostitution, whether or not the child is aware of what is happening. The activities may involve physical contact, including penetrative (e.g. rape, buggery or oral sex) or non-penetrative acts. They may include non-contact activities, such as involving children in looking at, or in the production of, sexual online images, watching sexual activities, or encouraging children to behave in sexually inappropriate ways. (HM Government, 2006a, para 1.32).

As with other categories of maltreatment, the above definition raises important threshold questions, including what may be deemed as 'sexual activities' or what constitutes 'sexually inappropriate' behaviour. It can also be seen to cover a wide range of activities, and arguably levels of seriousness. Debates on sex education and media content amply highlight the lack of consensus surrounding sexuality and childhood, as do studies of family norms with respect to nudity, bathing or sharing a bed with parents (Smith and Grocke, 1995). Professional judgements also have to take into account factors such as the age and level of understanding of the child, age and/or power imbalances and whether coercion was involved. Perpetrators resort to a wide variety of tactics to secure victims' silence, from bribery, deception and emotional pressure to threatened or actual physical violence (Bray, 1997). In the case of intra-familial abuse, children may well have ambivalent feelings towards the perpetrator. Dealing with alleged sexual abuse is rendered more difficult because there are often no physical signs or corroborating evidence. Hence, the credibility of children's narratives becomes crucial and this, in turn, has been influenced by ebbs and flows in the wider climate of 'belief' in relation to children making allegations.

EMOTIONAL ABUSE

Emotional abuse is the persistent emotional maltreatment of a child such as to cause severe and persistent adverse effects on the child's emotional development. It may involve conveying to children that they are worthless or unloved, inadequate, or valued only insofar as they meet the needs of another person. It may feature age or developmentally inappropriate expectations being imposed on children. These may include interactions that are beyond the child's developmental capability, as well as overprotection and limitation of exploration and learning, or preventing the child participating in normal social interaction. It may involve seeing or hearing the ill-treatment of another. It may involve serious bullying, causing children frequently to feel frightened or in danger, or the exploitation or corruption of children (HM Government, 2006a, para 1.31)

Intervention in the case of emotional abuse has risen steadily since the 1980s, boosted by a growing emphasis on children's development and research evidence on the damaging effects of low warmth/high criticism environments (DH, 1995). Once again, there are important issues of thresholds and patterns that mark out abuse from more isolated lapses in parenting. Recognition has built upon the idea that emotional abuse is involved in all types of maltreatment, while also occurring alone. It may take both 'active' – for example, calculated acts of hostility, cruelty, denigration and humiliation, threats and overt rejection – and 'passive' forms such as indifference, withdrawal, and a lack of affection or stimulation (Glaser, 2002; Iwaniec et al., 2006). Assessing emotional abuse can be challenging due to the difficulties of gathering evidence, taking into account cultural norms relating to expression of emotions and in the case of 'passive' forms of abuse gauging how far the maltreatment is deliberate or reflective of stress, preoccupation or a lack of awareness of children's needs (O'Hagan, 2006).

THE SCALE OF CHILD MALTREATMENT – INCIDENCE AND PREVALENCE

Gauging the scale of child maltreatment is important both to those involved in planning child welfare services and to those investigating it as a 'social

Table 5.1   Child protection registrations in the UK 2003–2007(*)

Category of maltreatment	2003	2004	2005	2006	2007(**)
Physical abuse	5882	5558	5268	5045	4530
Neglect	13,155	13,456	13,962	14,682	14,890
Sexual abuse	3366	3084	3037	2974	2400
Emotional abuse	6087	6182	6288	7115	8037
Two categories/other	4468	4034	3501	3177	2936
Total	32,958	32,314	32,056	32,993	32,793

(*) Figures collated from NSPCC Inform which gives links to the original sources for the four UK countries
www.nspcc.org.uk/Inform/OnlineResources/Statistics/ChildProtectionRegisterStatistics/CPR_asp_ifega2642
9.html
(**) 2007 England, Wales and Scotland only.

problem'. In quantifying maltreatment, it is common to distinguish between *incidence* – the number of new cases in a year – and *prevalence* – those affected at any time in their childhood. There are two principal sources of information on incidence and prevalence, namely official statistics and research evidence.

Official statistics for child protection

Figures from child protection registers constitute the main form of official statistics, although data are also collected on child deaths, through homicides or undetermined causes (Corby, 2005). Table 5.1 shows the snapshot numbers of children placed on child protection registers within the UK from 2003 to 2007.

Following the introduction of a register in the 1970s, the number of children whose names were placed on it in England and Wales rose rapidly from approximately 12,000 in the early 1980s to peak at over 45,000 in the early 1990s (Corby, 2005). This figure fell sharply in the 1990s – due to the Children Act 1989 and changes in registration practices – but as Table 5.1 shows, it has remained relatively stable in recent years. This overall stability, however, masks dramatic changes between the categories. Since the late 1980s, there has been a steady shift away from the 'incident-driven' categories of physical and sexual abuse to the more 'chronic' conditions of neglect and emotional abuse.

Like most official statistics, child protection register data have distinct limitations, not least as any estimate of the scale of maltreatment. This is partly a matter of the initial reporting, but also the operation of various 'filters' within the child protection system. For example, in the year to March 2007, there were 73,800 s47 enquiries in England, 39,400 cases (53 per cent) leading to conferences and 33,300 (45 per cent) children being made subject to a child protection plan (DfES, 2007a). The corresponding percentages in Scotland are lower at 39 and 27 per cent respectively (Scottish Government, 2007b). Similarly, registrations also appear to reflect local policy and practice thresholds within authorities (Gibbons et al., 1995a; Pugh, 2007). In terms of incidence and prevalence, while registration figures represent roughly 0.3 per cent of the population at one time, Sidebotham and Heron (2006) found that 1.1 per cent of their sample had been on the register during an eight-year period.

Research into the incidence and prevalence of maltreatment

Research into maltreatment within broader populations faces a number of major challenges, including the sensitivities of the topic and ethical dilemmas arising from any 'discovery' of maltreatment. Surveys broadly fall into two categories. The first, used mainly to gauge physical abuse, focuses on potential 'perpetrators', typically seeking information from parents on their attitudes and behaviour towards their children. Such studies rely significantly, however, on the willingness of participants to disclose sensitive material and as such are likely to under-report the scale or severity of abuse. The second survey method has rested on self-reporting by (potential) victims. This rarely involves children directly (especially in relation to intra-familial maltreatment) for ethical reasons (Gallagher et al., 2002). Young adults are often surveyed as their disclosures do not raise the same dilemmas of intervention as do those of children while they are seen as temporally closer to the maltreatment than older adults. Nevertheless, the period elapsed and consequent reliance on long-term memory, albeit perhaps of highly significant events, raises questions over the reliability of reporting.

The most authoritative study of prevalence in the UK was carried out by researchers for the NSPCC in the late 1990s (Cawson et al., 2000; Cawson, 2002). The postcode-based sample comprised 2,869 young adults although, as the authors note, the exclusion of homeless young people and those living in institutions may have produced an underestimate of the scale of maltreatment. The survey is important for its range and breadth of focus, setting findings on maltreatment in the context of family relationships as well as dealing with abuse outside the home. For each of the four main categories of abuse and neglect, the researchers utilised three levels – serious, intermediate and cause for concern. Respondents were also asked if they regarded themselves as abused, an exercise that typically yielded lower rates of abuse, perhaps due to factors such as self-blame, otherwise positive relationships with abusers, and a reluctance to identify as abused or experiencing abuse as 'normal'. In the following sections, findings from this study will be presented, supplemented where appropriate with those from other research.

Physical abuse

Cawson et al. (2000) adjudged 7 per cent of their respondents to have suffered serious physical abuse, defined as violent treatment resulting, or likely to result, in injury, such as being hit with an implement or fist, hit repeatedly, kicked or grabbed round the neck. Fourteen per cent were assessed as victims of inter-mediate-level abuse, defined as occasional violence without injury or regular treatment resulting in pain. Meanwhile, 5 per cent of the sample assessed themselves as having suffered physical abuse, although 17 per cent stated that they had been 'treated too harshly'. Roughly half of those self-assessing as abused were among those identified by researchers as suffering serious abuse. From surveys involving parents' self-reporting, Smith et al. (1995) found that 15 per cent of children suffered severe physical abuse, while in a later study Ghate et al. (2003) reported incidence and prevalence figures of 9 and 16 per cent respectively.

Neglect

Cawson et al. (2000) identified two distinct dimensions of neglect, namely an absence of physical care and supervision. They found an absence of basic phys-ical care, such as food and clothing, very rare (1 per cent of their sample), but adjudged 6 per cent to have suffered a serious lack of physical care, including too great a burden of self-care, abandonment and exposure to danger. A fur-ther 9 per cent were said to have suffered such problems at an intermediate level. Supervision was gauged primarily in terms of children being left at home alone, or being out without parental knowledge of their whereabouts. Five per cent of respondents were assessed as having suffered a serious lack of supervision as they had stayed out overnight without the presence or knowledge of an adult while under the age of 14. Those who did so aged 14 or 15 were deemed to have experienced lack of supervision at an intermediate level, and this affected 12 per cent of respondents. Only 2 per cent identified themselves as neglected, although many more agreed with statements implying a degree of neglect.

Sexual abuse

In attempting to operationalise definitions of sexual abuse, Cawson et al. (2000) focused particularly on experiences involving contact, when the respondent was aged under 16 or there was an age gap of five or more years between the child and the alleged perpetrator. Eleven per cent of respondents reported abuse involving contact (and in some cases abuse by more than one perpetrator), most frequently involving those outside the family but known to the victim. Six per cent of respondents assessed themselves as having suffered sexual abuse. Kelly et al. (1991) found that 4 per cent of women and 2 per cent of men reported having experienced serious sexual abuse as children, but the figures rose to 59 per cent and 27 per cent respectively when wider definitions were used. Gallagher et al. (2002) estimate that 9 per cent of children experience sexual abuse by strangers, typically involving indecent exposure, attempting to make the child go with, or touch them.

Emotional abuse

In their study, Cawson et al. (2000) utilised the following seven categories:

1   psychological control and domination;
2   psycho-physical control and domination (to cause distress rather than injury)
    e.g. locking up, making a child wear soiled clothes, forcing a child to eat;
3   humiliation/degradation;
4   withdrawal;
5   antipathy;
6   terrorising – including use of threats;
7   proxy attacks.

Employing a scoring system equivalent to some measure of abuse in at least four of these categories, 6 per cent of respondents were adjudged to have suffered emotional abuse. Three per cent assessed themselves as emotionally abused. These figures are broadly similar to the 1990s' estimate of 350,000 children living in low warmth/high criticism environments (DH, 1995).

Multiple forms of abuse

There is a relative paucity of research linking different forms of maltreatment but Cawson et al's (2000) study yields some interesting findings. Six per cent of the sample had experienced more than one form of serious maltreatment, including a small minority who were adjudged to have experiences indicating all four categories. While the above findings are indicative of widespread maltreatment, it is important to remember the happier childhoods of the majority. Over 90 per cent of Cawson et al's respondents reported that they came from a warm and loving family background.

WHO ABUSES WHOM?

In this section we offer a brief empirical overview of what is known about the social identities of the victims and perpetrators of child maltreatment. A number of these issues will also be discussed further in later sections on risk factors and the 'causes' of maltreatment.

Social class, poverty and social exclusion

One of the most consistent research findings in relation to child maltreatment is the over-representation of children from poor families among those diagnosed as victims.

Those placed on the child protection register or in care have been found to come overwhelmingly from social classes IV and V, and from families with relatively high levels of unemployment, occupancy of social housing and reliance on benefits as a main source of income (Corby, 2005; Sidebotham and Heron, 2006). This relationship has been found for all categories of maltreatment with the partial exception of sexual abuse, where any link has been found to be weaker and in some studies absent (Corby, 2005).

Given the socially constructed and often 'hidden' nature of maltreatment, there has predictably been much debate regarding whether its relationship with poverty is 'real' or a product of biases within child protection processes. In particular, it can be argued that poorer families are more open to surveillance, especially by welfare professionals, more likely to be regarded as potential abusers and less equipped to challenge professional judgements than their more affluent counterparts. While there is some evidence to support these arguments (Cobley and Sanders, 2003), this is unlikely to explain the consistently wide differences in maltreatment rates found between socio-economic groups. Crucially, in their study, Cawson et al. (2000) found strong class gradients in relation to *self-reported* physical abuse, neglect and exposure to domestic violence.

In line with interest in 'social capital' (see Chapter 3), increasing attention has been paid in recent years to neighbourhood effects, although relevant research is more developed internationally than in the UK (Coulton et al., 1999; Korbin, 2003.) This research suggests that a lack of community cohesion may contribute to higher levels of maltreatment both through the isolation of potentially abusive parents and less willingness on the part of others to intervene in protective ways. However, in policy terms, Jack (2006) argues that New Labour's emphasis on social investment has continued to prioritise formalised child protection systems over outreach and community involvement.

Gender

There are few headline gender differences among victims of maltreatment with the notable exception of those experiencing sexual abuse, where studies show girls' rates of victimisation to be between two and four times those of boys. Gender is equally relevant to perpetration, where it has been estimated that men commit roughly 95 and 80 per cent of the sexual abuse of girls and boys respectively (Finkelhor et al., 1986; Kelly et al., 1991). This strongly gendered pattern has formed the basis of a feminist analysis of sexual abuse, to which we will return. In other forms of maltreatment gender may appear less relevant, but this is misleading. For example, women form a small majority of perpetrators of physical abuse but, once living arrangements and time spent with children are taken into account, could be seen as less likely to become involved in such abuse. Men are also responsible for a clear majority of serious injuries inflicted upon children (Schnitzer and Ewigman, 2005). Neglect provides an even starker example, where assumptions regarding women's responsibilities tend to obscure any focus on men as perpetrators, or indeed as potential resources (Turney, 2000; Daniel and Taylor, 2006).

Ethnicity

Gauging links between ethnicity and child maltreatment is fraught with difficulty (see the discussion in Chapter 2) and predictably perhaps, research has yielded mixed results. (See Thoburn et al., 2004, or Chand and Thoburn, 2006, for reviews and Koramoa et al., 2002, on how to approach 'traditional practices' in relation to maltreatment.) Figures from the child protection register reveal an over-representation of black children and those of mixed parentage and an under-representation of those from South Asian backgrounds (DfES, 2007a: Table 4.D). However, these categories are notoriously slippery and may hide as much as they reveal (for example, in relation to socio-economic factors, religion, cultural practices or length of stay in the UK). Official statistics also crucially reflect policy and professional practices and there is some evidence that, once involved, BME families may be drawn more deeply into the child protection system than their white counterparts (Brophy et al., 2003). Equally important is the willingness of families and communities to report concerns. Here, it has increasingly been recognised that South Asian and to a lesser extent African communities may be reluctant to contact professional agencies for reasons such as family honour, ostracisation, unfamiliarity with the UK child care system or fear of racist treatment (Bernard and Gupta, 2006; Gillen, 2007).

Cawson (2002) found no link between ethnicity and maltreatment, while there have been mixed findings in respect of different forms of maltreatment, including the much-debated question of whether (harsh) physical punishment is more prevalent in certain BME communities (Barn et al., 2006).

Other child-related risk factors

Statistics from the child protection register suggest that young children are especially vulnerable to maltreatment, with the rate of registration being over twice as high for babies as for children aged 10–15 (DfES, 2007a: Table 3B). This is due almost entirely to the categories of physical abuse and neglect, as those of emotional abuse and, perhaps surprisingly, sexual abuse vary little with age. A key factor here is that young children may be seen as more susceptible to physical injury and developmental harm, including extreme cases such as 'shaken baby syndrome' and FII (Sheridan, 2003; Wheeler, 2003). Maltreatment of disabled children will be discussed more fully in Chapter 9, but at this point it can be noted that research studies show they are between one and a half and four times more likely to be victims than other children (Westcott and Jones, 1999). From their large-scale longitudinal study, Sidebotham and Heron (2006) also identify factors such as low birthweight, poor health and developmental problems as heightening the risk of maltreatment.

Familial and parental risk factors

Research studies have often found links between child maltreatment and family structure, with a higher incidence associated with lone parent and stepfamily households (Cawson, 2002; Corby, 2005). In a US study, Schnitzer and Ewigman (2005) estimated that children living with unrelated adults were almost 50 times more likely to die through inflicted injuries than children living with two biological parents. In relation to stepfamilies, attention has focused particularly on sexual abuse, where studies have found a relatively higher incidence (Corby, 2005). However, statistical correlations may hide a complex array of factors contributing to the maltreatment and hence demand extreme caution in interpretation. Young parental age has been a common research finding in cases of maltreatment, although some have expressed scepticism regarding this link (Corby, 2005). Mention has already been made in previous chapters of the risks associated with parental mental health, substance misuse and learning disabilities but, as with all identified risk factors, it is important to stress that child maltreatment occurs in only a small minority of families.

Children and young people who abuse

The focus on children and young people (hereafter children) who abuse has been almost entirely on sexual abuse, as other abusive behaviour between children is likely to be classified in other ways, e.g. as bullying (though see Hagell and Jeyarajah-Dent, 2006, for a discussion of children involved in serious interpersonal violence). Growing interest in sexual abuse by children in the late twentieth century drew on two separate themes, namely the inter-generational transmission of abuse (see below) and the recognition that many adult sex offenders had started their 'careers' or shown signs of deviant sexual behaviour as children (Brownlie, 2001). Over the past two decades, both official statistics and research evidence have shown fairly consistently that up to one-third of sexual offences are committed by those aged 17 or under (Corby, 2005). As is the case for adults, the overwhelming majority of these offenders are male. Although relatively little researched, abuse by siblings is also not uncommon.

Working with children who abuse poses particular challenges due to the bifurcation of child welfare and youth justice systems, especially in England and Wales (for handling within the Scottish hearings system, see Murray and Hallett, 2000). On the one hand, it has been estimated that between 20 and 60 per cent of the children have themselves been victims of sexual abuse (Lancaster and Lumb, 1999). More generally, they are frequently seen as having high levels of need, often including those arising from intellectual impairments (Fyson, 2005). Conversely, a 'no excuses' culture in youth justice combined with a wider social anxiety surrounding 'paedophiles' have ensured that the sanguine view of offending as a phase for many young people is often suspended in the case of sex offenders.

Against this grain, treatment programmes have been established that recognise children's needs and work through empowering rather than pathologising them (Myers, 2005; Durham, 2006). (Other helpful sources include Hackett et al's (2005) mapping exercise of services in the UK and Ireland, and Erooga and Masson, 2006, for the relevant legal, policy and practice issues.)

UNDERSTANDING CHILD MALTREATMENT

Understanding 'causes' of maltreatment holds out the promise of improving interventions through prediction and prevention although in practice, as will be explained, this is extremely difficult to achieve. If by no means mutually exclusive, there are two very distinct approaches to understanding child maltreatment. The first uses statistical analysis to identify 'risk factors', while the second involves the application of theories drawn from the social sciences, especially psychology and sociology. We consider each in turn.

Risk factors and prediction

The appeal of being able to accurately predict child maltreatment is obvious as it appears to clear the way for preventive interventions. Such efforts have generally taken an 'actuarial' form based on risk factors derived from research on known cases of (serious) maltreatment. Such checklists have been applied mainly to physical abuse and to a lesser extent sexual abuse (Hagell, 1998). One of the best-known examples comes from Greenland (1987), who identified the risk factors (shown in Box 5.1) relating to parents and children from an analysis of child deaths. High risk was defined as occurring when at least half the factors were present.

If the application of such 'checklists' has received official encouragement in recent years, it has also been subjected to significant critique. Crucially, it has been found that their predictive value in individual cases is low and that they generate significant 'false positives' – wrongly identifying maltreatment among those who score highly in terms of risk factors – and 'false negatives' – missing maltreatment among those who do not. As can be seen from Box 5.1, the risk factors are often at a high level of abstraction and may apply to large populations, only minorities of whom are (likely to be) involved in child maltreatment. On this basis, it has been suggested that such checklists are more useful for targeting family support measures than as a prediction of maltreatment (Farmer and Owen, 1995). Further criticisms include the danger of self-fulfilling prophecy, whereby the risk factors lead professionals to look for, and find, more maltreatment among particular groups of children and families. Wattam (1999) additionally suggests that despite some use of social categories, predictive approaches tend to generate narrow, individualised ways of understanding maltreatment.

Yet, as Hagell (1998) observes, prediction in some shape or form is unavoidable in child protection work and the challenge lies in how to draw on a knowledge of risk factors without doing so in a mechanistic or blinkered way. Munro (2002) offers an interesting account of different modes of decision making including the 'intuitive' and argues that there is a case for using more formalised, calculative methods.

Understanding the 'causes' of child maltreatment – theoretical contributions

Whatever its merits, a statistical correlation between 'risk factors' and child maltreatment does little to identify causal links that may help to develop effective interventions. Attempts to promote such understanding have drawn especially from the disciplines of psychology and sociology. In an excellent overview, Corby (2005: 154–180) divides theoretical perspectives into three broad groupings, namely psychological, social psychological and sociological, a schema that will be followed here.

Psychological perspectives

Explanatory accounts of child maltreatment have emanated from all the major schools of psychology. Their primary focus rests with individual perpetrators, but to a greater or lesser extent they also address ideas of 'intergenerational transmission' – examining the ways in which the childhood victims of maltreatment may become perpetrators as adults. Although they enjoy little support, there are also 'pre-psychological' theories rooted in biology and ideas of instinct (Corby, 2005: 156–158).

Psychodynamic perspectives (broadly derived from Freudian psychology) emphasise developmental stages and the formation of personality as these stages are negotiated (McCluskey and Hooper, 2000). In relation to child maltreatment, attention has focused on how a parent's own childhood may influence their capacity to recognise and meet children's needs, whether they have acquired a rigid personality, become easily frustrated or have difficulty in controlling aggression.

Attachment theory (see Chapter 2) has been increasingly applied to issues of child maltreatment in recent years (see especially, Howe, 2005). This application has focused on two key areas, namely how maltreatment can promote insecure (especially disorganised) attachments and how parents' own attachment histories may affect their responses to children. Of particular concern is the way in which those who were themselves insecurely attached may respond to children's needs with rejection, anger or helplessness, thereby increasing the risk of maltreatment.

Social learning theory focuses on how behaviour is learned through processes of observation, conditioning and reinforcement. In line with the theory, intervention would focus on identifying these patterns and seeking to modify them through behavioural therapy, perhaps by working on avoiding 'triggers' for maltreatment or reinforcing appropriate parental responses. Increasingly, behavioural approaches are linked to those that also reflect cognitive psychology. Here, maltreatment would be attributed to 'distorted thinking' on the part of an abuser, such as having unrealistic expectations of children, or mistaken beliefs about the effectiveness of discipline. For a guide to cognitive behavioural work, see for example the relevant chapters in Cigno and Bourn (1998) or Macdonald (1999).

Whatever their particular strengths, psychological approaches can be criticised for failing to take the social context into account, both in terms of the pressures that may have contributed to maltreatment and the limits of individualised 'treatment' in the absence of changing material circumstances.

Social psychological perspectives

Corby identifies three different social psychological approaches, whose common ground rests with seeing behaviour as situational, a product of particular relationships and environments. The first perspective is based on interactionism, within which abusive behaviour is seen to arise from the interplay of parental characteristics and the attributes and behaviour of children (as seen in Box 5.1). Any focus on child victims is controversial as it can appear to 'blame' children for their maltreatment. However, if the pattern of interaction can be identified and understood, this perspective holds out the possibility of a virtuous circle built upon mutual change.

A second perspective focuses on family dysfunction, extending the analysis of interactions to family roles, chains of communication and dynamics such as scapegoating or the 'proxy' involvement of children in adult conflicts. In relation to interventions, such models are closely linked to family therapy (Ben-Tovim et al., 1988). The family model has been utilised to explain (step)father–daughter incest. This is generally taken to arise as a response to difficulties in relations between parents, whereupon the (step)father 'turns' to his daughter(s) for sexual gratification. Mothers are often seen as colluding in this process to varying degrees. Predictably, the gendered assumptions of this model have been strongly criticised by feminists (see below).

A third social psychological perspective is the ecological, which, as discussed in Chapter 2, has been highly influential in child and family social care. In relation to child maltreatment, this perspective is particularly associated with the work of Garbarino et al. (1980) in the USA. While the importance of individual and familial factors is recognised, weight is also given to wider social networks as potential sources of both stress and support. In principle, strengthening networks represents an important means of reducing maltreatment, although in practice this remains challenging (Jack, 2006).

Sociological perspectives

Corby identifies two mainstream sociological perspectives on child maltreatment, the cultural and the structural. The former seeks to locate maltreatment within a wider cultural context and has been applied especially to physical abuse. Straus et al. (1980) link high levels of abuse with an embedded and culturally approved use of lower-level violence against children. This 'tip of the iceberg' analysis points to the need for wider cultural change to reduce maltreatment, and can also be applied to 'norms' that may increase the likelihood of sexual or emotional abuse (O'Hagan, 2006). The social structural perspective advocates understanding maltreatment in terms of the full range of factors impacting on child development (Gil, 1970). This entails going beyond the notion that factors such as poverty, unemployment, homelessness or racism act as stressors that lead to maltreatment, to recognise that they are in themselves harmful to children. This allows a radical redefining of 'perpetrators' of maltreatment to include those in powerful positions whose actions are damaging to children.

Although feminism has many variants (Williams, 1989), the common ground rests with the need to place gendered power relations centrally in analysis. We have seen earlier how this can serve to contextualise physical abuse and neglect perpetrated by women, but the influence of feminism has been strongest in relation to sexual abuse (Driver and Droisen, 1989; Cox et al., 2000). Here, it is argued that child sexual abuse must be understood in the context of a patriarchal society and a nexus of male controls over women and children, including 'rights' to sex. A particular target for feminist critique is the 'family dysfunction' theory described earlier, which is seen as employing gendered assumptions to 'excuse' male perpetrators and transfer blame to women who have doubly failed to properly nurture their partners or protect their children. Despite a broader political marginalisation and limited impact on social work practice (Scourfield, 2002), feminism has had some influence in certain areas, notably in according women key roles in dealing with the survivors of sexual abuse, and promoting the removal of perpetrators rather than children from the family home.

At a theoretical level, there is always the danger of reductionism, which may in part explain the relative lack of engagement of feminist perspectives with women as abusers. Ford (2006) provides an excellent and nuanced analysis of sexual abuse by women, including the tendency to question its occurrence or deny its seriousness.

Finally, sociological perspectives on childhood (see Chapter 1) may be used to examine children's lack of power as a contributing factor to maltreatment. From this stance, vulnerability may stem from factors such as whether children are given protective knowledge, or are encouraged to be too trusting of adults, or are believed when disclosing maltreatment (Kitzinger, 2004).

UNDERSTANDING CHILD MALTREATMENT – DILEMMAS AND IMPLICATIONS

The wide range of perspectives described above demonstrates that the 'causes' of maltreatment can be approached at different levels of analysis as well as through different theoretical lenses. Thus, the utility of competing perspectives may depend on whether in C. Wright Mills's terms, one is trying to explain child maltreatment as a 'private trouble' or a 'public issue'. If the primary focus rests on why maltreatment is perpetrated by particular individuals or within particular families, then more psychologically leaning theories may be the most relevant. If, however, it rests with levels, patterns or constructions of maltreatment, then sociologically informed approaches may have more to offer. There is a broad consensus among commentators that the 'causes' of maltreatment are multi-factorial, but significant challenges remain in attempting to understand how factors work in combination to produce maltreatment (Cawson, 2002).

Crucially, levels of analysis are also linked, albeit loosely, to different forms of intervention. More psychological explanations customarily inform individual or family-based treatment programmes while approaches such as the ecological may emphasise the value of work to strengthen local social networks. Sociological explanations point to the need for wider social change, for example, in areas such as the cultural acceptability of violence, gender relations, or class and ethnic inequalities. Although these perspectives may ultimately hold more potential for reducing child maltreatment, they are politically difficult, long-term projects, which pose distinct challenges to practitioners working for progressive change.

EXPLORING THE CONSEQUENCES OF CHILD MALTREATMENT

Knowledge of the consequences of child maltreatment is potentially valuable for several reasons. First, gauging harmful effects forms a crucial plank in both public and professional understanding of maltreatment. Second, it may aid detection by promoting greater awareness of the 'signs' or 'symptoms' of maltreatment. Third, such knowledge can engender important 'feedback' on particular forms of parenting. Fourth, understanding the consequences of maltreatment can guide policy makers and practitioners in terms of service provision for victims.

As is the case for the 'causes' of maltreatment, however, research on its consequences is fraught with methodological difficulties. The diverse nature of the main categories of abuse and neglect, their frequent overlap or co-existence and the adverse impact of factors other than maltreatment all make it extremely difficult to discern its specific effects. Once again, Corby (2005: 181–209) supplies the most useful overview of this area.

Despite the challenges, there is a significant body of research into the consequences of maltreatment, both in the USA and the UK. This relates particularly to physical and sexual abuse, reflecting their longer period of 'recognition' and, in the latter case, the focus on 'survivors'. While different forms of maltreatment sometimes have their own specific effects (see below), there is also considerable overlap in the domain of psychological problems. Anxiety, depression, substance misuse, eating disorders and self-destructive behaviours have been common findings in follow-up studies of maltreated children (HM Government, 2006a). Researchers have also found links with a later involvement in crime and prostitution, although these are often approached retrospectively and may therefore be overestimated. Other problem areas associated with a range of maltreatment include peer relationships and performance in education (Corby, 2005).

Physical abuse

The most obvious consequences specific to physical abuse are of course, the (serious) and sometimes fatal injuries that may occur. Children fearful of physical assault have also sometimes been found to show hyperconformity or a state of 'frozen watchfulness'. More broadly, while a range of negative out-comes is sometimes traced directly to physical abuse or physical punishment (see for example Afifi et al., 2006), these are more commonly attributed to the broader relational and emotional environment within which it takes place (Gibbons et al., 1995b).

Neglect

Like physical abuse, neglect can have extreme consequences on health and development, including fatality. In less severe cases, its specific impact is likely to be upon growth and/or intellectual development, with research studies particularly highlighting the problem of 'withdrawn' behaviour (Tyler et al., 2006). The especially damaging effects of chronic neglect and the difficulties of achieving rapid change have led to calls for long-term support-ive involvement in such cases (Tanner and Turney, 2003).

Sexual abuse

Based on the range of problems experienced as adults, Cawson (2002) argues that those who have been sexually abused as children face 'the direst situation'. From a review of research evidence, Corby (2005) identifies the following factors as heightening the harmful effects:

- penetration;
- persistence over time;
- father-figure as perpetrator;
- use or threat of violence or force;
- negative response from family.

Kogan (2005) found that prompt disclosure was beneficial to adolescents psychologically and in terms of avoiding revictimisation. Cawson et al. (2000), however, found that disclosures were often long delayed or never made and that a majority of victims felt that disclosures had failed to stop the abuse.

Beyond certain physical risks, including pregnancy and sexually transmitted diseases, two issues particularly associated with sexual abuse are the impact on sexual behaviour and self-harming behaviour. The former may include abusing other children, an early involvement in sexual activity, confusion over sexual and emotional aspects of relationships and an involvement in prostitution (Corby, 2005). Meanwhile, several studies have found high rates of self-harming and suicidal behaviour among victims of sexual abuse, with some evidence of particular vulnerability for young men (Durham, 2003; Martin et al., 2004).

Emotional abuse

Emotional abuse has probably been the least researched form of maltreatment in terms of its consequences, although there has been increasing recognition of its contribution to the psychological difficulties experienced by victims. Indeed, in a recent review of research, Iwaniec et al. (2006) have claimed that the effects of emotional abuse are the most damaging of all, identifying a higher incidence of a range of cognitive, social, behavioural and physical problems.

RESPONDING TO THE CONSEQUENCES OF MALTREATMENT – RESILIENCE AND INTERVENTION

Overall, despite the methodological challenges of demonstrating 'cause and effect', there is significant evidence of adverse consequences following child maltreatment. However, the effects on individuals of ostensibly similar types and degrees of maltreatment appear to vary widely, with longitudinal studies showing that many victims suffer no discernible ill effects in adulthood (Collishaw et al., 2007). This has prompted interest in the factors promoting resilience (see Chapter 2) in the wake of maltreatment. In addition to the well-known importance of education, supportive social networks, and family and adult relationships, Rutter (2007) highlights the importance of individual coping mechanisms and problem solving. He stresses how resilience must be seen as a changing phenomenon across the life course and how it can result from exposure to, and the overcoming of, adversity.

The consequences of maltreatment may of course depend on the availability and effectiveness of particular services and interventions. Their results have been found to be mixed, but to be beneficial to many survivors of maltreatment (for overviews, see Macdonald, 1999, or Doyle, 2006). Criticisms have, however, often been made regarding the availability, flexibility and timeliness of services, described by Cawson (2002) as 'a staggering indictment'. Mention should also be made of services, often on a group basis, available for non-abusing family members (Hill, 2001; 2003).

CONCLUSION

In this chapter, we have seen how building the 'knowledge base' in respect of child maltreatment faces significant challenges, arising from methodological issues and the contested nature of the subject matter. However, attempting to meet these challenges remains important for policy makers and practitioners seeking to prevent or ameliorate the undoubtedly damaging impact of maltreatment upon children. Recognition of its multifactorial genesis points to the importance of responses at all levels from the individual to the societal. As suggested earlier, the major intellectual challenge is to develop greater understanding of how factors interact within an ecological model.

GUIDE TO FURTHER READING

Although most child protection texts (see Chapter 4) have relevant material, Corby (2005) stands out, affording an excellent overview of issues covered in this chapter and a guide to other sources. For a global perspective on maltreatment, see the UN's *World Report on Violence against Children* – www.violencestudy.org/r229

Reading and resources for practice

Two recent additions to the literature offer useful accounts of the application of knowledge to practice assessment and intervention. They are Horwath's (2007) account of working with neglect and Iwaniec's *The Emotionally Abused and Neglected Child: Identification, Assessment and Intervention. A Practice Handbook* (Wiley). Although now somewhat dated, Glaser and Frosh's *Child Sexual Abuse* (Macmillan) provides an excellent overview, while Sanderson's *Counselling Adult Survivors of Child Sexual Abuse* (Jessica Kingsley) offers a good guide to the issues facing survivors, including those relating to recovered memories. The Association of Child Abuse Lawyers has a helpful internet guide to survivors' groups, available at www.childabuselawyers.com/linkssurvivors.asp

Discussion questions

What does it mean to say that child maltreatment is 'socially constructed'?

How useful are official statistics on child protection and what might be done to improve them?

To what extent is child maltreatment a 'male' problem?

What are the main strengths and weaknesses of sociological explanations of maltreatment?

What are the major challenges in conducting research into the consequences of maltreatment?

6

LOOKED AFTER CHILDREN – THE STATE AS PARENT

In this and the following chapter, the focus is on looked after children, the legal term adopted primarily for those living in public care. While Chapter 7 addresses the major settings within which children are 'placed', here we seek to review the main issues relating to their care.

It is important to note that the umbrella term looked after children hides great diversity in terms of care 'careers'. Children become looked after for a variety of reasons and under different legal circumstances, while their time in care may range from days or weeks to almost an entire childhood. A majority will return to their birth families, while significant minorities will be adopted or will leave for the 'independence' of adulthood. Experiences of public care are likely to be equally diverse, whether in terms of stability or quality of relationships. Our aim in this chapter is to map the diversity of care 'careers' and to examine the policies and practices that help to shape them. In so doing, cognisance must be taken of the challenges faced by the modern care system, in safeguarding children, listening to them, planning to meet their needs and preparing them for life beyond care. Our starting point, however, rests with the legal framework for entry into public care followed by a profile of looked after children.

LOOKED AFTER CHILDREN – THE LEGAL FRAMEWORK?

Legal pathways into public care essentially fall into two categories, the voluntary and the compulsory. The voluntary route involves parents requesting or sometimes agreeing that their children should be placed in care. Under the Children Act 1989 (s20) and its equivalents in Scotland and Northern Ireland, the term voluntary care was replaced by accommodation in an attempt to emphasise its function as a supportive service to families and to challenge the stigma attached to children being 'in care'. The provision of accommodation is intended to cover situations where there is no-one to care for a child (e.g. those abandoned, orphaned or UASC) or the parent is unable to provide care. It may also be offered when the local authority thinks it necessary to safeguard and promote the child's welfare. The principal legal effect of accommodation is that parents have the right to remove the child at any time and in practice have a major say over any decisions while the child is accommodated.

Despite the legal changes, however, accommodation can represent a difficult frontier for negotiation between families and the state, as the wishes of parents and professionals may conflict (Packman and Hall, 1998). Thus, social workers may encourage accommodation as a less confrontational alternative to compulsion, but this may be accompanied by the threat of coercion, whether veiled or not. Alternatively, they may resist parental requests for accommodation on the grounds that this does not serve the child's interests or as a 'gatekeeping' exercise to restrict numbers in public care. Crucially, children will also have their own wishes in respect of accommodation.

Although local authority care is utilised for remands and other criminal justice disposals (see Lipscombe, 2006), the major compulsory route to becoming looked after rests with care proceedings under s31 of the Children Act, or in Scotland, with parental responsibility orders (PROs) or supervision requirements, as described in Chapter 4. The effect of care orders and PROs is that parental responsibility is shared between parents and the local authority, with an expectation of partnership. However, in practice, the major powers of decision making rest with the authority.

Looked after children – a profile

In this section, a brief statistical profile of looked after children in the UK is given, focusing on both background socio-demographic variables and factors relating more directly to care careers. Aggregating statistics from the four UK countries, the total number of looked after children in March 2007 (2006 in the case of Wales) was approximately 81,000.[1] From its peak in the late 1970s, the looked after population declined sharply, falling in England and Wales from 95,300 in 1980 to 49,300 in 1994 (DH, 2001b), since when it has risen significantly, largely due to children being looked after for longer. The above population figures reflect annual snapshots and mask significant movement during each year. For example, in England a total of 84,300 children were looked after at some point during the year 2005-2006 (DfES, 2007c: Table S).

---

[1]Department for Children, Schools and Families (2007a) *Children Looked After in England (Including Adoption and Care Leavers) year ending 31 March 2007*, London: DCSF. Scottish Government (2007c) *Children Looked After Statistics 2006–7*, Edinburgh: Scottish Government. Local Government Data Unit, Wales (2006) *Personal Social Services Statistics Wales 2006: Children*, Cardiff: LGDU. Northern Ireland. Statistics and Research Agency (2006) *Children Order Statistical Bulletin 2006*, Table 2.8, Belfast: Community Information Branch.

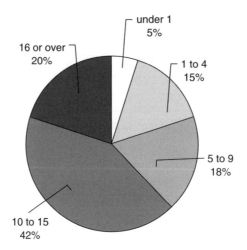

Figure 6.1   Ages of looked after children – England 2007 (adapted from DCSF, 2007a: Table A1)

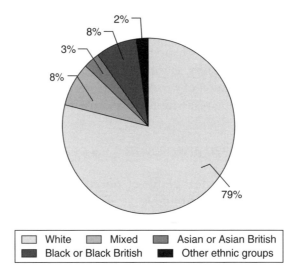

Figure 6.2   Ethnicity of looked after children – England 2007 (adapted from DCSF, 2007a: Table A1)

SOCIO-ECONOMIC FACTORS

Official statistics do not record the socio-economic background of looked after children, but research studies have consistently found that the latter come predominantly from the poorest sections of the community (Bebbington and Miles, 1989; Waterhouse and McGee, 2002). Across the UK, around 55 per cent of looked after children are male. The age distribution and ethnic make-up of looked after children in England can be seen in Figures 6.1 and 6.2.

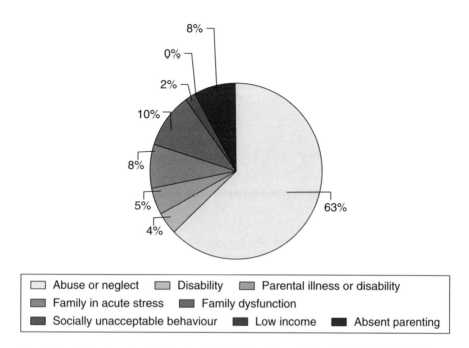

Figure 6.3 Categories of need for looked after children (adapted from DCSF, 2007a: Table A1)

Figure 6.1 shows that more than 60 per cent of looked after children are over the age of 10, the result both of those entering at older ages and those who have remained in care for significant periods of time.

The broad pattern revealed in Figure 6.2 is similar to that described in relation to child protection registration (see Chapter 4) with over-representation of black children and those of mixed parentage and under-representation of those from South Asian backgrounds. UASC comprise around 5 per cent of the looked after population.

CARE CAREERS

In terms of legal status, 64 per cent of looked after children in England in 2007 were subject to a care order, with 30 per cent accommodated under s20 (DCSF, 2007a: Table A2). (The remaining 6 per cent comprised those on child protection or criminal justice orders or children placed for adoption.) Roughly two-thirds of children start to be looked after on a voluntary basis, but those on care orders are on average likely to remain so for around four times longer than those accommodated (Table D5). In Scotland, almost 80 per cent of looked after children are subject to supervision requirements and 10 per cent are accommodated (Scottish Government, 2007c: Table 1.4).

Figure 6.3 shows the officially recorded categories of need for children being looked after in England. The dominant influence of maltreatment is

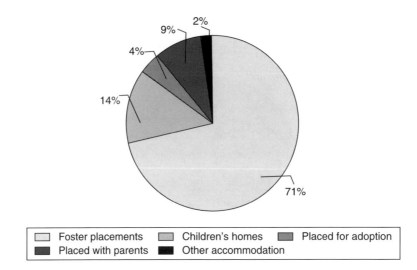

Figure 6.4 Placements for looked after children – England 2007 (adapted from DCSF, 2007a: Table A3)

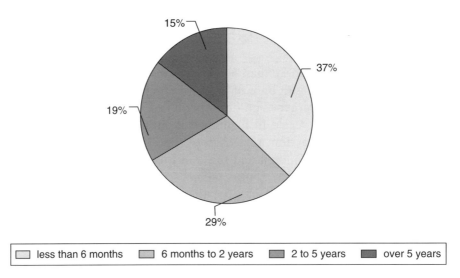

Figure 6.5 Time spent by looked after children – England 2007 (adapted from DCSF, 2007a: Table D5)

readily apparent, particularly for children aged 10 and below, but it is still the main category recorded for 33 per cent of those aged 10–15, with a range of family problems accounting for most of the remainder. The category of absent parenting is significantly inflated by UASC.

Placement of looked after children will be discussed more fully below and in the following chapter, but a brief overview is presented in Figure 6.4. Since the rapid contraction of residential care in the 1980s and early 1990s, foster care has been the dominant form of placement for looked after children, and this position has been consolidated over the past decade with the number of children in foster care in England rising from 33,700 in 1997 to 42,300 in 2006 (DCSF, 2007a. Table A3). With some variations, placements elsewhere in the UK follow a similar pattern, the notable exception being in Scotland where 43 per cent of looked after children are at home under a supervision requirement (Scottish Government, 2007c: Table 1.4).

Figure 6.5 shows the time spent being looked after for children leaving care in England during 2006–2007. As can be seen, there is wide variation, with almost 40 per cent spending less than six months in care, while 15 per cent were looked after for at least five years.

THE STATE AS PARENT – A LITANY OF FAILURE?

While policy interest in looked after children tends to be rather spasmodic, it can be argued that it has intensified fairly steadily since the 1970s. (For an earlier history see Hendrick, 2003, and the relevant chapters in Stevenson, 1999). This is partly due to the growing politicisation of child welfare, but also reflects powerful perceptions that public care has 'failed' in important respects. A significant trigger was the seminal research study *Children Who Wait* (Rowe and Lambert, 1973). The authors highlighted in particular the problem of 'drift', a term used to describe the situation of children in care, often for many years, without clear plans for their long-term futures. Efforts to address this problem drew on the concept of 'permanence', which emphasised the vital of continuity and both legal and emotional security for children. Equally vital was the idea that children's futures should be resolved speedily and decisively. If parents could meet the children's needs adequately, without damaging delay and with good long-term prospects, then permanence would be achieved within the birth family. If not, then it should be provided through substitute care, most usually adoption, as quickly as possible (Maluccio et al., 1986). Yet despite their apparent 'even-handedness', permanence policies were seen by family and parents' rights groups as punitive towards birth families – promoting 'adoption by the back door'. This perception gained ground during the 1980s and contributed to the 'partnership' philosophy of the Children Act 1989.

Around the same time, a number of other problems were identified within the care system, prompting the *Looked After Children* reforms (see Chapter 1). It was argued that an over-concentration on major planning objectives, such as achieving permanence, meant crucial aspects of children's lives were being neglected (Parker et al., 1991). This applied particularly to issues such as health and education, but also those of identity, development and skill acquisition. The phrase 'corporate parenting' was coined to emphasise expectations that the state should show similar levels of interest and concern to those of most birth parents. Increasing attention was paid by governments to the 'performance' of the care system, a trend accelerated when the New Labour government identified looked after children as a group who were particularly vulnerable to social exclusion.

The perception of the care system as 'failing' is a powerful one. In a recent polemical critique, Sergeant (2006: 1) describes this failure as 'catastrophic' and as perpetuating an underclass, suggesting that a successful system would reduce numbers of young prisoners, prostitutes and homeless people by up to half 'at a stroke'. In the following sections, we examine various aspects of perceived failure, starting with the phenomenon of the maltreatment of looked after children.

INSTITUTIONAL ABUSE AND SAFEGUARDING LOOKED AFTER CHILDREN

The term institutional abuse is an umbrella term encompassing several distinct though connected forms of maltreatment and may apply to a wide range of settings other than the care system (Gallagher, 2000). These forms can be divided into five categories, as follows.

Abuse of children by staff/carers describes situations where social care staff or foster carers, acting individually or with others, commit acts of physical, sexual or emotional abuse against children or neglect them. Although many foster carers have been involved in serious cases of maltreatment, public attention has tended to focus more strongly on that taking place in residential care (Corby et al., 2001).

Involvement of staff or carers in the abuse of *children by others* may occur in two ways. First, in extreme cases, they may actively recruit children for sexual abuse or exploitation by others. Second, they may be passive to the point of neglect when children are known or suspected to be involved in offending, substance misbuse and sexual exploitation, risks that are often heightened when looked after children go missing from their placements (Biehal and Wade, 2000).

Abuse of children by other children has been found to be widespread, especially in residential care. This may take different forms including peer violence, sexual harassment and homophobic bullying (Barter et al., 2004; Green, 2005). In a minority of cases, informal hierarchies among children have been enlisted by staff as a form of discipline within the home or are even incorporated into the latter's abusive activities. Such difficulties have been exacerbated by the placement of vulnerable children alongside those with histories of violence or sexually abusive behaviour (Farmer, 2004). In an interesting study of the links between care experiences and involvement in the sex industry, Coy (2007) highlights the role played by peers in introducing young women into prostitution.

There may also be *abusive regimes*, where maltreatment is officially sanctioned as treatment. Perhaps the most infamous was that of 'Pindown', where various forms of humiliation and deprivation – such as children being dressed in pyjamas or stripped, put in play pens, or kept in isolation or rooms with no furniture – were deployed to 're-establish control of the child' (Levy and Kahan, 1991). In the case of Frank Beck, controversial therapeutic techniques acted as a cover for serious sexual abuse over many years. More generally, concerns remain about measures such as strip-searching, segregation and techniques of 'distraction', used to control children's behaviour in residential care and young offender institutions (CSCI et al., 2005).

The final category may be termed *systemic abuse*, where, in line with broader definitions of maltreatment, any actions or inactions that have negative consequences for looked after children may be deemed 'abusive'. Examples might include multiple placement moves or failure to attend adequately to health or educational needs.

Believing allegations – empowerment or witch-hunt?

Widespread allegations of institutional abuse have proved extremely divisive. On the one hand, a common feature of almost all the major 'scandals' has been that victims told or tried to tell those in authority but had their concerns ignored or dismissed (Dalrymple, 2001). Their advocates see this as indicative of children's general lack of power and the 'troublesome' image attached to those in care (Stein, 2006). Conversely, there are critics who argue that the accused have faced a 'witch-hunt' (Webster, 2005). They accuse the police of 'trawling' for evidence by contacting potential victims, who may be motivated by revenge or the hope of financial compensation, and relying on the sheer volume of allegations as evidence rather than their veracity (Beckett, 2002). Colton et al. (2002), however, argue that the tactic is reasonable given the history of 'silencing' victims and that there is no evidence to support widespread malicious allegations. Research into institutional abuse has been relatively limited, but for a good review see Gallagher, 2000.

Tackling institutional abuse

In addition to several inquiries focused on specific instances of institutional abuse (see Corby, 2005: 55–60), there have also been those taking a broader view of safeguards for children living away from home (Kent, 1997; Utting, 1997). The proposed reforms from these reports and other commentators have reflected the diverse nature of the abuse and the view that good practice makes it much less likely to occur. Box 6.1 sets out the main measures that have been pursued to safeguard looked after children and others living away from home.

PLANNING FOR LOOKED AFTER CHILDREN

As noted earlier, permanency planning for looked after children emerged as a response to the problem of 'drift' but has been characterised by a tension between avoiding delay and allowing the time and resources potentially necessary to reunite children with their birth families. The tensions were exacerbated rather than eased by the Children Act 1989, contributing to a significant lengthening of care proceedings (Beckett, 2001).

Whatever the challenges, care plans have been seen as a key mechanism for achieving positive outcomes for children and providing clarity and transparency for all those involved. The route to permanence, whether through the birth family or a substitute family, or for older children through independence, lies at the heart of the plan. Timescales have been tightened in England and Wales to require that a permanency plan is agreed at the four-month review. (Statutory reviews should take place within four weeks, then after a further three months and thereafter six monthly.) Additionally, to avoid delay and drift, there should be alternative plans, some of which, such as twin-tracking or concurrency (see Chapter 7), may be pursued in parallel with the main goal. Equally important are the details of how the plan is to be realised, for example what changes or resources might be necessary to facilitate a return to the birth family. For children, the plan should incorporate separate, detailed education and health plans (see below), while there should also be a placement plan, including details of the contact arrangements with birth family members or others. In a study of care plans and their implementation,

Harwin et al. (2003) found a clear link between the detail of plans, their fruition and positive outcomes for children.

An important refinement has been to place the role of an independent reviewing officer (IRO) on a statutory basis (Adoption and Children Act 2002, s118). The intention is for the IRO to bring a more 'objective' perspective to bear on local authority plans, primarily through chairing statutory reviews but also by taking a wider co-ordinating and problem-solving role. As a last resort, IROs may refer cases to CAFCASS, but there are no known cases of this power being enlisted. While there are varying degrees of independence, the basic requirement is that the IRO has no part in either line management or resource allocation relevant to the child.

Part of the role is to facilitate the involvement of parents, so long as this is consistent with the child's welfare (see McCann, 2006). Children's participation in planning can be understood as part of a wider process of their empowerment, and is discussed below. Plans for substitute family care and independent living are discussed in chapters 7 and 8 respectively, but we now turn to examine the most frequent goal for looked after children, namely reuniting them with their birth families. At around 40 per cent of cases, this remains the most frequent destination for children ceasing to be looked after (DCSF, 2007a: Table D1).

PLANNING FOR REUNIFICATION

Biehal (2007) provides an excellent overview of research on reunification, noting that, after some major studies in the late 1980s and early 1990s, it has until recently attracted little research interest, despite major changes within the care system. She examines two key tenets that emerged from earlier research, namely that the chances of successful reunification were enhanced by an early return and frequent contact between the child and birth family. In both cases, Biehal argues that these variables do not in themselves influence the likelihood of reunification, but rather that they reflect other factors such as the easing of problems or the underlying strength of family relationships.

Prospects for successful reunification have also been found to be enhanced by continuity in terms of family composition, schooling and neighbourhood. Bullock et al. (1993) highlight the importance of the looked after child's 'sense of belonging' and how this may be aided where they retain a role and 'territory' (e.g., a bedroom, possessions) in the family home. Research findings also suggest that prospects may be better when children are looked after as a result of behavioural problems and family conflicts rather than maltreatment.

Biehal (2007) summarises evidence on the outcomes of reunification, which, for those children subject to care orders, often means a period placed with parents while the order is in place. The overall picture is mixed, with studies showing that roughly a third of children return to public care, while a significant minority suffer further maltreatment. Children reunited with their families also fare less well in terms of educational performance and offending behaviour than those who remain in care. In their study, Farmer and Parker (1991) adjudged reunification as beneficial to 45 per cent of the children in their study and detrimental to 19 per cent, with the remainder in between these poles. Interpretation of such figures clearly depends on underlying perspectives (see Chapter 1) and there remain powerful lobbies arguing either for more or for less emphasis on reunification. While social work practice has been found to be important in reunification work, it has frequently been criticised as too passive when children are placed at home, provoking an unfavourable comparison made of the work put into substitute family care (Murray, 2006; Biehal, 2007).

LOOKED AFTER CHILDREN – CONTACT WITH BIRTH FAMILY MEMBERS

An important element within the Children Act 1989, was a duty (s34) on the part of local authorities to facilitate 'reasonable contact' between looked after children and their parents or guardians unless this was detrimental to the child's welfare. Contact issues can be seen as important for almost all looked after children but these vary significantly in terms of form, pattern and purpose. Although contact may be indirect, by telephone, letter or email, attention is generally focused on direct (face-to-face) contact. As discussed above, contact is a vital ingredient in reunification, whether employed to assess risk in cases of previous maltreatment or to gauge the quality of family relationships following a (substantial) period of separation. Depending on the perceived risk to the child and legal status (for example, when care proceedings are ongoing), contact may be supervised, either in the placement setting or in 'neutral' venues such as family centres or specialist contact centres. Needless to say, parents tend to dislike supervised contact, feeling under scrutiny in an 'unnatural' situation (Freeman and Hunt, 1998).

For children in longer-term placements, there has been ongoing debate regarding the importance of contact. Following Jolowicz's (1973) notion of the 'hidden parent' (which stressed the psychological importance of parents to children even in the absence of contact), research appeared to show that those children who were in contact with birth family members fared better than those who were not (Cleaver, 2000). However, it has been argued that the relationship is not necessarily causal and that contact may be detrimental to some children. (See the research reviews of Quinton et al. (1997; 1999) and Ryburn (1999) arguing the 'sceptical' and pro-contact positions respectively.) For children not in contact with birth relatives, the Children Act 1989 introduced the role of independent visitor to provide outside contact, but this has not been widely used (Knight, 1998).

IDENTITY AND DIRECT WORK

Identity is one of the seven developmental dimensions identified in the *Looked After Children* materials but relatively little is known about how it is applied and interpreted in practice. Identity can be understood both in personal terms, focusing on biography, family history and relationships, or in social terms based on factors such as class, gender, ethnicity, religion, sexuality and disability. Recognition of personal identity issues has focused primarily on helping looked after children make sense of their life histories, for instance why they came into care or why it is not considered possible for them to return to their birth families. The latest edition of Ryan and Walker's classic (2007) text features an excellent account of the rationale and techniques of life story work, while Rose and Philpot (2004) examine its potential for traumatised children.

Life story work is perhaps the best-known example of what is more broadly termed 'direct work' with children. Promotion of direct work rests on the premise that planning for looked after children is adult-dominated and fails to engage children or address the complex issues they face. Direct work may encompass activities such as play, exercises or outings, aiming to help build relationships and facilitate more meaningful communication between the worker or carer and the child, in addition to any 'therapeutic' value. Social workers have regularly been exhorted to undertake more direct work but such aspirations have largely been thwarted by pressures of time and often a lack of confidence on the part of workers (Luckock et al., 2006). The therapeutic potential of direct work is also controversial, raising the spectre that, in arousing deeper feelings, it may take social workers beyond their limits of expertise.

Questions of social identity for looked after children have been dominated by ethnicity (for helpful discussion in a cross-cultural context, see Robinson, 2007). Many of the debates relate to placement in care (see Chapter 7), but there is also a well-developed literature on helping BME children to cope with the negative effects of racism in society and often within the care system itself (see for example Barn, 1999; Okitikpi, 2005). Kelly and Sinclair (2005) provide an interesting account of the challenges faced by looked after children in Northern Ireland from cross-community backgrounds in negotiating identities both within the care system and local neighbourhoods. There is relatively little literature on care identity issues related to sexual orientation, but see Bremner and Hillin (1993) for discussion and Mallon (1998) for research in the USA.

THE EDUCATION OF LOOKED AFTER CHILDREN

Over the past two decades, the education of looked after children has risen steadily up the policy agenda, being seen as a key site for tackling social exclusion as well as improving life chances (Social Exclusion Unit, 2003). This rise has been accompanied by a growing body of research into the factors that underpin low levels of attainment.

A key early finding was that social care services often gave little priority to education for looked after children (Parker et al., 1991). This was manifest in a lack of liaison with schools, the poor recording of educational information and a culture of low expectations. Moves within the care system often entailed (repeated) changes of school with all the attendant disruption. Facilities for study in terms of equipment and space were often poor, especially in residential care, where staff were also sometimes said to be too passive in tackling non-attendance or exclusion (Jackson, 2001). Moreover, there was increasing recognition of the potential for positive school experiences, including extracurricular activities, to foster resilience in children and contribute to stability in placements (Gilligan, 2001).

In explaining the poor educational performance of looked after children, there has been considerable debate on the relative influences of prior experiences and ongoing family relationships compared with treatment in the care system. Research evidence is mixed and open to different interpretations. As noted above, children remaining in care have been found to perform better than those returning to their families of origin, while statistics for care leavers show qualification levels rising with time spent in care (although this effect reaches a plateau after about four years: see DfES, 2007c: Table AM). However, any such effects are small, with minimal progress in narrowing the attainment gap between children and those in the general population.

Data on attainment have been gathered in England since 2000 and although this includes Key Stages 1 to 3 most attention is paid to GCSE results (for equivalent figures in Scotland, see Scottish Government, 2007c). Here, statistics show modest progress in raising the educational qualifications of looked after children, with 12 per cent of those in care for at least a year gaining five CGSE passes at grades A*-C and 63 per cent at least one GCSE (DfES, 2007d). However, these figures remain below the government targets set in 2000 (15 and 75 per cent respectively), and fall dramatically short of qualification levels in the wider population, where 61 per cent achieve five passes at A*-C. Exclusion rates for looked after children have also fallen (significantly) in recent years but, at 0.8 per cent, remain eight times higher than the national figure for England in 2006 (DfES, 2007d).

Official data also reveal that higher levels of qualification are linked to fewer, more local and fostering rather than residential placements, but it is difficult to establish any 'causal' relationships as these groups are not entirely comparable.

In response to the complex and seemingly intractable challenges, a wide range of measures has been introduced, with an emphasis on corporate parenting and 'joined up' working between social care and education services (Harker et al., 2004). Measures for England and Wales (summarised in Box 6.2) have been underpinned by a mixture of statutory responsibilities, official guidance and additional funding (Department for Education and Employment/ DH, 2000). (For Scotland, see HM Inspectors of Schools and the Social Work Services Inspectorate, 2001.) Further steps are also proposed under the Care Matters initiative (see below).

BOX 6.2

Measures to improve education for looked after children in England

- a statutory duty for local authorities to promote the educational achievement of looked after children (Children Act 2004, s52);
- personal education plans to record attainment, and identify needs, resources and responsibilities (see Hayden, 2005, for a review of implementation);
- designated teachers in schools with responsibility for looked after children;
- specialist co-ordinating roles within local authorities;
- guidance provided to lead members (see for example 'Champions for Children' series, www.rip.org.uk);
- guidance and training for social workers, residential staff and foster carers;
- priority (with certain exceptions) in admissions to schools (Education Act 2005, s106);
- improved grants for further and higher education;
- provision of computers in residential and foster care;
- government targets set for attainment and attendance;
- encouraging the use of boarding schools.

Closing the attainment 'gap' between looked after and other children has become a rallying cry for politicians, media commentators and children's charities (NCH, 2005). Such calls are located firmly within a 'no excuses' discourse, whereby any remaining 'gap' is indicative of failure in the care system. However, not only does this tend to ignore the impact of children's adverse experiences and often special educational needs (27 per cent of looked after children compared with 3 per cent of the school population (DfES, 2007d)), it also risks denigrating the slow but steady progress that has been made and undermining the efforts of those involved.

THE HEALTH OF LOOKED AFTER CHILDREN

Debates surrounding the health of looked after children share many parallels with those for education. In particular, health was identified in the late 1980s as an important but neglected area, characterised by poor corporate parenting. Responses, too, show strong similarities with a strong emphasis on joined up working and ensuring that professionals understand their responsibilities (DH, 2002). Newly designated health care roles for doctors and nurses have been created to oversee the issues relating to looked after children, and efforts have been made to incorporate health matters into planning processes at every stage, from assessment to review (see Dunnett, 2006). However, concerns remain about the effects of unco-ordinated organisational change and the place of paediatric health within the NHS. Performance indicators have been introduced but these have tended to focus on compliance with regulations – for example, on health and dental checks or immunisations. Similarly, the narrowness associated with an 'annual medical' has come under criticism, not least as concepts of health have widened towards greater participation and promotion through healthy lifestyles. Ward et al. (2002) provide a useful review of the issues and relevant research on the health of looked after children.

Mental health

A number of small-scale research studies in the 1990s highlighted high levels of mental health problems among looked after children, with up to 75 per cent found to be suffering from some form of psychiatric disorder (see Stanley et al., 2005, for a summary). A subsequent larger survey of 1039 looked after children found 45 per cent to have a mental disorder, five times the level in the general population, while the rate in residential care was over 70 per cent (Meltzer et al., 2003). The most common type of disorder related to conduct, especially among boys. Other studies have also found high levels of self-harming behaviour and suicidal tendencies among looked after children (Sinclair and Gibbs, 1998). There is also evidence from longitudinal research that such mental health problems often persist into adulthood, although it is important to emphasise that this affects only a minority of those formerly in care (Buchanan and Ten Brinke, 1997).

Looked after children are, of course, more likely to face risk factors for poor mental health, including genetic predisposition, erratic parenting, family conflict, lone or reconstituted families, maltreatment, physical ill health or impairment, substance misuse and socio-economic deprivation. However, these may be further exacerbated by instability and sometimes further maltreatment within the care system.

In a context of mounting concern about the mental health of children (Collishaw et al., 2004), services were widely seen as being in 'crisis' during the late 1990s, with vast local variation, funding and staffing problems, and often with long waiting lists and perceptions that the most needy were not receiving treatment (Smith and Leon, 2002). To address the particular problems faced by looked after children, many local authorities have introduced dedicated mental health posts as well as improving links with local Child and Adolescent Mental Health Services (CAMHS). Alongside issues of access are those involving the acceptability of services, where concerns about stigma, labelling and, for BME children, a lack of cultural sensitivity may make children less willing to engage with services. Survey data show that CAMHS services have expanded significantly in recent years and that relatively more resources have been devoted to looked after children, of whom one in six was seen by CAMHS during 2005 (D. Barnes et al., 2006).

Substance misuse

Numerous studies have shown a greater participation in smoking, drinking alchohol and drug taking among looked after children, with Meltzer et al. (2003) finding them roughly four times more likely to engage in one or more of these activities than their peers. Government survey data show similar multiples for frequent use of drugs, including Class A drugs (Home Office, 2007). Although there has been relatively little qualitative research on substance (mis)use among looked after children (Newburn and Pearson, 2002), it is clear that they experience many of the relevant social and familial risk factors, often including parental or sibling substance misuse. Misuse is often correlated with mental health problems and involvement in offending, but the nature of the links is clearly complex and worthy of further research. Growing awareness of the issue has prompted efforts to improve drug education for looked after children and training for staff, with closer liaison between children's services and specialist workers from Drug Action Teams (Ryan and Butcher, 2006).

YOUNG PARENTHOOD AND LOOKED AFTER CHILDREN

Responses to young parents (especially mothers) in the care system must be seen in the wider context of the UK's relatively high rate of teenage parenthood and the government's Teenage Pregnancy Strategy (TPS). Launched in 1999, this aimed to halve the number of conceptions among under 18s by 2010, and to increase young parents' participation in employment, education and training (SEU, 1999). Young parents in the UK frequently face a range of disadvantages linked to social exclusion but policies to promote their life chances are also underpinned by neo-liberal concerns regarding welfare dependency. (For a discussion of how policies vary between welfare regimes, see Daguerre and Nativel, 2006.) Such concerns have combined with norms of delayed parenthood to construct young parenthood as inherently problematic and young parents as 'undeserving'.

Research in the 1990s highlighted particularly high rates of teenage motherhood in and beyond the care system, with studies of care leavers finding between one in seven and one in four young women to have given birth or pregnant (SEU, 1999). Statistics for looked after children in England, however, show much lower figures, with roughly 5 per cent of 16–17 year-olds and less than 1 per cent of under 16s being mothers (DCSF, 2007a: Table A5). However, taking into account (unrecorded) terminations, this suggests that girls and young women who are looked after are roughly twice as likely to conceive as their peers. Reflecting wider demographic patterns, incidence of motherhood was highest among those of Black or Black British origin. Looked after children are, of course, exposed to many of the known risk factors associated with teenage parenthood, including socio-economic deprivation, educational failure or disaffection, being the child of a teenage parent, involvement in offending and a range of adverse experiences, often including sexual abuse. Additional risk factors arise within the care system, including instability, a lack of supportive adults and especially in residential care, peer pressure or even coercion into sexual activity.

In line with the TPS nationally, considerable effort has been put into prevention, including improving awareness and training among social care staff and carers, sex and relationship education and access to contraception and sexual health services (SCIE, 2004a). Important protective factors for young parents include the support received from families (especially mothers) and from partners, although research evidence shows mixed outcomes in both areas, with the birth of a child sometimes, but by no means always, improving relationships (Corlyon and McGuire, 1999). Study evidence suggests that relationships between young parents and social workers are often fraught, perhaps predictably given the parents' own care histories and the inevitable (sense of) scrutiny of their own parenting. The approach of the workers is crucial here in striking the balance between support and 'surveillance'. In line with its broader approach to young parenthood, government policy has also emphasised various forms of supported accommodation rather than independent living for young parents.

Yet, while much policy and practice is still premised on the disadvantages of early parenthood, there is a growing body of evidence that for many it has positive effects, promoting greater maturity and steering parents away from behaviours such as substance misuse and offending (see for example Cater and Coleman, 2006).

OFFENDING AND LOOKED AFTER CHILDREN

Since the 1980s, child welfare and what is now termed youth justice in the UK have become increasingly divergent, both in terms of legislation and philosophy with the latter dominated by 'tough' measures (for a discussion, see Muncie, 2004). This divergence is much less evident in Scotland due to the hearings system, but here too there have been pressures for greater separation (Tisdall, 2006). However, the position of young offenders merits at least brief coverage in this text for two main reasons. First, offending remains a target for intervention within the care system, where proportionately three times as many children are convicted or cautioned as in the wider population. Retrospective studies show up to a third of male and half of female prisoners have been in public care (Worsley, 2007). Although offending is regularly referred to in 'care' research, it only rarely represents the main focus (Taylor, 2006).

A second reason relates to recent struggles led by prison reformers and children's charities to reduce or abolish custody for young offenders and to humanise regimes in the 'secure estate' (an umbrella term covering all institutions where children are legally detained – Young Offender Institutions (YOI), Secure Training Centres (STC) and secure children's homes). While much of the campaigning rests on long-held principles, it has also received impetus from the high levels of mental health problems, self-harm and suicide in the secure estate. The Howard League for Penal Reform has been particularly active, winning important legal victories to establish that the protections of the Children Act 1989 apply in youth custody (although their practical implementation remains challenging) and that local authorities have duties in respect of former looked after children during and after custody (Stuart and Baines, 2004).

PARTICIPATION AND EMPOWERMENT

The participation and 'voice' of looked after children have received increased attention in recent years for a number of reasons. Some are contextual, such as the influence of children's rights and academic interest in children as social actors. Others arise from the recognition of institutional abuse, with empowerment seen as having protective value. The Children's Rights Director in England and Children's Commissioners elsewhere in the UK all have a particular brief for children living away from home.

Participation may vary widely in terms of 'levels' – from tokenism to shared decision making (Hart, 1997) – and may focus on individual or more systemic matters. Involvement in statutory reviews has been a major focus for research and recently official statistics. The latter reveal the following attendance figures for England in 2005–2006 (see Table 6.1).

Research findings suggest that, while levels of participation have risen significantly since the Children Act 1989, children's sense of being listened to and having influence over decisions remains highly variable with many feeling marginalised (Thomas and O'Kane, 2000). Improved participation may require wider cultural change, including ways of making meetings more engaging for children. It is also important to see participation as an ongoing, 'everyday' process rather than as confined to formal meetings and major decisions. (See Tisdall et al., 2002, for a discussion of participation in Scotland.)

Table 6.1 Looked after children's attendance at reviews in England 2005–2006 by age

Under 4	0
4–9	22
10–15	61
16 or over	72

In this respect, it is worrying that many children are still not spoken to alone during social work visits (Morgan, 2007).

One key development from the 1990s has been the growth in children's advocacy services, many of which focus on looked after children. Provision has become more formalised with national standards set out in 2002 and a requirement in the Adoption and Children Act 2002 (s119) that advocacy should be available to support children making complaints. More generally, the advocacy role should help looked after children formulate and express their views and, where possible, exercise choice. Empowering children through advocacy poses a number of challenges, some intrinsic, others relating to the way services are delivered – (see for example Dalrymple, 2004; Boylan and Braye, 2006, for discussion). These include a commitment to expressing the child's view irrespective of the advocate's own, and working to enhance rather than inhibit the child's confidence in self-expression. Tensions may also arise between children's desire for a confidante and advocates' duties to disclose information relating to (risk of) significant harm. Relationships between advocates and social workers (who may themselves aspire to an advocacy role) can be difficult when the child's wishes and the professionals' plan conflict. Similarly, independence of services is a concern, especially when provided or funded by local authorities, and working within a performance and audit culture (Boylan and Braye, 2006). Critics suggest that professional advocacy reflects a 'consumerist' view of empowerment rather than a collective model for change, although looked after children are now more widely involved in the planning and delivery of services (Dalrymple, 2004).

Complaints procedures have been strengthened progressively but are widely seen as ineffective, whether in terms of timeliness, outcome or being mostly adult-led (Parry et al., 2008). Research shows that complaints come much more frequently from residential than foster care (perhaps partly reflecting greater awareness of procedures) and predominantly relate to placement issues, bullying, contact and treatment by social care staff (Oliver et al., 2006).

CARE MATTERS – A NEW VISION?

One indication of the policy priority given to looked after children is the government's current plan for legislative reform in England, based initially on the

Care Matters Green Paper (DfES, 2006b; 2007e). (See DHSSPS, 2007b, for the related initiative in Northern Ireland.) Full details are beyond our scope here (though see also chapters 7 and 8), and discussion will be confined to the main proposals and broader thrust of the process.

By way of context, the importance of preventive services for those 'on the edge of care' is emphasised, but the primary focus rests with improving corporate parenting. Within the myriad proposals, it is possible to detect the trademark themes of New Labour such as 'joined up working', for example in the piloting of 'virtual headteachers' to oversee the education of looked after children. Arguably the two main themes are those of personalisation and externalisation, which are seen as vital in counteracting the impersonal and bureaucratic nature of state care. One example of personalisation comes from the introduction of budgets for individual children (one general, one devoted to educational needs) to be held by lead professionals (social workers). Senior managers and council members are encouraged to take a personal interest in (the education of) looked after children, with local authorities acting as 'pushy parents', wanting the best for 'their' children. This includes admissions priority to the best performing schools, free access to leisure facilities and possibly employment opportunities within the local authority, all of which raise interesting tensions vis-a-vis local children not in public care.

Externalisation comes in two main forms. The first relates to strengthening the role of independent reviewing officers (including the possibility of making this a national service) and overhauling the independent visitor scheme (see above) to provide more advocacy for looked after children. A second and more radical measure is the trialling of social care practices. Modelled on GP practices, these would be independent organisations, offering lead professional and other services for looked after children. Practices would be contracted by the local authority to deliver services and would be paid (at least in part) according to achieving successful outcomes such as reunification or adoption.

The rationale behind social care practices is that freedom from local authority bureaucracy will allow greater flexibility, a sharper focus on children's needs and, in theory, less turnover of lead professionals. However, this innovation is highly controversial, raising concerns about where responsibility for corporate parenting will ultimately lie, the possibly distorting effect of bonus payments and, for some, the threat of creeping privatisation.

CONCLUSION

In this chapter, we have seen that the care system has come to occupy a higher position on the policy agenda. Within this process it is possible to detect the influence of the 'victim' and 'threat' imagery associated with looked after children. On the one hand, awareness of a range of institutional abuses has grown, along with measures to safeguard children from their effects and to improve their life chances. Equally influential, however, has been the linkage drawn between the care system and a wide range of social problems, involving welfare dependency and deviant behaviour.

Negative perceptions of care have encouraged both preventive and exit strategies such as adoption but the relatively stable, if not growing, population of looked after children attests to their limitations. The crucial question is then how far the care system can yield compensatory experiences for earlier adversities. While some commentators hold unrealistic expectations in this regard, it is beyond dispute that for many children public care affords little in the way of compensation and may even add new adversities. Efforts over the past two decades have seen some progress, but there is clearly significant room for improvement. The delivery of such improvement depends in large measure on the quality of placements for looked after children and it is this that we address in the following chapter.

GUIDE TO FURTHER READING

The best overview text on the care system is Thomas's *Social Work with Young People in Care* (Palgrave). More specific texts mentioned above include Jackson (2001) on education and Dunnett (2006) on the health of looked after children. The latest two in a series of surveys on children's experiences are Shaw's *Remember My Messages* (Who Cares Trust) and Timms and Thoburn's *Your Shout* (NSPCC).

Reading and resources for practice

Walker's *Social Work and Child and Adolescent Mental Health* (Russell House) represents an excellent contextualised account of the social work role in relation to mental health issues for children, while Payne's *The Mental Health Needs of Looked After Children* (DfES) provides a useful summary of research and practice initiatives. Macaskill's *Safe Contact: Children in Permanent Placement and Contact with Their Birth Relatives* (Russell House) helpfully covers many issues relating to contact for looked after children. The National Children's Bureau has produced various resources relevant to looked after children, including the *Care Planning Toolkit, Healthy Care* and Hart's *Tell Them Not to Forget about Us: A Guide to Practice with Looked After Children in Custody*. In discussing the participation and empowerment of looked after children, mention should be made of the role of dedicated voluntary organisations, often run by those (previously) in care, such as the Who Cares Trust (www.thewhocarestrust.org.uk), Voice (www.voiceyp.org) and in England, A National Voice (www.anationalvoice.org), and in Northern Ireland, Voice of Young People in Care (www.voypic.org). Such organisations undertake a range of activities, including advice, representation, research and campaigns such as 'This Is Not a Suitcase', protesting at the use of binbags to move looked after children's belongings. Luckock and Lefevre's eidted collection Direct Work: Social Work with Children and Young People in Care (BAAF) offers a wide range of contributions on the theory and practice of direct work from leading figures in the field.

Discussion questions

Is there sufficient emphasis given to links between looked after children and their birth families?

In what ways might 'identity' be important to children in the care system?

Is Sergeant right to say that reforming the care system is the key to addressing many of the major social problems in the UK?

What would you see as the main requirements for improving the education of looked after children?

What are the main barriers to effective planning in the care system?

7

CHOICE, STABILITY AND PERMANENCE
Placements for Looked After Children

Having discussed broader issues relating to the care system in the previous chapter, we turn our attention to the issue of 'placement', essentially a jargon term for where the looked after child will live. The main body of this chapter comprises an examination of the three main placement options for looked after children, namely, adoption, foster care and residential care, but we start by looking at some of the more thematic issues relating to such placements.

PERMANENCE AND STABILITY

The issue of permanence has been considered previously (see Chapter 6) and remains the 'gold standard' for child care planning. In situations when it is not possible within the birth or extended family, the question arises as to how permanence can be achieved in substitute care. In relation to placements, permanence has two crucial aspects, namely an 'objective' durability (ideally at least until adulthood) and a subjective 'sense of belonging'. Although far from straightforward or uncontested, there is in the UK an identifiable hierarchy in respect of permanence, with adoption the most favoured route. As residential care is rarely seen as providing permanence, the major focus of debate has been whether foster care can offer permanence comparable to that of adoption. Triseliotis (2002) offers a useful review of the research, concluding that adoption does, on balance, have certain advantages – judged in terms of stability and the child's (including as an adult) sense of security and well-being – which he attributes to its greater legal security. However, there are two important caveats to this assessment. The first is that the 'gap' between adoption and foster care has narrowed dramatically in recent years as more children with troubled histories have been adopted and breakdown rates have increased. A second is that the general preference for adoption may be over-ridden in certain circumstances, for example, when the child is strongly opposed, has an attachment to existing (foster) carers who do not wish to adopt, or particularly close links with birth family members.

In the UK, adoption involves a complete and irrevocable transfer of parental responsibilities, but there is a history of legal measures that effect such transfers without the finality of adoption. The most recent example is the status of special guardianship, introduced under the Adoption and Children Act 2002 (see Jordan and Lindley, 2006, for a discussion).

While stability is a vital element in permanence, it has a broader relevance to all placements, namely, that 'unnecessary' moves can disrupt relationships, friendships and education, with the possibility of damaging self-esteem and the capacity to form attachments in the future (Ridge and Millar, 2000). Thus, while some placement moves are positive, for example, leading to permanence or provision that will better meet a child's needs, the general principle of minimising changes of placement holds. This has been reflected in the setting of government targets relating to both short-term (moves in a year) and longer-term stability (in a current placement for at least two years if looked after for more than two and a half years). As Schofield et al. (2007) contend, such indicators are fairly crude and hide highly complex situations. Nevertheless, both indicators have shown improvement in recent years, although many children continue to experience multiple moves (CSCI, 2006).

PLACEMENT CHOICE

Another major goal for the contemporary care system has been to offer greater placement choice, a concept that can be understood at the micro-level of individual placements, through the meso-level of service provision to the macro-domain of policy and legislation. In principle, individual placements should be attuned to meeting the needs of the child, a process often described as 'matching', especially in relation to family placements. Matching may cover a wide range of factors, and understandably perhaps tends to be more detailed in relation to permanent placements (Sellick et al., 2004). Based on an assessment of the child's needs (and wishes), relevant factors might include the size and make-up of the family, ethnic background, lifestyle, parenting style, and the capacity to meet special needs, facilitate contact with birth family members and take a sibling group. Locality may be important in order to ensure continuity in terms of education and networks (and the current Children and Young Persons Bill strengthens the duties of local authorities to secure placements local to home and school), or conversely, to provide a placement distanced from an abusive family or deviant peer group. Similar considerations may apply to residential care placements, including the size, regime or treatment programme offered.

A consistent research finding, however, has been that in practice, scope for matching is often limited by a lack of placement choice (Berridge and Brodie, 1998; Waterhouse and Brocklesby, 2001). Similarly, for older children with more troubled histories or complex needs, there may be very few, if any, families willing and able to offer a home, and hence limited scope for matching. Recruitment of substitute families has thus become a key concern for child social care agencies, but beyond the challenges of recruitment (and retention) themselves, it is also difficult to create and sustain 'spare capacity' on a scale that would significantly improve choice.

The most striking historical trend in relation to placement provision in the UK has been the progressive shift away from residential towards foster care, a trend also apparent to varying degrees in many European countries (Colton and Hellinckx, 1993). This began in the early postwar era, driven by concerns about both attachment and economy, but accelerated dramatically in the 1980s and 1990s, with residential care provision falling to around 10 per cent of placements. Research on the respective merits of foster and residential care is by no means unequivocal, although the broad consensus is that the former is preferable for younger children. The perceived advantages of foster care are those of more personal attention, closer relationships and a less 'institutional' lifestyle (Colton, 1988). Many teenagers, however, have reported a preference for residential care on the basis of offering more interaction with peers and 'space' from familial relationships (Sinclair and Gibbs, 1998). Outcome measures in areas such as education or offending appear to favour foster care, but it must be remembered that children's homes are on balance dealing with a more troubled, and sometimes disaffected, population.

PARALLEL PLANNING

As noted in the previous chapter, concern to prevent drift and damaging delay has led to tighter schedules for permanency planning. One perceived means of avoiding delay is through the parallel pursuit of other plans, also sometimes known as 'twin tracking'. Typically, reunification with birth parents is the preferred option, but should this not materialise, alternative plans for permanence will be in place, perhaps within the extended family or through substitute family care. While the advantages of parallel planning are obvious, there is a danger that work towards reunification may be undermined and that failure is somehow almost anticipated. Such tensions are perhaps sharpest in a form known as concurrency, pioneered in the USA and piloted in the UK in the late 1990s (Monck et al., 2003). Here, the foster carers looking after the child also agree to offer a permanent, usually adoptive, home for the child if reunification fails. In terms of attachment and continuity of care, concurrent planning potentially offers the optimum form of parallel planning, but it makes considerable demands on the substitute carers, who are asked to work wholeheartedly towards reunification while arguably standing to gain should it fail. Critics have argued that concurrent planning too easily becomes 'adoption by the back door', with perhaps insufficient effort at reunification and sometimes a lack of understanding of the process on the part of birth parents (Booth et al., 2006).

ADOPTION AND LOOKED AFTER CHILDREN

Adoption in the UK is governed by the Adoption Act 1976 as modified by the Adoption and Children Act 2002 (and similar legislation in Scotland (1978/2007) and Northern Ireland (1987)). Adoptions for looked after children are typically arranged by local authorities although they may engage specialist voluntary adoption agencies to recruit families and 'match' children to them. In this section of the chapter, we will be looking at the profile of looked after children who have been adopted, the processes involved and some of the key policy and practice issues. First, however, a brief historical context is in order.

The changing face of adoption

Since its statutory introduction in England and Wales in 1926 (Scotland in 1930) and more particularly in the period since the Second World War, adoption has undergone a number of important changes (see Thoburn, 1999, for a useful historical overview). One of these is the move from a 'closed' model of adoption towards greater 'openness' (see below). A second was to extend the scope of adoption to those previously deemed 'unadoptable' on grounds of age, disability or ethnicity. A third change relates to the overall scale of adoption. The number of adoptions rose steadily in the postwar era, peaking at an annual rate of almost 25,000 for England and Wales in the late 1960s, thereafter falling sharply to around 5,000 by the year 2000. This trend reflected two factors: first, a dramatic decline in baby adoptions due to more available contraception and termination, and changing attitudes towards illegitimacy and lone parenthood; and second, discouragement of adoption by step-parents due to its severing of legal ties with the other birth parent. The final change was a growing concentration on looked after children. This was in part simply a consequence of the decline in baby and step-parent adoptions, but from the 1990s, driven also by policies to promote adoption for looked after children.

The reform of adoption law

The effects of this changing climate are most evident in the process of reforming adoption law, a process lasting over a decade from its launch in the late 1980s. Originally focused on harmonising adoption law in England and

Wales with the Children Act 1989 and dealing with intercountry adoption, it was also widely expected that the reforms would reflect and support the trend towards greater openness in adoption. However, with a growing politicisation as discussed in Chapter 1, attention shifted progressively towards the promotion of adoption for looked after children, which became the focal point of the long-awaited legislation. The principal measures of the Adoption and Children Act 2002 are set out in Box 7.1.

BOX 7.1

Adoption and Children Act 2002 – key measures

- establishment of Adoption & Permanency Taskforce;
- setting of timescales for adoption;
- national register of adopters;
- improved support for adopters;
- independent review of approval decisions;
- amendment permitting cohabiting (including lesbian or gay) couples to adopt;
- placement orders (to replace freeing orders);
- new grounds for dispensing with parental consent;
- special guardianship.

These measures were underpinned by a government target that the annual number of adoptions from care should rise by at least 40 per cent from their 2000 level by 2004–2005. This target was effectively achieved with the number of adoptions in England rising to 3800 (or 6 per cent of looked after children) in 2004, although this has since fallen to 3300 and is predicted to fall further (DCSF, 2007a). The scale of adoption from care in Wales is fairly similar (5 per cent), but less frequent in Northern Ireland (3 per cent), where there is greater reliance on adoption by existing foster carers than elsewhere in the UK. In Scotland, the figure is lower still at 1 per cent, which is partly, but not entirely, explained by the lower proportion of its looked after population living away from home (see Chapter 6). In both Scotland and Northern Ireland, recent initiatives have sought to increase adoption of looked after children, through the Adoption and Children (Scotland) Act 2007 and the 'Adopting the Future' consultation respectively.

A breakdown of the figures shows an even gender split and some under-representation of both South Asian and Black British children who, according to official figures, account for 11 per cent of those looked after but only 5 per cent of those adopted (DCSF, 2007a). The reasons for this are complex and include preferences in some communities for foster care as well as any failings

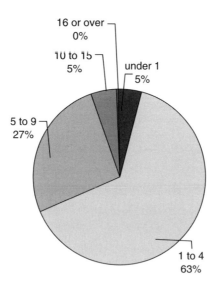

Figure 7.1 Ages of looked after children adopted – England 2007 (adapted from DCSF, 2007a: Table E1)

in relation to recruiting families. As can be seen from Figure 7.1, a majority of those adopted from care are young children, although baby adoptions comprise only a small minority.

Efforts to expedite the processes of adoption more quickly have brought only marginal falls in the average age at adoption (4.2 years) and the duration of the final period looked after (2.8 years) between 2003 and 2007. Ward et al's (2006) study found that long periods were common even for those originally looked after as babies.

Decision making in adoption – key stages

The path towards adoption in England and Wales comprises a set of agency (normally local authority) and court decisions operating in tandem. (In Scotland, where the child is subject to a supervision requirement, decision making also involves the hearings system: see Plumtree, 2005). The initial step will be a review decision that adoption is the preferred plan for the child, based on the view that there is no realistic possibility of reunification with the birth parents or an appropriate placement within the extended family. Particularly for older children, the desirability of remaining looked after (e.g. in long-term foster care) will also be considered, along with the child's own views on adoption (in Scotland children's consent is formalised for those over 12). The proposed plan will then be referred to the local authority's adoption panel (see Box 7.2) and, in turn, to the court. Assuming both approve the plan, the local authority will then make what is known as a 'best-interests' decision, which, as the name suggests, indicates that adoption is in the child's best interests.

This is followed by identifying prospective adopters who will also have to be approved as adopters by an adoption panel. Crucially, the panel must also decide that the adopters and the child form a 'match', as described earlier.

BOX 7.2

Adoption panels

All adoption agencies, whether state or voluntary, must appoint a panel to make recommendations as outlined above, in relation to children, adoptive parents and the matching process between them. Panels may have up to 11 members, but core membership should comprise:

- two experienced (three years post-qualifying) social workers;
- a local authority councillor (or in voluntary agencies a director or manager);
- a medical advisor;
- three independent members, including at least two with personal experience of adoption.

Note: The 2002 Act introduced an independent review mechanism (effectively a second opinion) for applicants who wish to challenge a panel decision turning them down as adopters.

Source: Adoption Agencies Regulations 2005 (England)

Under the Adoption and Children Act 2002 (s21), a placement order is required before the child can be placed with the family (or where a placement e.g. fostering, becomes a planned adoptive one). If the birth parents do not consent, the order requires the court to dispense with this, either on the grounds of parental absence or incapacity, but most frequently because the welfare of the child requires it (s52). In the case of a new placement, there should be carefully planned introductions, starting with shared information, followed by meetings, and short stays before the final move. The final stages of the adoption process involve the prospective adopters formally applying to the court and, with rare exceptions, the adoption order being made.

Contested adoptions – law and practice

There is arguably no more contentious area within child welfare than adoption without the consent of birth parents, or 'contested adoptions', a phenomenon that has become more frequent with the growing concentration of adoption on the care system (Ryburn, 1994a). Reflecting the different perspectives outlined in chapter 1, there are often sharp, even bitter, divisions on the appropriateness of adoption in such situations. Adherents to both laissez faire and state paternalist perspectives may favour adoption on the grounds that it offers parenting superior to that provided by birth parents (Morgan, 1998). By contrast, the modern defence of the birth family is fundamentally antipathetic towards adoption without consent, often seeing it in terms of state-sponsored 'child-snatching'. Critics argue that the adversarial system is damaging to all parties, tending to unnecessarily denigrate birth parents in order to justify the adoption (Ryburn, 1994a).

Adoption, openness and contact

As noted earlier, there has been a long-term historical trend away from the 'closed' model of adoption which developed in the early postwar years. This emphasised the anonymity of adopters, often secrecy (including from the adopted child) and a complete severance of ties with the birth family, this being seen as best for all members of the 'adoption triangle' – children, adoptive parents and birth parents. (Some prefer wider terms such as circle or network to denote those affected by adoption.) Under mounting challenge, the first major step away from the closed model in England and Wales (this right already existed in Scotland) came in the Children Act 1975. This allowed adopted adults access to their original birth certificate, and thereby the chance to search for birth family members, as well as discover more of their own personal and family history. (See Howe and Feast, 2000, for research on the outcomes of searching and reunion.)

Subsequently, however, the concept of openness was extended significantly, focusing on the child's life before the age of 18, on the basis that openness helped to meet identity needs (Ryburn, 1994b). Openness can be seen as a continuum, from the involvement of a birth parent in selecting adopters, through an exchange of information (including so-called 'letter box' contact), telephone calls or emails, to continued face-to-face contact between the child and birth family members. While attention is generally focused on the birth parents, this contact frequently involves members of the extended family and, importantly, siblings, when they are living separately (Mullender, 1999).

There is now a growing body of research in the UK and USA on the most controversial aspect of openness, namely adoption with contact, much of which is helpfully summarised in Neil and Howe's edited (2004) collection. Without minimising the challenges involved, research studies paint a broadly positive picture of adoption with contact, identifying the benefits for children, the birth relatives and, perhaps surprisingly, for many adoptive parents also.

However, such findings demand cautious interpretation, given that sampling methods tend to engage agencies and adopters who are more positive about contact. As with contact more generally, it is important that its costs and benefits are carefully considered for each child. Although it is possible for contact to be ordered in the case of adoption, there is a strong consensus that relationships built on trust between the parties offer the key to successful contact (C. Smith, 2005). Argent's edited (2002) collection offers helpful guidance on managing contact in adoption.

Post-adoption support

Efforts to promote adoption for looked after children have highlighted the need to offer better support to members of the adoption triangle, especially adoptive parents, who are increasingly seen as supplying a service, and even treated as part of the children's *workforce* (HM Government, 2005), although this sits uneasily with a view of adoption as rooted in family autonomy vis-a-vis the state (Luckock and Hart, 2005). The Adoption and Children Act 2002 requires local authorities to deliver a range of services including:

- **financial help through adoption allowances;**
- **support groups for adoptive parents, children and birth parents;**
- **assistance with contact;**
- **therapeutic services for children;**
- **general assistance including short breaks.**

An earlier survey by Rushton and Dance (2002) found that support for adoptive families was patchy and often lacking. It is perhaps too early to know how far implementation of the 2002 Act has rectified this situation. For birth parents, despite a body of research outlining the (ongoing) difficulties faced by many (see Triseliotis et al., 1997: 91–113), post-adoption support remains a neglected area, heavily reliant on a small number of voluntary organisations or mutual support groups. There is a paucity of research on children's experiences of adoption but for an excellent study, see Thomas and Beckford (1999).

Choosing adoptive families – approved parenting and 'political correctness'?

The approval of parents as suitable adopters is an emotive issue, not only because of the high stakes involved and applicants' sense of being judged, but also because the process is articulated with highly sensitive political issues. Depending on one's viewpoint, the protracted and painstaking approval process is entirely appropriate, given state responsibilities and the enormous complexities of adoption, or over-intrusive and offputting to applicants. Importantly, however, such debates have become embroiled with concerns, articulated in the media and by politicians, that adoption from public care has been thwarted by 'political correctness' (PC) on the part of social workers and agencies (Morgan, 1998). As applied to adoption, PC comprises disparate elements, finding common ground in the notion that 'deserving' families are (allegedly) being rejected, while the 'undeserving' are given preference. Thus, unwarranted restrictions are allegedly placed on families on the basis of age, smoking or weight, while agencies are too willing to approve lone parents and lesbians or gay men as adoptive parents.

The context for these attacks is the declining number of 'normative' heterosexual married couples and the desire to increase the scale of adoption from public care.

The latter has seen a steady rise in adoption by lone parents (Owen, 1999), while an amendment to the 2002 Act permitted cohabiting (including same-sex) *couples* to adopt, replacing the previous situation, where only one became the legal adoptive parent. Hicks (2005) presents an interesting account of how lesbians and gay men have increasingly been accepted as adopters and foster carers (although their numbers remain very small) while the traditional norms of gender and sexuality remain strongly entrenched in policy and practice. Moreover, far from a situation of equality or even 'positive discrimination', there is evidence of a hierarchy, where children such as healthy babies or toddlers are placed with married couples, while those with more complex needs are likely to be placed in less traditional families.

'Race', ethnicity and adoption

The controversy over PC has been greatest, however in relation to BME children and their placement in white families or 'transracial adoption'. Here, agencies' preferences for ethnic matching on the grounds of meeting racial and cultural identity needs have variously been attacked as unjustified, over-rigid and denying children good homes. The core issues in this debate (see Kirton, 2000, for a fuller discussion, including their broader political context) relate to children's needs in respect of identity, cultural heritage and coping with racism and the capacities of families from different ethnic backgrounds to meet these needs. A 'liberal' view tends to play down their importance, while simultaneously emphasising the capacities of white families to meet such needs. Conversely, a 'Black radical' perspective places such needs centrally for BME children and argues that few, if any, white parents can adequately meet them. The UK's only major study comparing transracial with 'ethnically matched' placements concluded that the former should be used only rarely in the light of the considerable additional challenges faced by white parents of BME children (Thoburn et al., 2000b).

Controversy also surrounds the apparent shortage of BME adoptive families, which tends to be taken as a 'given' by the supporters of transracial adoption, while its opponents argue that the 'shortage' stems largely from failures and even institutional racism on the part of recruiting agencies.

Readers interested in similar debates in relation to intercountry adoption (which does not involve looked after children) should see the edited collection by Selman (2000).

FOSTER CARE

As already described, foster care has come to occupy a dominant role in providing placements for looked after children, not least due to the rapid decline of residential care dating from the 1980s. (See Triseliotis et al., 1995, for an earlier history.) This role has also undergone A significant transformation for several reasons. First, catering for a higher proportion of what is widely seen as a more troubled population has meant many more challenging fostering placements. Second, the impact of the Children Act 1989 and efforts to improve planning have led to increased demands upon foster carers: for example, facilitating contact or working with birth parents, providing assessments or giving evidence in court and, more recently, improving education for looked after children. Third, the performance management regime has inevitably focused largely on foster care, given its dominant position, as the principal site for meeting targets. Collectively, these developments have tended to create pressure towards a greater 'professionalisation' in foster care (see below), but wider social changes have also contributed. In particular, growing female participation in paid employment has diminished the pool of families willing or able to foster on a voluntary basis. Pressures on placements and increased recognition of (family) networks as a resource have also led to a growth in the involvement of family and friends as carers (FFAC), also known as 'kinship care' (see below).

Types of foster care

By contrast with adoption, the unifying feature within foster care is that it is (with the exception of 'permanent fostering') regarded as temporary, legally and to a greater or lesser extent by those involved. However, the umbrella term hides a wide range of placements, which vary according to length of stay and purpose, although these may change in line with circumstances. Carers may be approved for a certain number of children, an expected length of placement, age range and sometimes gender, but a lack of placement choice can lead to children being placed outside the carers' terms of approval. A by no means exhaustive list of types of foster care for looked after children might include:

- emergency;
- short-term/intermediate;
- long-term/permanent;
- specialist foster care – (e.g. offenders, disabled children, treatment/therapeutic);
- remand foster care.

The timescales and boundaries between placements have tended to become more fluid over time. A short-term placement usually denotes a period of up to six months, with the assumption that the child will either return home or move to another placement fairly quickly. Intermediate placements typically relate to more complex situations, where it is recognised that such a return or move is likely to take longer. Similarly, the distinction between a long-term and permanent placement is a much debated one, with the principal difference being that the latter implies a placement at least until adulthood (Sinclair, 2005).

OUTCOMES IN FOSTER CARE

Judging success in foster placements is a challenging task, and open to different interpretations. Historically, one of the most commonly used measures has been to analyse the 'breakdown' or premature ending of placements (Berridge and Cleaver, 1987), although it must be remembered that such placements may still have positive aspects and that continuity is no guarantee of satisfactory care or experiences. Research studies have sought not only to gauge the incidence of breakdowns, but also to identify risk factors with a view to future prevention. Wilson et al. (2004) helpfully review this research, but at this point it should be noted that factors may relate to foster carers, children, the interaction or 'match' between them and the quality of professional support. Some of the strongest risk factors are those of the child's age (with breakdown rates for teenagers at around 50 per cent), emotional and behavioural problems, foster carers taking placements reluctantly, and a lack of social work visits or other forms of support. Despite improvements, at a time of more challenging placements, stability remains elusive, with many children continuing to experience 'serial parenting' (Sinclair et al., 2005).

An alternative approach to assessing outcomes is to consider whether placement goals have been met. These may relate to major objectives such as reunification or adoption or more day-to-day concerns with behaviour or educational performance, but particularly in relation to the major placement goals, it can be difficult to weigh the contribution made by the foster placement. Sinclair et al. (2005) found mixed evidence of success in relation to major placement goals.

A third approach to outcomes is to gauge these more directly. Largely self-selected samples mean that there are few reliable data on foster children's perspectives, but both quantitative and qualitative studies show wide variations in experience (Ward et al., 2005). Much of this is positive, particularly in comparison with life in birth families, but a significant minority of children report feelings of not being accepted in foster families, or treated less favourably than the carers' children. Sinclair (2005) highlights how, alongside concerns with their birth families and care careers, children particularly value the opportunity to live 'ordinary' lives through foster care. Schofield's (2003) study of 40 adults who grew up in foster care paints a generally positive picture and offers an interesting account of the factors that help or hinder successful outcomes in the longer term.

Alongside outcomes for children, attention has also increasingly been paid to the needs of foster carers and how they can be helped to cope with 'stressful events' – such as placement breakdowns, allegations of maltreatment, and conflicts with birth parents or social workers (Sinclair et al., 2005). Similarly, a growing body of research has focused on carers' birth children or 'children who foster', their support needs, the impact of fostering upon them, and their contribution to its success (see Wilson et al., 2004, for a summary).

THE PROFESSIONALISATION OF FOSTER CARE

Since the 1970s, there has been a clearly discernible, if uneven, trend towards professionalisation in foster care. Some of the key factors behind this process were outlined earlier, but it has also been boosted by the aspirations of many foster carers, led by representative organisations such as the Fostering Network (and its predecessors).

The term professionalisation in foster care can describe both distinct processes of innovation and their wider permeation. Historically, the changes can be traced to the pioneering schemes of the 1970s, mostly targeted at 'troublesome' teenagers (Shaw and Hipgrave, 1983). The key innovations were that foster carers would receive training, intensive support from a dedicated social worker and their peers, and crucially, that they would be paid a fee in addition to maintenance allowances for the children. These features, with the partial exception of payment, were progressively adopted for all forms of foster care during the 1980s and early 1990s. A 'second wave' of professionalisation was spearheaded in the 1990s by independent fostering providers (IFPs), many formed by ex-local authority foster carers. IFPs re-emphasised the importance of payment, training and support, crucially extending the latter in areas such as counselling, education, respite care and out-of-hours assistance (Sellick, 2002). IFPs have grown rapidly and number over 250, accounting for 23 per cent of fostering placements England (DCSF, 2007a).

The principles of professionalisation, including payment and a career structure, have received significant endorsement in recent policy documents, especially as a means of improving recruitment and retention (DfES, 2006b). While the controversy surrounding professionalisation has arguably diminished over time, there remain complex questions about the role of foster carers, the relationship between 'love and money', family and 'work', or 'detachment' in relationships (Kirton, 2007).

FAMILY AND FRIENDS AS CARERS (FFAC)

Under the Children Act 1989, care by extended family and friends was promoted as the most desirable alternative to living with parents and this has been strengthened in the current Children and Young Persons Bill. However, this care may take place under a variety of legal circumstances and with differing degrees of state involvement. These include private arrangements without state support, assistance for a 'child in need' under s17 of the Act, and our main focus here, occasions when a looked after child is placed with FFAC, who then become approved foster carers for the child. Although relatively low in international terms (Hunt, 2003), such placements have increased significantly in the past decade and in 2007 accounted for 17 per cent of all foster placements in England and 25 per cent of all looked after children living away from home in Scotland (DCSF, 2007a; Scottish Government, 2007c).

Research has identified several *potential* advantages for children in placements with FFAC, including continuity of relationships, bonds based on kinship, avoiding aspects of public care, contact with birth parents and, in the case of BME children, meeting racial and cultural identity needs (Broad, 2001). Some studies have also found such placements to afford greater stability, although evidence is mixed on this (see Farmer and Moyers, 2005).

Yet there are also potential areas of difficulty. Aside from the possibility of placements being affected by intra-family conflicts, the challenges tend to relate to the place of FFAC within the child welfare system. Here, questions have focused particularly on whether FFAC should be treated in a similar manner to unrelated foster carers. Advocates of equal treatment have argued that, as carers for looked after children, FFAC (who often make significant financial sacrifices) should be entitled to the same support as other carers, and successful campaigns have been waged against discrimination in payments. However, equal treatment sits uneasily within a professionalising framework that emphasises a participation in training and payment according to the skills and experience of the carer. (There may also be concerns about the principle of being paid (beyond expenses) to look after a related child.) Understandably perhaps, FFAC may not (though some do) identify themselves with the professional project nor meet the criteria for approval as carers for children outside the family. The government has acknowledged this uneasy relationship by proposing a revision to assessment processes and support for FFAC to recognise the probability that they will only ever care for one child (DfES, 2006b).

AN ADDENDUM ON PRIVATE FOSTERING

Although private foster care does not involve looked after status for children, it is mentioned briefly at this point because of its relevance for child welfare in the UK (see Holman, 2002, for an excellent analysis). Private foster care covers situations where parents arrange to have their children fostered by someone other than a close relative (defined in the Children Act 1989, s105, as a step-parent, aunt/uncle, grandparent or sibling) for over 28 days. For reasons explained below, there are no reliable figures for the number of privately fostered children, but it is estimated to be at least 10,000 (Philpot, 2001). The largest grouping involves the children of West African parents, while other children involved may be teenagers living away from parents, UASC, language and exchange students.

The primary concerns surrounding private fostering have been the vulnerability of children and the regulatory framework in place to safeguard them and promote their welfare, including the identity needs of BME children. Private foster carers are required to notify the authorities of any placement and, in turn, the authority must visit and satisfy itself as to the child's welfare, offering support if required (HM Government, 2006a: 195–196). However, compliance is minimal, estimated at around 10 per cent of placements being notified, while many local authorities give this work little or no priority.

RESIDENTIAL CARE

As described earlier, contemporary residential (child) care has been shaped by a history of rapid contraction in scale and accompanying negative imagery. (For a good postwar history, see Bullock, 1999). According to Milligan and Stevens (2006), residential care reached its nadir in the early 1990s, after a decade of home closures and a succession of abuse scandals, since which time the sector has made a slow but steady recovery.

The contraction of residential care can be located within the wider processes of 'deinstitutionalisation', driven by a desire for cost savings and a long-standing critique of the 'institutional' environment (Bowlby, 1953). Internally, institutions are said to suffer from regimentation, a lack of individuality (bulk-buying, rules against customising bedrooms) or privacy, physical barriers (locks on doors, fridges) and bureaucratic decision making. Externally, there may be geographical isolation, a discouraging environment for visits from family or friends, a lack of external scrutiny and social stigma. This relative 'closure' is seen as increasing the potential for institutional abuse. As we shall see, efforts to (re-)establish residential care as more than simply a 'last resort' have focused significantly on ameliorating its 'institutional' features. Before considering these policy and practice measures, however, a brief profile of contemporary residential care may be helpful.

Residential child care – a profile

Two trends stand out in the recent development of the UK's residential child care sector, namely, a trend towards smaller units and a growing 'mixed economy' in terms of providers. CSCI (2006) lists 2025 children's homes in England providing over 11,500 places. Over 60 per cent of these homes are privately owned, supplying an average of five places each, but are often smaller, including some single-place homes. Many now also offer education and are registered as schools. While some see advantages in smaller units, this market has also prompted fears of fragmentation, damaging placement choice. One possible indication of this is the high number (roughly 35 per cent) (DCSF, 2007a) of residential placements outside of local authority boundaries, with their potential adverse effects on networks and the quality of social work support offered.

Over 95 per cent of those in residential care are aged 10 or over and, on a range of indicators, this population is likely to include many of the most troubled and troubling of looked after children. Children's homes may deliver a range of services, from respite and emergency accommodation to (more rarely) long-stay and support for semi-independent living as preparation for leaving care. Some may offer specialist treatment regimes, including therapeutic communities (Ward et al., 2003), although overall there has been a decline in specialisation (Bullock, 1999). Secure children's homes operate at the somewhat diffuse boundary between social care and custody and are discussed further below. Finally, it is worth noting that disabled children and those with emotional, behavioural or health problems may be placed in residential facilities under the auspices of education or health authorities, also giving rise to difficult boundary issues (see Chapter 9).

Residential care – last resort or positive choice?

The embattled position of residential care within child welfare in the UK has significantly framed debates in terms of whether it can represent more than the 'darkened door at the end of the line' (DH, 1998b: 39). Despite reforms and improvements, it is not difficult to find negative reportage. Reference has already been made to relatively poor educational outcomes, the high incidence of mental health problems and levels of formal complaints compared with children in foster care (see Chapter 6). In their study of running away among looked after children, Biehal and Wade (2000) found that the vast majority of flights occurred from residential care, while research has also identified children's homes as 'magnets' for those seeking to involve young people in drug-taking or prostitution (Berridge and Brodie, 1998). Sinclair and Gibbs (1998) found significant levels of bullying, sexual victimisation by other residents (experienced by almost one in four girls) and suicidal feelings (reported by around 40 per cent of children).

Several aspects of the regimes found in residential care have come under critical scrutiny. Their common ground rests with an alleged failure to engage adequately and build relationships with children, instead emphasising the maintenance of control (Berridge and Brodie, 1998). This failure may take different forms, including confrontation, as well as forms of distancing and withdrawal. Several studies have found evidence of 'macho' cultures among staff and, while this may be partly explained as a response to challenging and sometimes violent behaviours, it can exacerbate such difficulties and arguably serve to legitimise violence and (homophobic) bullying among residents (Barter et al., 2004; Green, 2005). For their part, distancing and withdrawal may take physical forms, such as remaining in the staff room, or may be evidenced in defensive practices, where staff may prioritise their own vulnerabilities to allegations over understanding children's behaviour, generating what Horwath (2000) describes as 'childcare with gloves on'. (See also Piper et al., 2006, on 'paranoia' relating to the dangers of touching children.) In their follow-up study, Berridge and Brodie (1998) found that homes had become less 'institutional' in some respects, such as in provision of food and clothing, but that this was partly offset by a decline in live-in staff and a greater turnover of residents.

Despite the challenges faced, however, there are also many encouraging tales to tell from residential care. These reflect the experiences of many looked after children, their preferences and the contribution of children's homes to the wider care system. Positive aspects identified in studies include enjoyment of peer relationships, aspects of group living and sometimes levels of activity available (DH, 1998b). From her small-scale study, Emond (2003) also counters the often negative view of peer relationships by highlighting their potential for mutual support and solidarity. While policy makers and professionals retain their clear preference for foster over residential care, there is no such consensus among looked after children.

Thus, residential care can play an important role in a number of situations. These may include providing emergency placements, dealing with the aftermath of fostering breakdowns or situations where foster care is not deemed appropriate, allowing sibling groups to live together and offering specialist therapeutic services. There has been significant research into 'what works' in residential care (DH, 1998b). From their more recent literature review, Clough et al. (2006) identify seven key factors linked to safer and more effective care. These are set out in Box 7.3. To these could be added good external links with families, communities and professionals. As with foster care, there is an important social work role in supporting residential placements and facilitating links with the external environment.

BOX 7.3

Key factors in high-quality residential care

- the culture and ethos of residential establishments – underlying values, teamwork, communication;
- quality of relationships between children and carers – informal, respectful, frank, confidential, reliable;
- staffing and training – qualifications, training, stability (see below);
- leadership – management with clear vision;
- listening to children;
- size of home – majority view that smaller homes provider better care;
- information-recording and -sharing.

Working in residential child care

Issues relating to staffing in residential care have often been linked to the sector's difficulties, both as cause and effect. Staffing levels have increased significantly over the past two decades but, as noted above, this has not necessarily led to closer relationships being formed with residents (DH, 1998b). Low pay and status and a lack of career prospects have all been cited as reasons for a high turnover among staff, although much of this is within the sector (Colton and Roberts, 2007). The scandals of the 1980s and early 1990s prompted a focus on increasing levels of qualification among residential workers (and especially managers) on the grounds that better training would improve confidence in dealing with challenging behaviour and in 'whistle-blowing' when witnessing malpractice among colleagues. Efforts to increase qualifications have met with modest success (Campbell, 2006) but research studies have found no link between qualification levels and quality of care or child outcomes (Sinclair and Gibbs, 1998). A more radical move to improve the status and quality of residential child care has come from plans (under *Care Matters*) to pilot the European model of the social pedagogue, which combines an education and social care role in what advocates see as a more holistic and creative approach to work with children (Cameron, 2004).

Secure children's homes

Some of the tensions surrounding residential care are at their sharpest in relation to secure accommodation. Children may be placed in secure homes in England by a court order under the Children Act 1989, s25 (and by a children's hearing or court in Scotland), when they have a history of absconding and are consequently at risk of significant harm or pose a risk to themselves or others. As O'Neill (2001) argues, this creates a hybrid, and arguably mismatched, population based on gender divisions, with mostly male young offenders alongside female residents placed due to perceived sexual risks. Thus, while many child welfare professionals favour secure accommodation over custodial alternatives in the secure estate (see Chapter 6) because of its relatively more welfare-based regime, they face a number of challenges. These include high levels of mental health problems among residents, a limited availability or duration of therapeutic programmes, an often distant geographical location, and poor after-care (Walker et al., 2005).

CONCLUSION

In this chapter, we have seen both continuity and change in the provision of placements for looked after children over the past two decades. An important area of continuity from the 1980s has been the shift away from residential to substitute family care in the forms of adoption and fostering. However, this has taken place against the backdrop of a seemingly more troubled population of children and an apparent decline in the 'altruistic' provision of family care. This context has prompted a significant increase in the material, practical and professional supports offered to substitute families, although these are still widely regarded as insufficient in certain respects.

An important area of change has been the progressive emergence of a mixed economy of placement provision, with a substantial private sector presence in foster and residential care. However, entry into this market by private equity firms has raised concerns about its longer-term stability (Samuel, 2007).

There is no doubt that New Labour's substantial investment in services has yielded improvements in relation to permanence and stability as well as in education for looked after children. However, this investment has been accompanied by a burgeoning bureaucracy with myriad standards, guidance and targets. It is perhaps too early to assess the longer-term impact of this strategy but it may be that it serves to undermine other government goals in respect of workforce development and the recruitment and retention of carers.

GUIDE TO FURTHER READING

Although now somewhat dated, the most comprehensive book on adoption is that of Triseliotis and colleagues (1997), while Hill and Shaw's edited collection *Signposts in Adoption: Policy, Research and Practice Issues* (British Agencies for Adoption and Fostering (BAAF)) also gives a wide coverage of relevant issues. Another useful source is Rushton's *The Adoption of Looked After Children* (SCIE). For foster care, the best texts are those by Sinclair (2005) and Hill (ed.) *Signposts in Fostering: Policy, Research and Practice Issues* (BAAF). SCIE has produced two relevant knowledge reviews, Sellick and Howell's *Innovative, Tried and Tested: A Review of Good Practice in Fostering*, and Wilson et al. (2004). For overviews of residential care, see Clough et al. (2006), Crimmens and Milligan (eds) *Facing Forward: Residential Child Care in the 21st Century* (Russell House), or Mainey and Crimmens (eds) *Fit for the Future? Residential Child Care in the United Kingdom* (National Children's Bureau).

Reading and resources for practice

Iwaniec (ed.) *The Child's Journey through Care: Placement Stability, Care Planning and Achieving Permanency* (Wiley) examines relevant topics, with a particular focus on looked after children in Northern Ireland. BAAF (www.baaf.org.uk) and the Fostering Network (www.fostering.net) are the major organisations in the fields of adoption and foster care. Both furnish a wealth of information, including practice guidance, policy analysis and research, for all 'stakeholders' in family placement. Schofield and Beek's *Attachment Handbook for Foster Care and Adoption* (BAAF) explores the relevance of attachment for many facets of substitute family care. For residential care in England, the National Centre for Excellence in Residential Child Care (www.ncb.org.uk/ncercc) can help with practice guidance, while the longer-established Scottish Institute for Residential Child Care (www.sircc.strath.ac.uk/) features a range of information and library resources. The Secure Accommodation Network (www.secureaccommodation.org.uk/) provides useful practice guidance relating to secure children's homes.

Discussion questions

What are the most effective ways to provide permanence for looked after children?

Does the recent drive to promote adoption from care serve the best interests of children?

Is a professional fostering service feasible or desirable?

What are the strengths and weaknesses of placements with family and friends?

How would you explain the declining use of residential child care in recent years?

YOUNG PEOPLE LEAVING CARE

Since their identification as a vulnerable group in the 1980s, there has been copious research into the plight of care leavers, much of it highlighting their difficulties and inadequacies in service provision for them, though arguably obscuring more positive outcomes. In this chapter, we review this research and policy and practice developments relating to care leavers, including proposals under the *Care Matters* initiative.

The term care leaver is a complex one and is applied only to a minority of all the children and young people who leave care. Above all, it is an age-related category, reserved for those aged 16 or over, who have spent more than a minimal time in care. In 2006–2007, roughly 8000 of the 24,700 leaving care in England fell into this category (DCSF, 2007a: Table D1). While some may return to their families or even occasionally be adopted, the dominant assumption is that care leavers are embarking upon the independence of adulthood. Care leavers also comprise a heterogeneous group in several respects – including pre-care experiences, length of time spent as a looked after child, number, type and 'quality' of placements, preparation for leaving and the handling of transitions from care. Their experiences are also significantly shaped both by social divisions – based on class, gender, ethnicity, sexuality and disability (see Chapter 9) – and by the wider context of youth transitions.

HISTORICAL BACKGROUND

In certain senses, addressing the needs of 'care leavers' has a long history, with efforts made by the Poor Law authorities and children's charities to assist young adults into employment and accommodation, sometimes involving emigration to the countries of the British Empire (Stein, 2004). The Children Act 1948 introduced a legal duty for local authorities to 'advise, assist and befriend' those leaving care, together with powers to provide accommodation and offer financial assistance, especially to support education and training. In his excellent historical overview, Stein (2004) argues that after-care work suffered following the formation of social services departments in England and Wales in 1971, with a loss of specialist skill and priority relative to child protection work. By the 1980s, there was growing recognition of the difficulties faced by many care leavers, with the Short Report (House of Commons, 1984) calling for stronger duties both to prepare those in care for leaving and to support them thereafter. Such calls were backed by a growing body of research highlighting the particular vulnerability of care leavers to unemployment and homelessness at a time when these problems were increasing generally for young people (Stein and Carey, 1986). They were also bolstered by campaigning groups, including the formation of First Key in the early 1980s, which broadened its initial focus on housing and homelessness to encompass a range of issues relevant to care leavers, being renamed as the National Leaving Care Advisory Service (NLCAS) in 2003. The Children Act 1989 contained new, if modest, measures to support young people leaving care. These included a duty (s24) to *prepare* looked after children for leaving care and a power to request assistance from other (local) authorities in respect of housing, education and health (s27).

Although the 1989 Act gave fresh impetus to services for care leavers, its effects were limited, and research studies continued to reveal widespread problems in areas such as education, employment, housing, health and the high incidence of young parenthood (Biehal et al., 1995; Broad, 1998). One particular problem highlighted was the wide variation in provision between local authorities, notably in the availability and level of financial support and, importantly, the establishment of specialist services. Building on, and sometimes in collaboration with, voluntary sector initiatives, some local authorities introduced leaving care teams to provide a dedicated service. Although not without their difficulties (discussed below), these were generally found to offer a better service to care leavers than generic child care teams, which tended to give this work a low priority (Broad, 1998).

The election of the New Labour government with its social investment approach brought a new policy focus on care leavers, who were seen as one of the groups most vulnerable to social exclusion and for whom successful investment might reap rewards in terms of reductions in unemployment, crime, early parenthood and homelessness. A government consultation paper (DH, 1999) was followed by the Children (Leaving Care) Act 2000, the principal measures of which are summarised in Box 8.1. Elsewhere in the UK, broadly similar legislation was introduced in Northern Ireland in 2002 and Scotland in 2004. For studies of services for young people leaving care in those countries, see McAuley and Bunting (2006) and Dixon and Stein (2005) respectively.

These provisions will be discussed in more detail below, but at this point the key themes can be identified as follows. First, the Act made the duties in respect of assessment and planning much more specific than under the Children Act 1989. Although not formally required, these duties led almost all local authorities to establish specialist leaving care teams where these were not already in place. Second, there was to be a more proactive approach, evident in the duty to keep in contact with young people after they leave care. Third, the 2000 Act's provision can be seen as extending the period of support, building on a presumption that leaving care would not ordinarily take place before the age of 18. This compared with the pattern of leaving at 16, which had become widespread during the 1990s, often based on a convenient marriage of local authority resource constraints and a desire for 'freedom' on the part of young people (Broad, 1998).

LEAVING CARE AND YOUTH TRANSITIONS

The experiences of care leavers cannot be adequately understood outside the broader context of youth transitions and here it is important to note significant changes that have occurred in the past two decades or so. It is customary to identify three aspects of western youth transitions – from school to work, from the family home to independent accommodation and family of origin to the formation of adult relationships. While these may in practice be linked in various ways, there are no necessary or sequential relationships between the three. Jones (2002) argues that in the late twentieth century, transitions became significantly extended, due to increasing participation in higher education, high housing costs, relatively low wages for young workers and social norms regarding 'settling down'. Importantly, extended transitions rest on assumptions that young adults will receive support from their families and should not be reliant on state benefits. However, within this broad trend towards extension, Jones also argues that there has been a polarisation between what she refers to as 'slow-track' and 'fast-track' transitions. The former characterises the new 'norm' of extended transition prior to the establishment of careers and new families. Conversely, the latter (found more frequently among working-class youth) may occur when a young person leaves education at the earliest opportunity, lives independently or becomes a parent.

Many of the problems faced by care leavers stem from their 'accelerated and compressed' transitions (Stein, 2004), which have historically entailed facing the various aspects of transition much earlier than other young people while frequently lacking adequate support from either their birth family or the public care system. Thus, while extended transitions offer many young people a 'protected space' (Furlong and Cartmel, 2007), this is rarely the case for care leavers.

EDUCATION, EMPLOYMENT AND TRAINING

Two of the starkest findings from early studies of care leavers were the very low levels of educational attainment and high levels of unemployment. The educational difficulties and relative lack of qualifications of looked after children have been described in Chapter 6, and these in part explain their subsequent lack of participation in further and higher education. However, studies of those who do enter higher education have also highlighted the importance of young people's aspirations, encouragement from family, carers or teachers and practical support in relation to books, equipment, finances and accommodation (Martin and Jackson, 2002). Current statistics indicate 6 per cent of care leavers in England attending higher education (3–4 per cent in Scotland: see Scottish Government, 2007c), representing a rise in recent years, but still a very low proportion in comparison with the general population (DCSF, 2007a: Table G1).

Unemployment among care leavers has, however, fallen significantly over the past decade, falling from over 50 to around 30 per cent (Broad, 2005a), with corresponding rises in employment, education and training from 44 to 63 per cent between 2002 and 2007. The shift clearly reflects wider trends in education and unemployment but also the effect of specific measures such as financial incentives when in education, employment or training (Wade and Dixon, 2006).

ACCOMMODATION

Suitable and settled accommodation is a vital element in successful transitions, with recent research highlighting its importance in providing a platform for engagement with education, training and employment (Wade and Dixon, 2006). Earlier studies consistently identified the instability of housing careers for many care leavers, often involving serial moves and both short- and long-term experience of homelessness (Stein, 2004). Vulnerability may take other forms, such as feelings of isolation, and fears of harassment or exploitation from neighbours or associates (Sergeant, 2006). In broad terms, the challenges are twofold: first, questions of availability and suitability of accommodation and second, the readiness of care leavers to cope with the varied demands of independent living.

Care leavers in many areas have suffered from wider shortages of social housing and good rented accommodation (Broad, 1998). Recent government statistics show that, at age 19, the most common housing status is independent living (43 per cent) followed by living with parents or relatives at 12 per cent. Other types of accommodation include (supported) lodgings, foyers and bed and breakfast. Wade and Dixon (2006) suggest that overall the housing situations of care leavers have improved in recent years but remain fragile, with 35 per cent of their respondents having experienced at least temporary homelessness. Similarly, a survey by Rainer (2007) highlights the gap between policies that should guarantee satisfactory accommodation for care leavers and the reality for a significant minority, estimated at one in six. Particular problems identified include issues of co-ordination between children's trusts and housing departments and the way in which rules relating to 'intentional homelessness' often work against care leavers.

HEALTH

Further to the health difficulties of looked after children discussed in Chapter 6, Broad (2005a) found health input to be the weakest element within leaving care teams while noting the variable experiences of care leavers in dealings with medical professionals. Dixon and Stein (2005) found deteriorating levels of mental health among young people in the year after leaving care, while Buchanan and Ten Brinke (1997) have demonstrated from longitudinal data the enduring effects of mental health problems for those growing up in care. Ward et al's (2003) study of drug use among care leavers found that, although this was higher than among the general population, it tended to decline rapidly, with care leavers 'maturing out' of drug use more quickly than other young people. Nevertheless, links have been found to persist, with May et al. (2005) reporting that almost half of the drug dealers in their study had experience of care. Broad (2005b) provides the most wide-ranging discussion of care leavers' health and well-being, including difficulties sometimes experienced in gaining access to services. Issues relating to young parenthood have been discussed in Chapter 6 and will not be repeated here.

OFFENDING AND CARE LEAVERS

The over-representation of care leavers in custody was noted in Chapter 6. However, there is a paucity of research mapping offending careers during transitions from care and hence a limited knowledge of the factors that stimulate or constrain such careers. Studies in the USA have also found that care leavers experience high levels of victimisation, although to date there is no comparable UK research (Stein, 2004). In relation to service provision, some of the major issues have been those surrounding the interface between public care and the criminal justice system. As outlined in Chapter 6, particular concerns have arisen in respect of 'throughcare' which are equally pertinent for care leavers. Young offenders in custody may be particularly prone to losing contact with local authorities, which in the case of care leavers also means the loss of entitlement to assistance. This may, in part, be due to the complex legal situation of young offenders in relation to the Children (Leaving Care) Act 2000, but has also been seen by some as 'convenient' for local authorities in terms of cost savings (Sergeant, 2006).

MAKING THE TRANSITION FROM CARE – PSYCHOSOCIAL ASPECTS

The areas of challenge and often difficulty catalogued above may both reflect and, in turn, shape the psychosocial well-being of care leavers. In this regard, it is important to note the many success stories, even if these are often represented in the literature as 'absences' amid the discussion of problems. As is the case for victims of maltreatment and looked after children, variations have prompted considerable interest in understanding resilience among care leavers.

Stein (2004) identifies three broad groupings of care leavers – 'moving on', 'survivors' and 'victims' – based on the balance of risk and support factors. The first group comprises those who make the most successful transitions, a majority of whom are young women. The group's principal characteristics are those of relative stability and continuity while looked after; the presence of secure attachments either with birth family members or substitute carers; a positive sense of identity; a measure of educational success; and a gradual, planned process of leaving care. Typically, the transitions of the second group lack most or all of these features, but an image of being 'tough and self-reliant' helps them to 'survive', albeit in less than ideal circumstances. The final group also lack the requisite factors for benign transition, but here damaging experiences, usually starting prior to being looked after, have weakened their capacity to cope. As a consequence, they are likely to experience numerous areas of difficulty, not only in relation to work, accommodation and relationships but also with added vulnerabilities to mental health problems, substance misuse and offending.

Some of the factors identified, such as stability in care and educational attainment, have been discussed previously, but at this point it may help to examine others a little more fully. The idea of preparation for leaving care has been firmly on the UK child welfare agenda for at least two decades but remains challenging, not least because it can be understood in different ways. It can, for instance, be seen largely in terms of task performance but may also signify a much more holistic notion of 'readiness'. Stein (2004) highlights the distinction between notions of *independence* – understood in terms of key practical skills for survival – and *interdependence*, where the emphasis is on interpersonal skills. A common criticism of 'preparation' work for looked after children is that it is often started too late and condensed into what Stein disparagingly describes as a 'domestic combat course'. Similarly, moves into (more) independent living may be abrupt and triggered by crises rather than carefully planned and phased (Dixon and Stein, 2005).

The idea of providing a secure base for transition brings together ideas of attachment and relationship with those of continuing support and availability. In attachment theory, a platform based on felt security allows exploration and engagement with new challenges. However, this is linked to the possibility of return to the secure base in cases of stress. For many young people, their birth family affords such a base, often including regular returns before transition is 'completed' and at an older age. Such support, especially from birth parents, is available only for a minority of care leavers, although Marsh and Peel (1999) argue that the potential of support from family networks remains significantly underestimated and underused. With rare exceptions among social workers or residential staff, the only group from within the care system to endow its graduates with a secure base is that of foster carers. However, in a majority of cases, this pattern of continued residence or contact tends to be fairly shortlived (Wade and Dixon, 2006). In this respect, specialist leaving care teams have proved a mixed blessing. For while they have undoubtedly brought greater focus and resources to work with care leavers, transfer to such teams has often entailed changes of placement and the loss of links with previous carers.

Issues of both personal and social identity are important for care leavers. Research has consistently found that many young people leave care having lost contact with parents or other close relatives and are without any clear understanding of why they became looked after (Stein, 2004). In some cases, this may have significant effects later in the life course, but adults formerly in care lack many of the rights and services afforded to those who are adopted when accessing files (Goddard et al., 2005). Barn et al's (2005) study features an interesting account of the post-care experiences of young people from a range of ethnic backgrounds, highlighting the complexities of both issues of identity and patterns of disadvantage and discrimination.

UNACCOMPANIED ASYLUM-SEEKERS AND 'LEAVING CARE'

Services for care leavers represent a particular site of struggle over the treatment of UASC, not least as two-thirds are aged 16 or 17. At the heart of such struggles lies a conflict between principles of equal treatment with other looked after children and pressures both of cost saving (at national and local government levels) and immigration control.

Prior to 2003, local authorities often made use of support for UASC under s17 of the Children Act 1989 as an alternative to accommodation under s20, an option that saved both direct and indirect costs arising from statutory responsibilities. Following a successful legal challenge known as the 'Hillingdon judgment', new guidance was issued stating that there should be a presumption of accommodation under s20 (DH, 2003). The judgment also clarified the entitlement of UASC to assistance under the Children (Leaving Care) Act 2000; previously often denied them. However, there have been continued instances of UASC being 'de-accommodated' at the earliest opportunity (often aged 16) in order to save local authority costs (JCHR, 2007) and evidence of them receiving poor quality services (Wade et al., 2005). The Joint Committee on Human Rights (JCHR) is also highly critical of new Home Office plans that appear to further enshrine the priorities of immigration policy, with tougher tests to verify age (despite frequent evidence of their inaccuracy) and planning based much more clearly on the likelihood of deportation and the latter taking place earlier, in some cases even before the age of 18. Work with UASC has been a significant focus of efforts for voluntary sector organisations such as Save the Children and the Refugee Council.

'IN THE MANNER OF A GOOD PARENT?' – IMPLEMENTING THE CHILDREN (LEAVING CARE) ACT

The 2000 Act specified four categories of young people entitled to services if they have been looked after since the age of 14 for at least three months. These are shown in Table 8.1.

As noted earlier, the Act laid particular emphasis on planning processes built around needs assessment, the role of the personal advisor and the pathway plan (except for the 'qualifying' group, reliant on support under the Children Act 1989). The pathway plan was to cover issues such as education, training and employment, accommodation, health, financial assistance, practical skills acquisition and support needs, and also included contingency plans in the case of placement breakdown or other major difficulties.

The broad message emanating from studies of the 2000 Act's implementation is one of increased resources and often significant improvements in service

Table 8.1 Designations under the Children (Leaving Care) Act 2000

Designation	Age	Care status
eligible	16–17	looked after
relevant	16–17	left care
former relevant	18–21	previously eligible or relevant
qualifying	under 21	left care after age 16

provision but continuing wide, and perhaps widening, variation between local authority areas. Broad (2005a) describes these variations in terms of faster-and slower-running services, and argues that it has been those already performing poorly that have made the least progress. Cameron et al. (2007) found that the Act's planning framework has been generally well received by stakeholders and the role of personal advisors appreciated by a majority of care leavers. In support of the improvements in education, training, employment and accommodation noted above, the authors also conclude that care leavers were faring better in these areas than a comparison group of disadvantaged young people who had not been in public care. However, there have been significant implementation gaps or delays, with Broad (2005a) reporting around 35–40 per cent of leavers not having a needs assessment or being allocated a personal advisor. More recently, Morgan and Lindsay (2006) report that a significant minority of care leavers did not feel that they actively participated in the planning process.

The local authority duty to keep in contact 'in the manner of a good parent' with care leavers can also be seen as broadly beneficial but may be experienced as an unwelcome intrusion by those who do not want such contact.

Financial support

An important measure in the 2000 Act was to transfer responsibility for financial support to 'relevant' 16 and 17 year-olds from the social security system to the local authority. This could in part be seen as introducing a more paternalistic regime, within which young people had effectively to 'earn' the right to handle their own financial affairs, while local authority discretion gave professionals and agencies more influence and control. The Act's guidance does, however, make clear that young people should ordinarily receive financial treatment more generous than the benefit payments to which they were previously entitled. Yet from his survey, Broad (2005a) found that benefit-level payments were the norm, with little account being taken of wider needs. The notable exception to this rule was that incentive payments to care leavers for participation in education, training or employment were widespread, offered by around two-thirds of authorities. Nevertheless, this leaves many without such assistance and studies have found continuing financial difficulties linked to further and higher education courses and lack of awareness in respect of entitlements (Cameron et al., 2007).

Leaving care grants, designed to help with the start-up costs for independent living, have become more widely available since the 1990s, but their levels have been found to vary by a factor of five between authorities (Broad, 2005a).

FAREWELL TO 'LEAVING CARE'? – *CARE MATTERS*

The Green Paper on looked after children contained a number of measures relevant to young people leaving care, which collectively signal that the broad thrust of the 2000 Act needs to be reinvigorated and extended. An overarching aim is to move further away from abrupt transitions.

> It is time to leave behind the unhelpful idea of 'leaving care' and recognise that every young person needs continuing help to make a smooth transition to adulthood. (DfES, 2006b: 84)

Key practical measures include improving placement stability and extending support in various ways, especially in relation to further and higher education. The principal proposals are summarised in Box 8.2.

BOX 8.2

Care Matters – principal measures regarding leaving care

- piloting a veto for young people over any decisions about moving on from care before they turn 18;
- piloting allowing young people to continue to live with foster carers up to the age of 21, receiving the support they need to continue in education;
- access to support through a personal advisor until the age of 25;
- providing a top-up to the Child Trust Funds of young people in care;
- creating more supported accommodation for young people;
- introducing a national bursary for young people in care going to university.

Source: DfES (2006b)

Delaying moves from care placements and the system itself reflects research evidence in both the UK and USA that those who leave later have better outcomes, although it is difficult to demonstrate a causal link (Pecora et al., 2004; Wade and Dixon, 2006). Official statistics reveal that there is considerable work to be done in relation to later leaving, with a quarter of those leaving care in England doing so at age 16 (DCSF, 2007b: Table F1). Questions also remain about how some of the measures, such as the 'veto' and remaining with foster carers until aged 18 or beyond, will work in practice or be resourced.

CONCLUSION

In this chapter, we have charted policy and practice developments over the past two decades in relation to young people leaving care. There is little doubt that service provision has improved significantly during this time, as have outcomes in a number of areas. However, these improvements have taken place within a difficult context for youth transitions and at a time of rising expectations, whether in respect of education and employment or avoiding the pitfalls of social exclusion. As discussed, recent policy has been framed by New Labour's 'social investment' approach, with support and resources closely tied to monitoring and performance targets. While further effort is needed to promote 'joined up working', arguably greater challenges arise from the psychosocial aspects of transition. Crucially, in addition to the supports offered to care leavers, this requires extensive improvements for looked after children, in terms of stability, achievement and participation.

GUIDE TO FURTHER READING

Two valuable overview texts on policy in practice in relation to leaving care are those of Stein (2004) and Wheal (ed.) *The RHP Companion to Leaving Care* (Russell House). Broad (2005b) also helpfully covers the areas of health and well-being.

Reading and resources for practice

The above texts all contain useful practice guidance, as does Wheal (ed.) *The Leaving Care Handbook* (Russell House). The main representative organisations for looked after children (see Chapter 6) are all involved to varying degrees in supporting and campaiging on behalf of care leavers. Dedicated organisations include NLCAS www.leavingcare.org and the Care Leavers Association www.careleavers.com, both of which provide a wide range of relevant information, guidance and links to other bodies. In relation to offenders, the National Association for the Care and Resettlement of Offenders' *The Children (Leaving Care) Act 2000: Implications for the Youth Justice System, Youth Crime Briefing* features good guidance. Clayden and Stein's *Mentoring for Care Leavers: Evaluation Report* (Prince's Trust) discusses the role of mentors for those leaving care.

Discussion questions

Assess the strengths and weaknesses of New Labour's 'social investment' approach to care leavers.

What are the main challenges in creating a 'secure base' for care leavers to make their transitions to adulthood?

Does the duty of local authorities to keep in touch with care leavers until they are at least 21 raise civil liberties issues?

What is meant by preparation for leaving care and how might it be improved?

DISABLED CHILDREN AND
YOUNG PEOPLE

In this chapter, our focus rests with the major concerns of the book – assessment, family support, child maltreatment, looked after children and leaving care – as they relate to disabled children and young people (hereafter shortened to children unless specifically addressing the older age group). Although coverage here will often stress the common experiences of disabled children and families, it is important to remember that they comprise a heterogeneous group in terms of the nature, extent and sometimes combination of impairments, and the impact of social divisions based on class, gender or ethnicity.

TERMINOLOGY AND MODELS OF DISABILITY

The discursive domain of disability is a controversial and contested one. It is customary to talk in terms of two contrasting models of disability, the medical and the social, which can be summarised briefly as follows (for a fuller discussion see for example Campbell and Oliver, 1996). The former tends to construe disability as a direct consequence of physical (or intellectual) impairment and to focus on (para-)medical treatment aimed at maximising physical functioning and fostering adaptation to that which cannot be restored or attained. By contrast, the social model, favoured by disability activists, emphasises the importance of social processes. These may relate to the generation of impairment – for example, the greater vulnerability of poor people to accident, disease etc. – but crucially highlight failure to cater for the needs of those with impairments. Hence, the social model draws a clear distinction between impairment and the disability that arises from social barriers and exclusionary practices. Tensions between medical and social models have given rise to those over terminology. Historically, within a medical model the term 'disabled' (or predecessors such as 'handicapped') denoted the direct effects of impairment. In an effort to re-frame this label and emphasise similarities with other children, some commentators have preferred the term 'children with disabilities'. However, writers operating within the social model often favour the term 'disabled children' so long as this is understood as the result of disabling processes. It is this construction that will be used here.

In discussing the social model, it is important to recognise its internal debates. These include questions of whether the model enshrines the concerns of those who are relatively young, fit, physically impaired and mostly white and male and how to understand the perspectives of those who do not fall into these categories or may not identify with the model. It has also been argued that, in its resolutely political stance, the social model has neglected or even suppressed the significance of impairment as a lived experience, while giving insufficient weight to the effects of cultural barriers (Riddell and Watson, 2003). Similarly, for Connors and Stalker (2007), the social model has paid little regard to children or the applicability of the model to their experiences. It should be noted that, while support for the social model tends to be endorsed in official pronouncements and sometimes those of the voluntary sector, the degree of social change envisaged falls well short of that sought by disability activists.

HISTORICAL BACKGROUND

Many recent developments in policy and practice regarding disabled children and their families can be seen as attempts to address the legacy of segregation and institutionalisation that began in the nineteenth century. (For short historical accounts, see Hendrick, 2003: 49–56, or Fawcett et al., 2004: Chapter 7). Of particular importance was the pattern of separate educational institutions (often including boarding schools) and the role of philanthropic organisations.

In the latter part of the twentieth century several factors combined to create pressure for moves away from specialised/segregated provision, notably in schooling under the Education Act 1981 but also more broadly. These factors included a wider pattern of deinstitutionalisation, driven by cost concerns and a belief in the value of community living, an awareness of institutional abuse and the disability movement's emphasis on civil rights and opposition to exclusion through the 'segregation' of separate provision.

Disabled children were recognised in the UNCRC, with Article 23 referring to rights to 'a full and decent life', 'dignity' and 'active participation in the community'. Disability was specifically included among the criteria for children in need under the Children Act 1989, which also mandated the compilation of a register of disabled children but, as described in Chapter 3, the impact of the Act was blunted by problems of interpretation, inconsistent definitions and a lack of new resources.

In the years following the Act, a succession of inspection reports painted a picture of widespread difficulties in gaining access to services and a lack of co-ordination between relevant agencies (Goodinge, 1998). The New Labour government has devoted considerable policy attention to improving services for disabled children and their families (DH, 1998a; 2001a; PMSU, 2005). Yet a report by the Audit Commission (2003) referred to families facing a 'jigsaw puzzle' in accessing services, while the Children's Commissioner for England has described the plight of disabled children and their families as 'nothing short of a national scandal' (Ad Hoc Parliamentary Committee, 2006: 10). In a tacit admission of limited progress, the government has recently undertaken a wide-ranging review of services for disabled children, which will be discussed further below (HM Treasury/DfES, 2007b).

Some commentators have suggested that disabled children may be vulnerable in a social investment state, where they are seen neither as an economic opportunity nor a social threat and where the emphasis on children's rights is relatively weak (Fawcett et al., 2004). This is reflected in a tendency in policy documents for the needs of disabled children to be subsumed within the wider population without recognising the particular challenges and barriers they may face (Every Disabled Child Matters, 2006a).

DISABLED CHILDREN IN THE UK – A PROFILE

Calculating the number of disabled children in the UK is a challenging task due to problems of definition and data collection. Under the Disability Discrimination Act 1995 (s1), disability is defined in terms of:

> A physical or mental impairment which has a substantial and long-term adverse effect on [his] ability to carry out normal day-to-day activities.

However, as Pinney (2005: 1–2) describes, agencies working with disabled children operate different forms of classification. In the case of education, the focus is on 'special educational needs', while health services concentrate on specific diagnoses. There may also be debates about whether emotional and behavioural problems should be classified in relation to disability.

Official estimates have also been sought by means such as the census, analysis of government data sets and commissioned surveys, which have produced figures in the range of 320,000–777,000 (Pillai et al., 2007). A recent government publication has suggested that there are 570,000 disabled children in England, of whom around 100,000 have complex care needs (HM Treasury/DfES, 2007b). What is widely recognised is that this has been a growing population, almost doubling in the last quarter of the twentieth century (Langerman and Worrall, 2005), for two main reasons. First, medical and technological advances have meant that more children with life-threatening conditions survive and for longer. Second, certain impairments, such as those associated with the autistic spectrum (ASD) or attention deficit hyperactivity disorder(s) (ADHD), have increased dramatically, although it is unclear how far this is due to diagnostic factors (Russell, 2003). Specifically on learning disabilities, *Valuing People* estimated that there were 65,000 children and young people with severe and profound learning disabilities, and over 300,000 with mild or moderate disabilities.

Disabled children, families and social exclusion

To contextualise the social care needs and experiences of disabled children and their families, it is necessary to look at their vulnerabilities to poverty and social exclusion. As Langerman and Worrall (2005) document, there is a two-way relationship between disability and poverty. On the one hand, children from poor families are more likely to be born with, or develop, certain impairments, while on the other, disabling barriers make families more vulnerable to poverty (Gordon et al., 2000). This is partly due to the impact of caring duties on employment. Only 16 per cent of mothers of disabled children are employed compared with 61 per cent of all mothers (Langerman and Worrall, 2005). Alongside lower incomes, families with disabled children also face markedly higher costs, estimated as between two and three times the average for all children (Langerman and Worrall, 2005). The pressures may be particularly acute for families with more than one disabled child (Lawton, 1998). Higher costs may reflect a range of factors, linked to diet, clothes, 'wear and tear', transport, equipment or adaptations and have been found to be (significantly) above the level covered by disability or carer benefits (Dobson et al., 2001). Studies have also found that housing problems are extremely widespread among families with disabled children, whether in terms of access, space (including for equipment), suitability for lifting, toileting and bathing, and safety (Beresford and Oldman, 2002).

Social exclusion is, of course, more than simply a matter of material deprivation, but also extends to participation in formal and informal activities such as play, leisure, holidays, transport, neighbourhood networks and community organisations. It may also entail experiences of stigma and discrimination, while BME families with disabled children have been found to be particularly vulnerable to exclusion (Chamba et al., 1999). Although all family members may face elements of exclusion, for disabled children there are often particular difficulties in making and sustaining friendships due to lack of transport or other restrictions on movement (Connors and Stalker, 2007).

DISABLED CHILDREN, COMMUNICATION AND PARTICIPATION

Disabled children share with others many of the challenges outlined in previous chapters in relation to participation, but they may also be hampered by communication difficulties. These arise from the interaction of impairments, professional and organisational practices and, arguably, wider societal values.

Some children with sensory or cognitive impairments may require particular forms of communication such as sign language(s) and visual methods such as pictures, photographs or cards in addition to possible technological help. However, research suggests that these challenges are often avoided rather than embraced, with professionals instead relying on parents'/carers' accounts to gauge children's views. Such reliance is often rationalised on the basis that workers lack time or in some cases the necessary skills and confidence but it represents a worrying example of the routinised discrimination faced by disabled children and the absence of a strong rights emphasis in work with them (Connors and Stalker, 2002). Lack of communication may also be underpinned by assumptions that the views of disabled children, especially with intellectual impairments, have little value or significance. A recent survey found that, although involvement and consultation with disabled children had increased, progress had been slower than that for children more generally and remained 'fragile' (Franklin and Sloper, 2006). It can therefore be argued that the case for advocacy, including that supplied by other disabled people, is particularly strong for disabled children (see Mitchell, 2007 for a review of services). Research interest in the perspectives of disabled children is relatively recent and still underdeveloped in certain areas, not least in relation to experiences of BME children (Ali et al., 2003). Proposals in the *Care Matters* initiative will require independent reviewing officers to demonstrate skills in communicating with disabled children in care, or to commission specialists with such skills.

ASSESSMENT FOR DISABLED CHILDREN AND THEIR FAMILIES

Both the impact of impairment and the wider social context of disability pose challenges for assessment and raise issues relevant to all three domains of the Assessment Framework (see Chapter 2). Interesting commentaries can be found in Marchant and Jones (2000) and Kennedy and Wonnacott (2003).

In the case of child developmental needs, the challenges include assessing the impact of impairment on development, looking at educational needs in the light of provision for disabled children, examining the place of disability in relation to identity and recognising the pressures on children to present socially as 'normal' (Marchant and Jones, 2000). All are contentious areas and must be assessed sensitively, ensuring that the views of the child are ascertained.

Assessing parenting capacity requires judgements as to what a reasonable parent might offer in terms of physical care, stimulation, boundaries or the management of risk. This requires a delicate balancing act, between setting unattainable standards for parents or accepting lower standards of parenting due to sympathy with them (Kennedy and Wonnacott, 2003). As described above, environmental factors might include a range of disabling barriers in relation to local facilities, services and support networks, and the impact of structural inequalities, poverty and poor housing. Fawcett et al. (2004) contend that, while there have been some improvements under the Assessment Framework, families with disabled children still often experience assessment as an intrusive process. This may reflect the spectre of child protection concerns and often poor co-ordination between professionals and agencies in health, education and social care.

FAMILY SUPPORT AND DISABLED CHILDREN

Family support provision for disabled children and their families has been framed by two key sets of relationships. First, the level of support offered by the state is linked to constructions of the 'reasonable parent' and what s/he might be expected to provide. Second, the needs and rights of disabled children are interconnected, in complex ways, with those of other family members. Debates in both areas reflect the wider issues and tensions relating to family support and those of 'disability politics'.

Advocates of greater support emphasise the high levels of unmet need within families and often the paucity of state provision. Despite being over-represented among those living away from home, an overwhelming majority (variously estimated at 85–98 per cent: see Langerman and Worrall, 2005) of disabled children are cared for within their families. Particularly for those with more severe impairments, the 'extra care' in looking after them - in areas such as feeding, dressing, bathing, keeping children occupied, dealing with challenging behaviour, suffering sleepless nights, or providing forms of medical attention - may be substantial (Roberts and Lawton, 2001). A survey by Mencap (2001) reported 60 per cent of parents undertaking such tasks for more than 10 hours a day, with further hours spent in therapeutic and educational activities. Importantly, only around half received any help from outside the home, and this was often of very limited duration. Dobson et al. (2001) write of how families must often develop a 'new paradigm' in which relationships, obligations, aspirations and responsibilities are redefined.

A comparison of data from Children in Need surveys (see Chapter 3) with wider population estimates suggests that less than 10 per cent of disabled children are in receipt of social care services in any one week, while there are huge variations between local authority areas (HM Treasury/DfES, 2007b). Even allowing for the snapshot nature of the surveys and some disabled children being 'hidden' in other categories of need, the message that only a minority receive help is fairly clear. As with family support more generally, critics argue that resources tend to be targeted at those deemed most at risk, i.e. where there may be child protection concerns or an immediate likelihood of entry into care (Middleton, 1999). However well founded, such perceptions may add to the stigma associated with asking for help and fears that interventions are driven more by 'surveillance' than 'support'. They may also encourage parents to exaggerate difficulties in order to receive help (Middleton, 1999). From a professional standpoint, the challenge in most cases is to be supportive without being intrusive, with research studies highlighting the importance for parents of feeling that their input and knowledge are valued (Roberts and Lawton, 2001; Beresford et al., 2007). A further challenge in relation to parents of disabled children is to acknowledge the parental alongside the 'carer' role (Dobson et al., 2001).

Unsurprisingly, studies have found very widespread dissatisfaction with services among parents of disabled children, especially in relation to social care (Ad Hoc Parliamentary Committee, 2006). Difficulties often start with diagnoses of impairments, which are often felt by parents to be delayed and poorly handled in terms of sensitivity and explanation (Mencap, 2001; Russell, 2003). Thereafter, diagnostic labels often 'overshadow' other problems, with physical and mental health problems being wrongly seen as symptoms of the diagnosed impairment (Emerson and Hatton, 2007). Many parents also complain about a lack of clear, consistent information either about their children's impairments or available service provision (DH, 2001a). In response, the government has funded a national information centre Contact a Family (see 'Reading and resources' at the end of this chapter). Dissatisfaction with statutory services is also a key factor behind an extensive self-help and charitable sector working in the field of childhood and disability (Langerman and Worrall, 2005)

Another important aspect within family support is the implicit construction of 'family'. For example, what weight should be given to parents' own needs or those of siblings? (In Scotland, explicit recognition is given in law to needs arising from having a disabled family member, although this tends to be exercised to support young carers: see Banks et al., 2001.) Here, the challenge is to recognise the wider impact of impairment and disability upon whole families without losing sight of the needs of disabled children or casting them as a 'burden' (Connors and Stalker, 2002).

Early intervention and prevention

New Labour policy for disabled children and their families has been shaped by the broader government push towards early intervention and prevention. An Audit Commission (2003) report referred to provision that was 'too little, too late', while the government has acknowledged that too often crises are allowed to develop, necessitating more costly interventions such as expensive residential placements (HM Treasury/DfES, 2007b). As always with prevention, however, there are questions about how to transfer resources from high-cost services to broader-based provision and whether the desired effects for families and government finances will materialise.

Initiatives to combat social exclusion such as SureStart and the Children's Fund have both included a focus on disabled children and their families (see reviews by M. Barnes et al., 2006, and Pinney, 2007) while there have also been more targeted measures such as the Early Support Programme linked to children's centres and Together from the Start (see www.earlysupport.org.uk for details). Core themes include those of 'joined up working' and the involvement of a key worker to lead and co-ordinate provision, improved information for parents and the latter's participation in service planning and delivery.

In more substantive terms, provision focuses on equipment, play facilities, parenting support, specialist services such as speech and language therapy, short breaks (see below) and childcare. Despite some improvements, child care has been identified as a particular area of difficulty for disabled children, with problems of availability, suitability in terms of skills and facilities and costs. A report by Every Disabled Child Matters (2006b) has argued that a higher profile must be given to disabled children in childcare planning arrangements and that increased funding (including more generous tax credits) is necessary to meet their needs. For BME families of disabled children, there have also been concerns about the shortage of culturally sensitive services (Hatton et al., 2004).

Direct payments and individual budgets

Originally introduced in 1996, direct payments were extended to the carers of disabled children and to young disabled people aged 16–17 under the Carers and Disabled Children Act 2000. As the name suggests, direct payments involve money transfers to recipients following an assessment of need, with the service user then able to purchase goods or services (including those of a personal assistant) directly rather than through the local authority. Direct payments are seen as having the advantages of greater flexibility and control for service users, and, despite certain (potential) pitfalls, have generally been viewed as a positive development (Leece and Bornat, 2006). Uptake has been slow, but tripled in the year to 2004–2005 to involve over 2200 carers, almost 500 16–17 year-olds and a budget of over £11 million (CSCI, 2006). In line with its broader social policy, the government has signalled a wish to increase the use of individualised budgets, with the possibility of drawing on funding from other agencies as well as social care services (HM Treasury/DfES, 2007b).

SHORT BREAKS FOR DISABLED CHILDREN

Further to the discussion of short breaks in Chapter 3, our focus here is upon disabled children and their families, who comprise the majority of those who receive them. Provision of short breaks has been a focal point for family support campaigners (including ongoing attempts to establish a minimum entitlement) but, as will be explained, is also open to different interpretations of needs. Cramer and Carlin (2007) report that having a break from caring is the most frequently reported unmet need amongst parents of disabled children, estimating that only one in three 'eligible' families receives them.

Short breaks may occur in the home (through sitting services) day-time care or activities outside the home but most commonly involve overnight stays away from home, in families, residential care, hospices and hospitals. Children, especially boys, with complex health needs, ASDs or challenging behaviour and children from BME families are the most likely not to be catered for or to be placed in more 'institutional' forms of care (SCIE, 2004b). Despite a general preference for family-based short breaks, and government endorsement of their value, provision falls significantly short of demand. Indeed, Cramer and Carlin's (2007) national (excluding Scotland) survey indicates a slight fall in recent years, with roughly 5,000 carers looking after 6760 children. This appears to result both from funding restrictions and difficulties in recruiting carers. The survey also found a shift in schemes towards more 'professionalised' care, with a fall in sitting and befriending services and increased recourse to contracted carers. Beyond availability, other problems identified in research have been those of bureaucracy, lack of choice and flexibility.

Respite or segregation? – the politics of short breaks

While short breaks tend to be seen as beneficial for all concerned, some commentators are more critical. The concern expressed is that short breaks may lend support to parents and other family members 'at the expense of', or to the detriment of, the child receiving the break. In the case of disabled children, this danger may be heightened by an ideology that casts them as a 'burden' or of lesser value. Clearly, there are difficult balances to strike - recognising the extra care demanded of parents without seeing them as martyrs or saints and weighing carefully the needs of the child as an individual and as a family member. Several writers argue that short breaks constitute an example of disabled children being treated in ways that would not generally be regarded as acceptable for non-disabled children (see for example Middleton, 1999). This might include situations where 'short breaks' become semi-permanent, a point to which we will return later. Cocks (2000) contends that disabled children are subjected to a pattern of segregation, albeit cloaked in the garb of helping and caring, that presages their later treatment as disabled adults.

Research on the outcomes of short breaks for disabled children has tended to be positive in terms of expressed satisfaction, especially among parents, but it has proved difficult to demonstrate positive outcomes in more 'objective' terms. Studies have found that children value the chance to meet and make friends, the variety of activities and opportunities to develop independence and the break from their family (SCIE, 2004b), but there remains scope for further research on their perspectives.

Palliative care

Palliative care for those with life-threatening or life-limiting conditions has also come under the policy spotlight in recent years throughout the UK. A recent review in England has highlighted the lack of strategic planning and co-ordination between agencies (Craft and Killen, 2007). Although there have been positive developments, such as the creation of specialist children's hospices, there remain major difficulties in relation to long-term funding and the enormous local variations in provision. Problems also arise, however, from a lack of recognition of palliative care as a specialist area of practice with appropriate training and career development. Recently launched guidance in England emphasises community nurses, short breaks and palliative care networks as the key funding priorities (DH, 2008).

INTER-AGENCY WORK WITH DISABLED CHILDREN AND THEIR FAMILIES

Nowhere are the challenges of 'joined up' working more acute than in relation to disabled children, who are likely to have higher levels of contact, relative to other children, with a range of state agencies and sometimes voluntary organisations. Families with disabled children have been estimated to have contact with an average of 10 professionals and to make over 20 hospital and clinic visits annually (Langerman and Worrall, 2005). In addition, as will be described below, transition to adulthood often entails a shift from children's to adult provision in most or all these services, creating a complex nexus for co-ordination.

A report by the Audit Commission (2003) referred to families negotiating a 'maze' and having to jump through a series of hoops to try to gain access to support. The difficulties relate in part to gaining information but perhaps more so to the process(es) of assessment, which historically have been carried out separately by each agency, requiring families to repeat their stories and requests, sometimes on several occasions (PMSU, 2005). Policy measures to improve co-ordination have included the development of the Common Assessment Framework (see Chapter 2), an emphasis on the role of key workers and a 'team around the child', co-location, and abundant exhortation for professionals and agencies to work in partnership. (See also DH, 2004, for official guidance on the co-ordination of services.) Research studies paint a picture of progress, with positive effects arising from the co-location of workers and improved co-ordination of assessments (Abbott et al., 2005). However, the improvements have been slow and fairly modest to date. Greco et al. (2005) report that only a minority of families had key workers and argue that there are significant resource implications in developing this role fully. Moreover, studies point to a lack of evidence that more 'joined up working' leads to improved outcomes for children and families.

It is also important to consider how 'outcomes' are judged, and in particular the way in which wider population norms are applied to disabled children (e.g. see Beresford et al., 2007, for a discussion of the *Every Child Matters* outcomes). There also remain certain crucial shortfalls in capacity for effective inter-agency working, for example, CAMHS's lack of dedicated provision for children with intellectual impairments despite high levels of mental health problems among the group (Emerson and Hatton, 2007).

MALTREATMENT AND THE SAFEGUARDING OF DISABLED CHILDREN

Growing awareness of the vulnerability of disabled children can be seen as an important theme within the broader (re-)discovery of maltreatment in the late twentieth century. In a wide-ranging historical review, Westcott and Jones (1999) map a shift from research that appeared to reflect little more than 'medical curiosity' to studies underpinned by clear notions of disabled children's rights to protection. Studies have evolved in two key areas, first taking greater account of social context and second, exploring the dynamics of maltreatment, including the experiences of victims.

The overarching message that emerges from prevalence studies is that disabled children are significantly (between one and a half and four times) more vulnerable to maltreatment than their peers. Sullivan and Knutson (2000) offer further analysis, suggesting that there is a broad gradient of risk arising from ASD via physical and sensory impairments, health problems and intellectual impairments to the highest risk category, children with speech and language difficulties. (Those with intellectual impairments were found to be most at risk of sexual abuse.) It is also important to recognise that, in addition to such vulnerabilities, disabled children also face distinctive types of maltreatment. These might include being subjected to excessive restriction under the guise of protection and in some instances painful medical procedures in highly questionable efforts to make them more 'normal'.

Risk factors

While it is important to remember that maltreatment can itself lead to a range of impairments, our focus here is on the heightened risks faced by those already impaired. These risks reflect complex interactions between the effects of impairment, relationships with carers and others, and broader social and political factors (Westcott and Jones, 1999; HM Government, 2006a). Disabled children can be vulnerable, for example to bullying, in schools and public spaces but crucially also in intra- and extra-familial settings where care is being provided.

Depending on the nature and degree of children's impairment, vulnerability may arise from a need for intimate physical care and resultant 'boundary' issues in respect of control over their bodies. Disabled children may also have a reduced capacity to resist maltreatment. Similarly, any reporting of maltreatment may be rendered more difficult by fear of, or threat from, carers and limited communication. When efforts to report are made, the testimony of disabled children may be regarded as less reliable, whether initially stages or in more formalised stages of investigation and court appearance. Howe (2006a; 2006b), while emphasising that only a minority of disabled children are maltreated, examines the heightened risks that may arise from insecure (especially disorganised) attachments. This may partly be a matter of 'attunement', as problems in verbal or non-verbal communication hinder the cycle of meeting needs and mutual satisfaction (see Chapter 2). Howe suggests that some parents may respond to communication difficulties with more punitive discipline. Powerful evidence on the importance of communication also comes from research showing that deaf children are more likely to be insecurely attached to hearing parents than to parents who are also deaf. While the additional demands of caring for a disabled child can be regarded as (potentially) stressful, Howe (2006a) points out that there is no simple relationship either between demands and stress or between stress and the risk of maltreatment.

Safeguarding disabled children

The risk factors outlined above pose significant challenges for safeguarding disabled children. In addition to the communication difficulties described, workers may also find it more difficult to recognise signs of maltreatment, for example attributing self-mutilation or repetitive behaviours to impairment (Westcott and Jones, 1999). Equally important is the assessment of parenting, where higher thresholds for maltreatment may be applied on the basis of the pressures and demands facing parents. Historically, this can be seen as part of a wider pattern of institutional neglect and discrimination, whether in terms of a lack of resources or implicit assumptions that disabled children are less in need of, or even worthy of, protection. One organisational manifestation of this is the undue separation between disability teams (focused on family support measures) and child protection work (Middleton, 1999). This can mean that disability teams may fail to detect or act effectively upon maltreatment, while conversely, mainstream child protection services may lack disability awareness and will consequently make poor decisions (Cooke and Standen, 2002). Data are often collected in either/or categories, making it difficult to know, for example, the proportion of disabled children on the child protection register. As with all anti-discriminatory work, there is a need to tackle problems at a range of levels, from personal prejudices through to professional (including communication skills) and organisational practices. It may also necessitate adapting models of prevention where messages of 'say no and tell someone' may not be appropriate for children with communication impairments (Westcott and Jones, 1999). Similarly, relatively little attention has been paid to therapeutic or other support measures for the disabled survivors of maltreatment.

DISABILITY AND LOOKED AFTER CHILDREN

The 1990s can be seen as a time of increasing awareness of the needs and experiences of disabled children living away from home. This was in part prompted by duties under the Children Act 1989 but perhaps more so by wider recognition of their vulnerability to institutional abuse (Utting, 1997). What also became apparent was that disabled children living away from home had 'only a shadowy presence on major policy and research agendas' (Read and Harrison, 2002: 211). One of the key emerging problems was fragmentation and a lack of co-ordination between the main agencies involved, social care, education and health, in relation to their definitions of disability, data collection, funding arrangements and information-sharing. As we shall see, in the case of residential placements, this gave rise to significant concerns about safeguarding children.

Despite improvements in data collection, it remains difficult to establish accurate figures for disabled children who are looked after. However, while the estimated degree of over-representation varies enormously (between factors of two and ten), it is widely accepted that disabled children are significantly more likely to become looked after than their non-disabled peers (Read and Harrison, 2002; HM Treasury/DfES, 2007b). This may be for reasons of maltreatment or because families cannot provide the necessary care, fail to cope or reject disabled children, although data categorisations do not facilitate deeper analysis. Once in public care, there is also evidence that disabled children may receive less favourable treatment in certain respects. Stuart and Baines (2004) argue that there is a link between the everyday abuses of the rights of disabled children (abuse with a small 'a') and their vulnerability to more harmful treatment (abuse with a large 'A').

THE PLACEMENT OF DISABLED CHILDREN

Permanency and substitute family care

Finding families for disabled children was an important plank in the drive to expand substitute family care in the late twentieth century. However, despite substantial progress, significant challenges remain. Baker (2007) draws on a larger-scale study of foster care to argue that disabled children face a 'reverse ladder of permanency', being less likely to be returned home or adopted and, even when achieving permanence, experiencing longer delays. While in public care, they are also less likely to be placed in foster care than non-disabled peers. Baker suggests that 'clearly disabled' children, i.e. those with more visible often physical impairments, fare better in terms of permanence than those with intellectual impairments and/or challenging behaviour. Cousins (2005) acknowledges that disabled children are affected by the 'hierarchy' in adoption and are more likely to be placed with lone parents or same-sex partners. She also argues that problems in recruiting families arise from the labelling of children in ways that arguably give too much emphasis to issues of disability/impairment over their personalities and attributes.

Some writers have argued that institutional discrimination can be detected in the difficulties faced by disabled adults seeking to adopt or foster (Wates, 2002b). This can also be related to issues of disability and (cultural) identity. For example, should deaf children be placed with deaf substitute carers where possible and what importance should be attached to a Deaf culture and identity built around the use of sign language? Issues of ethnic identity are also important in relation to disability in different ways. For example, Cousins (2005) notes how ethnic identity is often downplayed for disabled children, while Jones et al. (2002) argue the need for disabled identities to recognise (ethnic) diversity more fully. (See Connors and Stalker, 2007, for interesting qualitative research into how disabled children identify themselves.)

Residential care

The historical legacy of institutionalisation and the safeguarding agenda have ensured that contemporary residential care for disabled children remains controversial. Is, for instance, provision often regarded as a 'last resort' for others used too readily for disabled children? Placements may be made under the auspices of social care services, education and health authorities with variable sole and joint funding arrangements. In her survey in England, Pinney (2005) reported a total of 13,300 residential placements for disabled children. The majority were boys of secondary school age, with the largest groupings being those with behavioural, social and emotional difficulties and

ASDs, but there was also a significant over-representation of those with sensory impairments. Of the total, around 1500 were looked after children. Research has found wide variation between areas in recourse to residential placements, with local policies and the availability of services seemingly more influential than individual needs assessments (Read and Harrison, 2002).

Studies in the 1990s raised questions about whether the welfare of children was being adequately safeguarded when many children were living away from home for lengthy periods without the legal status of looked after children (Morris, 1995). Duties on the part of education and health bodies to notify social care services of placements lasting over three months (Children Act 1989, s85–86) appeared to be widely ignored. Even when notified, social care services interpreted their responsibilities quite differently, notably on according children looked after status, and often failed to make the required visits and reviews (Morris et al., 2002). This may reflect gatekeeping concerns with regard to costs and workload, but also fits with parents' desire to avoid the trappings and stigma of looked after status. However, it can also create a dangerous vacuum with respect to safeguarding and planning, minimising engagement with both children and their families, especially when placements are often distant and the children may face communication difficulties. Knight (1998) reports that only a small minority of disabled children had independent visitors.

DISABLED YOUNG PEOPLE AND THE CHALLENGES OF TRANSITION

For disabled young people, transition carries two distinctive meanings, which, as will be explained, often sit uneasily alongside each other. The first is the process of transition to adulthood (see Chapter 8) while the second describes a move from children's to adult services. All three major components of the transition to adulthood – gaining employment, securing independent accommodation and forming adult relationships – may be more difficult for disabled young people. Similarly, the links between these components may pose different challenges from those faced by non-disabled peers, for example, in both sustaining full-time employment and managing accommodation (Pascall and Hendey, 2004). Particularly for those with complex care needs[1] the 'adulthood' implicit within transition models may be (severely) restricted.

Studies have consistently shown that, while the aspirations of disabled young people are very similar to those of their peers, they are aware of facing

---

[1] Complex care needs are often defined in terms of two or more of the following factors: acute and chronic medical conditions, multiple and profound impairments, behaviour problems and learning difficulties (CSCI, 2007).

numerous barriers to realising them (Russell, 2003). For instance, disabled young people are at least twice as likely not to be in employment, education or training, while many of the remainder will face poorer prospects within these sectors (Ad Hoc Parliamentary Committee, 2006). Priestley et al. (2003) found that suitable housing or related support is also often lacking, leading to an over-reliance on institutional care, sometimes including nursing homes with overwhelmingly elderly residents. They also contend that disabled young people may also be more vulnerable to social isolation, with limited transport, smaller friendship networks, and fewer opportunities to form sexual relationships, which may be actively discouraged or prevented.

For Morris (2001), the seeds of such difficulties are sown in the patterns of segregation experienced by disabled children, especially those in institutional care, which often leads to educational disadvantage and limits opportunities for 'ordinary' social interaction. Instead, the children inhabit a world largely dominated by adult care staff, while peer friendships rarely survive beyond institutional residence. The importance for disabled children of such relationships and the support that they may offer is often overlooked (Priestley et al., 2003).

Transitions and 'joined up' working

Many commentators argue that, too frequently, transition for young disabled people is approached in terms of transfer(s) from children's to adult services rather than as a pathway from childhood to adulthood (Beresford, 2004). The danger of a service-led approach can be linked to clashes over the term 'independence', which tends to be understood within a medical model in terms of self-care, whereas autonomy and the ability to make life choices are paramount in the social model. While these difficulties are given official recognition in policies to promote 'person-centred planning' (see below) and 'joined up working', studies indicate slow progress in meeting these aims, with a consensus that transitions are 'not being handled well' (PMSU, 2005).

Transition for disabled young people represents one of the most challenging areas for the co-ordination of provision, for two main reasons. First, transfers from children's education, social care and health services (often with both statutory and voluntary sector involvement) to their adult counterparts generate an extremely complex nexus of relationships with the attendant potential for disruption, conflict and institutional neglect. Second, within child social care services, the difficulties may be exacerbated by the separation of disability services from the mainstream. Thus, for example, disabled young people tend to be dealt with separately from care leavers, irrespective of whether they have been looked after.

Numerous studies have shown that transition plans are either not made or formulated reactively at the point when a placement move is required (Stein,

2004; Hudson, 2006). This is despite a requirement under the Disabled Persons Act 1986 to start transition planning at the age of 14. The difficulties described earlier in respect of residential placements are often replicated at transition, with confusion over responsibilities and tensions surrounding eligibility criteria and budgets. For instance, as is the case for those of school age, educational provision sometimes effectively functions as a form of social care or even 'warehousing' (Priestley et al., 2003). As Hudson (2006) suggests, transition often ends up being 'everyone's distant relative'. Lack of co-ordination between agencies is both reflected in, and generated by, poor data collection, for example, in ethnic monitoring or follow-up after the transfer to adult services (CSCI, 2007). Beyond generating confusion and stress on the part of many disabled young people and their families, the transition from children's to adult services also frequently results in the loss of (hard-won) services. In particular, specialist educational and health provision for children is often not available once adulthood is reached (Beresford, 2004).

The involvement of disabled young people and their families

Despite being emphasised in legislation and guidance, the participation of disabled young people and their families in transition planning has often been limited, including at the strategic level (Beresford, 2004). For those with intellectual impairments, *Valuing People* promoted 'person-centred planning' (PCP), an individualised approach placing the service user's values and per-spective centrally (DH, 2001a). However, a recent review has concluded that the principles of PCP have not been widely adopted for disabled young people (CSCI, 2007).

While a minority may eschew involvement in their children's lives, parents usually represent the most consistent and committed support for disabled young people. In profiling successful transitions, Pascall and Hendey (2004) highlight the crucial role of 'exceptional parents', while noting that they tend to be either socially advantaged or to have experience relevant to disability issues. However, there are sometimes tensions relating to perceived 'overprotection' on the part of parents and mixed evidence on how far professionals challenge or collude with this by prioritising security over risk (Hudson, 2006).

Improving transitions - policy responses

Recent policy towards disabled young people has been framed by familiar New Labour themes. These include the promotion of direct payments, which to date have been little used but are seen as a means of improving continuity during transition as well as empowerment (CSCI, 2007). Beyond general duties to co-ordinate services and identify key workers, various specific requirements have been introduced relating to transition. These include 'transition champions' under the Valuing People programme and more recently the establishment of a new Information Network and dedicated funding for a Transition Support Programme. The creation of transition teams is intended to bring greater 'ownership' to this work and to avoid 'cliff-edge' moves between services (HM Treasury/DfES, 2007b). However, as Hudson (2006) notes, there is a long history of such initiatives that have subsequently had limited impact.

CONCLUSION

The period since the Children Act 1989, especially under New Labour, has been one of considerable policy development for disabled children, but this has arguably owed as much to continuing weaknesses in provision as to the commitment of government. The 'Cinderella services' described by the Audit Commission (2003) still await their handsome prince.

At the heart of this situation lie the partial gains of the social model and the question of human rights. While official rhetoric routinely endorses the tenets of the social model, the understanding of discriminatory barriers is crucially shaped by the priorities of the social investment state. In particular, social inclusion remains largely a matter of labour-market participation. As Morris (2001) contends, there are limits to this strategy for those with severe impairments, not least for those unlikely to offer obvious 'returns' on investment beyond their improved quality of life. She rightly argues the need to see service provision in human rights terms rather than those of social investment. In the social care field, such tensions can be found in a history of permissive legislation backed by limited funding, with rights only to assessment. Similarly, there is significant reliance on voluntary sector provision and, while this makes a valuable contribution, it is often dependent on time-limited funding. In this context, it remains to be seen how far the government's current emphasis on 'transparency' and a proactive duty on the part of public bodies to ensure fair treatment for disabled people will deliver real progress (HM Treasury/DfES, 2007b).

GUIDE TO FURTHER READING

Read et al's *Disabled Children and the Law: Research and Good Practice*, second edition (Jessica Kingsley) constitutes an invaluable guide to the legal framework and welfare entitlements of disabled children, but also sets this in its wider political context. Middleton (1999) still offers a useful examination of childhood disability in relation to social exclusion. Burke's recent book *Disability and Impairment: Working with Children and Families* (Jessica Kingsley) is helpful in its coverage of relevant practice issues and their wider contexts.

Reading and resources for practice

Safeguarding Disabled Children: A Resource for Local Safeguarding Children Boards from www.everychildmatters.gov.uk/search/IG00048/ gives excellent guidance relating to child maltreatment. Although now a little dated, Argent and Kerrane's *Taking Extra Care: Respite, Shared and Permanent Care for Children with Disabilities* (BAAF) represents a comprehensive practice guide to supporting placements for disabled children. Useful websites include Contact a Family (www.cafamily.org.uk/) and Every Disabled Child Matters www.edcm.org.uk, which, apart from its own information on policy, campaigns etc., features good links to other sites. See also the relevant section of the Every Child Matters website (www.everychildmatters.gov.uk/socialcare/disabledchildren/).

Discussion questions

What are the major challenges in adequately safeguarding disabled children?

Are short breaks good for disabled children?

What changes would most improve the lives of disabled children living away from home?

How influential has the social model of disability been in shaping policy for disabled children and their families?

What should be done to promote social inclusion for young disabled people?

10

GOVERNING CHILD SOCIAL WORK
Contemporary Issues and Future Directions

While some of the major issues within child social work have an enduring quality, the landscape for policy and practice has changed dramatically since}the time of the Children Act 1989. Mirroring wider trends in the public sector, much of this change stems from efforts to improve management and co-ordination among those working with children and families. The fruits and ambition of this endeavour are well captured in the government's recent *Children's Plan* for England, discussed further below. In this chapter, we consider key cross-cutting issues linked to the delivery and governance of what is now termed 'children's services'. Discussion will focus particularly on developments in England, where they have arguably been strongest and most formalised.

MANAGERIALISM

Although in certain respects, the Children Act 1989 was atypical of Conservative legislation (see Chapter 1), its implementation was significantly shaped by wider developments in the public sector. One of the most important of these relates to government faith in management as a key to delivering the three 'E's of economy, efficiency and effectiveness (see Clarke and Newman, 1997). Greater emphasis was placed on the management of budgets and resources, with managers increasingly involved in areas previously regarded as the preserve of professionals. These responsibilities relied upon the collection (and utilisation) of data relating to service provision. Improving information systems, however, has proved a protracted process, with, for example, implementation of the *Integrated Children's System* stretched over several years. Despite its promise, social work's 'electronic turn' has tended to add to bureaucracy, and for some exerted an unhealthy influence over practice (Garrett, 2005).

PERFORMANCE MANAGEMENT AND THE AUDIT SOCIETY

The internal dyanamics of managerialism were to be monitored and enforced by an external regime emanating from central government. Its favoured levers were those of setting standards and a range of targets, compliance with which would form the basis of inspection and external audit and, in turn, be reflected in star ratings and published 'league tables' of authorities. The role of the Audit Commission expanded in the 1990s from a relatively narrow concern with the use of public money towards a broader involvement in assessing the effectiveness of policies. This new role also entailed undertaking joint reviews with the social services inspectorate.

These processes began under the Conservative government as a means of ensuring 'value for money' and disciplining what they regarded as a profligate welfare state. However, they were adopted enthusiastically under New Labour, determined to show that its substantial investment was being properly used and yielding results. The government's 'modernising' agenda included the setting of a wide range of national minimum standards (NMS) under the Care Standards Act 2000 and the establishment of a *Performance Assessment Framework* (PAF) in England and Wales. Introduced in 1999, the PAF employed performance indicators and targets in areas such as time spent on the child protection register, the use of adoption and foster care for looked after children, stability in placements, and the completion of reviews or assessments within timescales and spending on family support.

Many of these indicators (and compliance with NMS) have shown improvements over time, but their value and impact remain controversial (Tilbury, 2004). On the one hand, it can be argued that such a framework improves performance by concentrating minds and offers external transparency. On the other, there may be concerns about the accuracy of data and the extent to which they are meaningful or a case of 'measuring the measurable'. Targets may also be seen as distorting professional judgements or creating 'perverse incentives'. CSCI (2006) has acknowledged that there is often little link between the star ratings given to authorities and outcomes for children, while an independent study concluded that children's social care reporting and inspection afforded low value in terms of financial cost and management time (DCLG, 2006). If the problems are widely recognised, solutions prove much more elusive. Reducing the number of targets (as in the new National Indicator Set) has obvious attractions, but may lead to even fewer meaningful data. Similarly, despite initiatives such as outcome-based accountability, it remains easier to identify changes in ways of working than to demonstrate links to the outcomes themselves (McAuley and Cleaver, 2006).

A MIXED ECONOMY

Unlike adult community care reforms, the Children Act 1989 did not require any large-scale contracting out of services but instead encouraged partnership with voluntary agencies, especially in the provision of family support services. However, many authorities adopted elements of the adult social care model by dividing functions between 'purchasers' and 'providers'. Although the latter were often to be found in-house, the 1990s saw a steady growth in private provision, especially for looked after children in foster and residential care. Under New Labour, local authorities were required to consistently 'challenge' their service provision and promote competition between internal and external providers in order to achieve 'Best Value'. As Sellick (2006) observes, this period has witnessed a steady, if uneven, shift towards commissioning services for children from outside the public sector.

Commitment to a mixed economy of provision has remained strong, with the government engaging consultants to analyse the functioning of the market in children's services (see for example PricewaterhouseCoopers, 2006). Identified 'market barriers' include a lack of information on costs and outcomes, but crucially also suggest a conflict of role for local authorities as both commissioners and providers, implicitly pointing towards a concentration on the former role. Responding to persistent criticism of the quality of commissioning, the government is proposing regional units to commission placements for looked after children (DfES, 2007e), despite the first such experiment having recently folded. The government has also underlined the importance of the voluntary and community sector (VCS) in delivering its ECM outcomes (DfES, 2004). This includes roles in relation to policy formation at a national level and local strategic planning as well as providing commissioned services. However, the position of the VCS, especially its smaller organisations, remains vulnerable, with funding often fairly short term and liable to cuts. (See Packwood, 2007, for an analysis of the role of the VCS in relation to commissioning, including issues of capacity and its role as 'critical friend' in relation to state provision.)

Managing the mixed economy presents a number of challenges. While all stakeholders call for transparency and a 'level playing field', they tend to understand these in different ways. As providers, local authorities may often feel under pressure to 'externalise', while private and VCS bodies often feel themselves to be at the mercy of a commissioning body that will favour its own in-house provision. Equally, at the planning level, local authorities may struggle with how to engage the VCS in a 'representative' fashion, while from the latter's point of view, their involvement may be seen as limited and 'selective' (Vallender, 2006)

'JOINED UP' WORKING? – CHILDREN'S TRUSTS

The New Labour government's enthusiasm for 'joined up' working has been discussed at various junctures in the book and, as described in Chapter 1, its most radical manifestation came in the establishment of Children's Trusts in England and Wales under the Children Act 2004. Section 10 of the Act required local authorities to co-operate with 'relevant partners' and others to deliver the five ECM outcomes. Relevant partners comprise the following:

- district councils in two-tier authorities;
- police authority;
- local probation board;
- youth offending team;
- Strategic Health Authority and Primary Care Trust;
- Connexions Partnership;
- local Learning and Skills Councils.

Beyond these mandatory inclusions, local authorities should also involve service users, including children, families and communities, VCS agencies and private sector bodies and those responsible for delivering services such as childcare, culture, sport and play.

The co-operation is envisaged as operating at four different levels (DfES, 2005b). First, frontline service delivery should be child-centred and co-ordinated, facilitated by measures such as effective multi-agency working, the co-location of services and joint training. Second, processes are to be integrated as far as possible, for example, through the CAF and information-sharing. Third, there should be an integrated strategy based on joint assessments of need, planning and commissioning, drawing on pooled budgets where appropriate. This strategy should be reflected and articulated through the production of a Children and Young People's Plan (see below). Finally, effective inter-agency governance arrangements are needed to identify and implement the necessary changes. While co-ordinating responsibility rests with local authorities, there should be a governing board with senior representation from participating agencies and clear lines of accountability. The key local authority roles are those of Director of Children's Services and Lead Member for Children's Services. The Children Act 2004 measures marked the final chapter in the break-up of the social services departments established in England in 1971 (although the role of Director of Social Services still remains in Wales). While co-operation between adult and child social care services is expected, the latter's dominant links are seen to be with other agencies supplying services for children and families. To reflect the breadth of the new arrangements for children's services, inspection is to be by Joint Area Review (JAR) of the performance of local authorities and their partners in improving outcomes for children.

Children's Trusts are still in their infancy (and only formally required from 2008) but a number of Pathfinder trusts were evaluated between 2004 and 2006 (O'Brien et al., 2007). The evaluation presents mixed evidence but is cautiously optimistic in tone. Improvements are noted in terms of integration, training and staff (including the creation of some new posts) working across traditional boundaries. Joint commissioning practices were seen to have developed but from a low base, while similarly, the involvement of children, parents and communities had increased but remained limited. Although noting some promising signs of improved outcomes, O'Brien et al. also identified significant barriers to effective integration, including differences of philosophy and complexities arising from individual agency responsibilities and funding arrangements.

The challenges of joined up working

Other commentators have expanded on the complexities involved in partnership working and in particular the need to address cultural issues among professionals and agencies. Horwath and Morrison (2007) argue that both government policy and often academic study tend to focus on the objective, rational or structural domains, whereas engaging with the irrational, unconscious or subjective aspects of organisational life, or 'people issues', is equally vital for successful change. Similarly, in a wide-ranging and thought-provoking report on leadership, Lownsbrough and O'Leary (2005) contend that policy on joint working has been dominated by top-down prescription that is at best likely to secure compliance rather than the necessary (internal) commitment. Rather than seeking technocratic solutions, they argue the need to engage fully with the complexities of working and agency practices, and especially those of entrenched risk aversion.

There are also more sceptical views of the 'joined up' enterprise. Percy-Smith (2006) argues from a review of strategic partnerships that, despite a growing literature on the factors linked to successful partnerships, there is very little evidence to suggest that they improve outcomes for children. She argues that an uncritical assumption that they are 'a good thing' has tended to stifle questioning of both their costs and limitations.

Children and Young People's Plans (CYPPs)

The imperative to plan services for children has strengthened significantly over the past two decades. Introduced originally on a voluntary basis in the early 1990s, Children's Services Plans (CSPs) were made mandatory for local authorities in 1995 (Scotland), 1996 (England and Wales) and 1998 (Northern Ireland). Although anchored by a focus on services for 'children in need', authorities were encouraged to look at a broader range of services for children with a view to promoting co-ordination. To an extent, CSPs were overtaken by planning requirements from the Quality Protects initiative and this, allied to a burgeoning number of related plans under New Labour, led to pressures for rationalisation. This culminated in the requirement under the Children Act 2004, s17, to produce Children and Young People's Plans (CYPP) in England and Wales, while there have been related developments in integrated service planning elsewhere in the UK.

Understandably, at this early stage research has largely concentrated on the content and formulation of plans rather than their impact. Particular attention has been given to the involvement of service users and especially children and young people themselves. Although inevitably varying between authorities, participation (including that of disabled children) has generally been significant, with the Children's Commissioner's (2006) review giving case-study examplars of extensive and often creative engagement. Overall, CYPPs have covered a wide variety of sub-groups, with looked after children and disabled children the most frequently mentioned (Lord et al., 2006). Other sub-groups figuring widely within plans included: BME children (including Travellers), teenage parents and lesbian, gay and bisexual young people. Lord et al's analysis found that, while commissioning was very prominent within CYPPs, this was often in the context of identifying the need for significant development.

DEVELOPING THE CHILDREN'S WORKFORCE

The emergence of the children's workforce as a policy domain can be seen to reflect both the safeguarding agenda and its vetting procedures and the quest for 'joined up' working in services for children. This development has seen the establishment of the Children's Development Workforce Council and initiatives throughout the UK (see for example Children in Scotland, 2005; HM Government, 2005). Building on earlier work in the social care sector, the scope was dramatically widened to cover early years, schools and health, along with the VCS. A major concern was to refashion the workforce in line with the new priorities, entailing a degree of harmonising in training with a Common Core of Skills and Knowledge and greater integration between qualifications. These measures aim to promote better understanding between professionals; to facilitate work (including new posts) that crosses traditional boundaries; and to offer greater career opportunities within the broader children's workforce.

Alongside these contemporary concerns are issues of longer standing such as recruitment, retention and qualification levels. In the case of social care, these are to be addressed under the *Options for Excellence* review (DfES/DH, 2006). Suggested measures include a publicity campaign to improve the image of social care work, protected workloads for newly qualified social workers and improved supervision and management. However, it remains to be seen whether the relatively modest funding earmarked will be sufficient for an ambitious programme relating to a workforce of around 125,000 in social care or the estimated 2.8 million in the children's workforce overall. Unlike its Scottish counterpart (Scottish Executive, 2006b), which refers to the importance of professional autonomy for social workers and therapeutic relationships with service users, *Options for Excellence* is overwhelmingly managerial in tone and fails to engage meaningfully with the widely recognised problems of proceduralisation, risk aversion and administrative burdens.

VISIONS OF CHILD SOCIAL WORK

New Labour and the Children's Plan

To understand the contemporary nature, and at least short-term future, of child social work in England, it is necessary to locate it within the New Labour government's approach to childhood and children's services. This has recently been set out in the *Children's Plan* (DCSF, 2007b), which seeks to draw together a wide range of relevant policy into a coherent vision, with the stated aim 'to make England the best place in the world for children and young people to grow up'(2007b: 3).

The specific child social care measures are essentially those of the *Care Matters* agenda (see Chapter 6) and need not be repeated here. More broadly, what is clear from the *Plan* is that they remain nested within a broadening and deepening of New Labour's social investment approach. Addressing some of the concerns raised about children's lifestyles, there is to be a promotion of play and exercise alongside investigations (and the promise of policy measures) into the influences of the internet, video games and the commercial world. Although there is to be some easing on staged educational testing, this remains set within a framework of higher targets in respect of 'school-readiness' and qualifications on leaving.

In relation to service provision, the watchwords remain those of early intervention and joined up working. The underpinning philosophy is one of 'progressive universalism', attempting to combine provision for all children and families with a particular focus on the disadvantaged. Early intervention is especially targeted towards the latter, for example, in the proposal to give free child care places to two year-olds in deprived areas. While the government argues that the *Plan* is built around partnership with parents, the strong emphases on parents' engagement with services and monitoring of children have led to claims from the political right of a 'nationalisation of childhood' (Kirby, 2006).

In a critical analysis, Garrett (2006) has argued that New Labour's transformation agenda is firmly rooted in neo-liberal principles that effectively constrain any progressive elements. This can be seen most easily within the *Children's Plan*'s coverage of poverty, which is discussed without reference to the (growing) inequalities of the labour market, ignoring both their effects on parents and on young people's career paths and aspirations. Tellingly, poverty is seen purely in terms of mobility and the escape from intergenerational patterns, rather than something that is structurally (re)produced. Garrett further contends that the tone of New Labour policy is essentially promotional, exploiting branding techniques to excite and conceal the superficial and often contradictory nature of the policies themselves. Once again, this is readily apparent in the *Plan*, where the phrase 'world class' appears repeatedly and aspirations are stated as if certain to be realised. The performance of all professionals and agencies must be 'brought up to the standard of the best' without any consideration of the feasibility of this goal or the means of achieving it. While it can sometimes be difficult to untangle policy intentions from 'political spin', it seems clear that New Labour remains firmly wedded to a top-down managerialist vision of children's services including those linked to social care. In the context of an international survey in which the UK was ranked bottom of a table of 21 rich nations in terms of children's well-being (United Nations Children's Fund, 2007), there appears little sense that a different approach may be necessary.

Alternative visions?

In the political arena, alternative visions to those of New Labour are relatively undeveloped. The Conservative Party has attacked New Labour policy along fairly traditional grounds, namely those of failing to deliver on promises and having little to show for a substantial investment of resources (Social Justice Policy Group, 2006). Such failure is partly portrayed in terms of mismanagement but also as a misguided belief in the power of state intervention. However, alongside a longstanding commitment for greater input from faith and community groups, the Centre for Social Justice does make a specific proposal for a Minister for Looked After Children. The Conservatives have also sought to position themselves as supporters of the professional autonomy and development of social workers (Conservative Party Commission on Social Workers, 2007). For their part, the Liberal Democrats (2006) have expressed support for the principles of early intervention, partnership working and a range of specific policies such as the use of FFAC, concurrency, and fostering for young offenders. However, they have also identified 'people issues' as important for effective service provision, highlighting problems of low morale, overload, and poor training, supervision and management. The influence of children's rights is evident in a commitment to make all new UK laws compatible with the UNCRC.

From within social care, there have also been calls to move away from technocratic approaches, which according to Blewett et al. (2007: 36), 'while superficially impressive are bureaucratically oppressive'. Instead, the authors call for social work's traditional emphasis on the therapeutic relationship to be placed centrally and for priority to be given to direct work with children and families. Meanwhile, the Commission for Families and the Wellbeing of Children (2005) has argued for a renewed focus on child welfare (especially in the treatment of young offenders) within a stronger 'ethic of care' and human rights framework in the policy arena. The influence of children's rights within the UK remains modest, though arguably stronger in countries outside England (see for example Croke and Crowley's (2007) analysis of rights in Wales). This difference of emphasis highlights the importance of devolved government and the potential for more diverse approaches to develop within the UK.

In a compilation from his recent reports, the Children's Rights Director has highlighted a number of 'messages from children' (Morgan, 2007). These include the importance of choices, being listened to and having input into decision making that is not reliant on participation in formal meetings. Information also figures prominently, whether in terms of knowledge of siblings and birth family or sensitivity to issues of privacy and confidentiality. To an extent, these messages are well known but it is clear that many looked after children do not feel that their concerns are always acted upon.

CONCLUDING COMMENT

These are 'interesting times' for child social work and its future direction. As discussion of competing perspectives has shown, tensions are almost inherent in areas such as the balance between family support and safeguarding, and in balancing the needs and rights of children and those of their families. Yet tensions have also arisen in recent years as successive governments have attempted to improve performance within climates of relative budget constraint. Particularly in England under New Labour, much of this effort has taken a managerialist form, with a significant emphasis on 'command and control' from central government. On the positive side, this has been accompanied by, and arguably used to justify, much-needed investment into child social care. However, research studies have suggested that this has failed to deliver the kind of face-to-face service supported by children and professionals alike. The reasons for this are complex but almost certainly owe a good deal to an increasingly bureaucratic, target-driven system, in which the 'human qualities' referred to earlier take second place. Turnover of social workers alone ensures that meaningful social work relationships with children will tend to be the exception and planning will often be blighted. In this context, Parton (2006) has argued that the New Labour goals of regulation and individual self-realisation make uneasy bedfellows.

To a greater or lesser extent, these problems have been recognised and there are signs that the tide may be turning away from a reliance on targets and tight procedural control over professionals. However, at present this is largely at the level of rhetoric and it remains to be seen how far any government will risk loosening the reins in this area and placing greater trust in professionals and local managers. Delivering improved outcomes for children will almost certainly depend significantly on 'people issues' within social care, but achieving change here represents a longer and arguably riskier route to politicians than schematic planning.

Disscussion questions

Have recent 'performance management' regimes improved services for children and families?

Would child social work be better served by greater involvement of the private and/or voluntary and community sectors?

Is the quest for more 'joined up' working misguided?

How would you seek to improve the quality of the children's workforce?

What policy measures would most improve the lives of children in need and their families?

BIBLIOGRAPHY

Abbott, D., Townsley, R. and Watson. D. (2005) 'Multi-Agency Working in Services for Disabled Children: What Impact Does It Have on Professionals?', *Health and Social Care in the Community* 13(2): 155–163.

Ad Hoc Parliamentary Committee (2006) *Parliamentary Hearings on Services for Disabled Children.* London: National Children's Bureau.

Adam, E., Gunnar, M. and Tanaka, A. (2004) 'Adult Attachment, Parent Emotion, and Observed Parenting Behavior: Mediator and Moderator Models', *Child Development* 75(1): 110–122.

Adams, C. and Horrocks, C. (1999) 'The Location of Child Protection in Relation to the Current Emphasis on Core Policing', in Violence against Children Study Group, *Children, Child Abuse and Child Protection.* Chichester: Wiley. pp. 143–158.

Adcock, M. (2001) 'The Core Assessment Process: How to Synthesise Information and Make Judgements', in J. Horwath (ed.). (2001b) *The Child's World*, pp. 75–97.

Advisory Council on Misuse of Drugs (2007) *Hidden Harm Three Years On: Realities, Challenges and Opportunities.* London: ACMD.

Afifi, T., Brownridge, D., Cox, B.and Sareen, J.(2006) 'Physical Punishment, Childhood Abuse and Psychiatric Disorders', *Child Abuse and Neglect* 30(10): 1093–1103.

Ahmed, S., Cheetham, J. and Small, J. (eds) (1986) *Social Work with Black Children and Their Families.* London: Batsford.

Ainsworth, M., Blehar, M., Waters, E. and Wall, S. (1978) *Patterns of Attachment: A Psychological Study of the Strange Situation.* Hillside, NJ: Erlbaum.

Aldgate, J. and Bradley, M. (1999) *Supporting Families through Short Term Fostering.* London: Stationery Office.

Aldgate, J. and Tunstill, J. (1995) *Making Sense of Section 17: Implementing Services for Children in Need within the 1989 Children Act.* London: HMSO.

Aldgate, J., Jones, D., Rose, W. and Jeffery, C. (eds) (2005) *The Developing World of the Child.* London: Jessica Kingsley.

Aldridge, J. and Becker, S. (2003) *Children Caring for Parents with Mental Illness: Perspectives of Young Carers, Parents and Professionals.* Bristol: Policy Press.

Ali, Z., Fazil, Q., Bywaters, P., Wallace, L. and Singh, G. (2003) 'Disability, Ethnicity and Childhood: A Critical Review of Research', *Disability and Society* 16(7): 949–968.

Allen, N. (2005) *Making Sense of the Children Act 1989* (4th edn). Chichester: Wiley.

Archard, D. (2004) *Children: Rights and Childhood* (2nd edn). London: Routledge.

Aries, P. (1962) *Centuries of Childhood: A Social History of Family Life.* London: Jonathan Cape.

Argent, H. (ed.) (2002) *Staying Connected: Managing Contact Arrangements in Adoption.* London: British Association for Adoption and Fostering.

Armstrong, C. and Hill, M. (2001) 'Support Services for Vulnerable Families with Young Children', *Child and Family Social Work* 6(4): 351–358.

Audit Commission (2003) *Services for Disabled Children: A Review of Services for Disabled Children and Their Families.* London: Audit Commission.

Ayre, P. (1998) 'Significant Harm: Making Professional Judgements', *Child Abuse Review* 7(5): 330–342.

Ayre, P. (2001) 'Child Protection and the Media: Lessons from the Last Three Decades', *British Journal of Social Work* 31(6): 887–901.

Baker, A. and Duncan, S. (1985) 'Child Sexual Abuse: A Study of Prevalence in Great Britain', *Child Abuse and Neglect* 9(4): 457–467.

Baker, C. (2007) 'Disabled Children's Experience of Permanency in the Looked After System', *British Journal of Social Work* 37(7): 1173–1188.

Bancroft, A., Wilson, S., Cunningham-Burley, S., Backett-Milburn, K. and Masters, H. (2004) *Parental Drug and Alcohol Misuse: Resilience and Transition among Young People.* York: Joseph Rowntree Foundation.

Banks, N. (2001) 'Assessing Children and Families who Belong to Minority Ethnic Groups', J. Horwath (ed.), (2001b) *The Child's World.* pp. 140–149.

Banks, P., Cogan, N., Deeley, S., Hill, M., Riddell, S. and Tisdall, K. (2001) 'Seeing the Invisible Children and Young People Affected by Disability', *Disability and Society* 16(6): 797–814.

Bannister, A. (2001) 'Entering the Child's World: Communicating with Children to Assess Their Needs', in J. Horwath (ed.), (2001b) *The Child's World.* pp. 129–139.

Barn, R. (1993) *Black Children in the Public Care System.* London: Batsford.

Barn, R. (ed.) (1999) *Working with Black Children and Adolescents in Need.* London: British Agencies for Adoption and Fostering.

Barn, R., Andrew, L. and Mantovani, N. (2005) *Life after Care: The Experiences of Young People from Different Ethnic Groups.* York: Joseph Rowntree Foundation.

Barn, R., with Ladino, C. and Rogers, B. (2006) *Parenting in Multi-Racial Britain.* London: National Children's Bureau.

Barnardo's (2006) *Hidden Lives: Unidentified Young Carers in the UK.* Ilford: Barnardo's.

Barnes, D., Wistow, R. and Dean, R. (2006) *Child and Adolescent Mental Health Service Mapping 2005.* London: Department of Health.

Barnes, J., Katz, I., Korbin, J. and O'Brien, M. (2006) *Children and Families in Communities.* Chichester: Wiley.

Barnes, M., Evans, R., Plumridge, G. and McCabe, A. (2006) *Preventative Services for Disabled Children: A Final Report of the National Evaluation of the Children's Fund.* London: DfES.

Barrett, H. (2004) *UK Family Trends 1994–2004.* London: National Family and Parenting Institute.

Barter, C., Renold, E., Berridge, D. and Cawson, P. (2004) *Peer Violence in Children's Residential Care.* Basingstoke: Palgrave.

Batchelor, J. (2007) 'Parents' Perceptions of Services for Young Children with Faltering Growth', *Children and Society* 21(5): 378–389.

Bates, S. and Coren, E. (2006) *The Extent and Impact of Parental Mental Health Problems on Families and the Acceptability, Accessibility and Effectiveness of Interventions.* London: Social Care Institute for Excellence.

Baumrind, D. (1991) 'The Influence of Parenting Style on Adolescent Competence and Substance Use', *Journal of Early Adolescence* 11(1): 56–95.

Bebbington, A. and Miles, J. (1989) 'The Background of Children Who Enter Local Authority Care', *British Journal of Social Work* 19(1): 349–368.

Becher, H. and Husain, F. (2003) *Supporting Minority Ethnic Families – South Asian Hindus and Muslims in Britain: Developments in Family Support.* London: National Family and Parenting Institute.

Beck, U. (1997) 'Democratization of the Family', *Childhood* 4(2): 151–168.

Becker, S. (2000) 'Young Carers', in M. Davies (ed.), *The Blackwell Encyclopaedia of Social Work.* Oxford: Blackwell. p. 378.

Becker, S., Aldridge, J. and Dearden, C. (1998) *Young Carers and Their Families.* Oxford: Blackwell.

Beckett, C. (2001) 'The Wait Gets Longer: An Analysis of Recent Information on Court Delays', *Adoption and Fostering* 25(4): 60–67.

Beckett, C. (2002) 'The Witch Hunt Metaphor (and Accusations against Residential Care Workers)', *British Journal of Social Work* 32(5): 621–628.

Beckett, C. (2007) *Child Protection: An Introduction*, (2nd edn). London: Sage.

Beddoe, C. (2007) *Missing Out: A Study of Child Trafficking in the North-West, North-East and West Midlands*. London: ECPAT UK.

Bell, M. (2002) 'Promoting Children's Rights through the Use of Relationship', *Child and Family Social Work* 7(1): 1–11.

Bell, M. and Wilson, K. (2006) 'Children's Views of Family Group Conferences', *British Journal of Social Work* 36(4): 671–681.

Belsky, J., Barnes, J. and Melhuish, E. (eds) (2007) *The National Evaluation of Sure Start: Does Area-Based Early Intervention Work?* Bristol: Policy Press.

Ben-Tovim, A., Elton, A., Hildebrand, J., Tranter, M. and Vizard, E. (1988) *Child Sexual Abuse within the Family: Assessment and Treatment*. London: Wright.

Beresford, B. (2004) 'On the Road to Nowhere? Young Disabled People and Transition', *Child: Care, Health and Development* 30(6): 581–587.

Beresford, B. and Oldman, C. (2002) *Housing Matters: National Evidence Relating to Disabled Children and Their Housing*. Bristol: Policy Press.

Beresford, B., Rabiee, P. and Sloper, P. (2007) *Priorities and Perceptions of Disabled Children and Young People and Their Parents Regarding Outcomes from Support Services*. York: University of York.

Bernard, C. and Gupta, A. (2006) 'Black African Children and the Child Protection System', *British Journal of Social Work*, Advance Access, 13 December.

Berridge, D. and Cleaver, H. (1987) *Foster Home Breakdown*. Oxford: Blackwell.

Berridge, D. and Brodie, I. (1998) *Children's Homes Revisited*. London: Jessica Kingsley.

Berthoud, R. (2007) *Work-Rich and Work-Poor: Three Decades of Change*. Bristol: Policy Press.

Biehal, N. (2005) *Working with Adolescents: Supporting Families, Preventing Breakdown*. London: British Association for Adoption and Fostering.

Biehal, N. (2007) 'Reuniting Children with Their Families: Reconsidering the Evidence on Timing, Contact and Outcomes', *British Journal of Social Work* 37(5): 807–823.

Biehal, N. and Wade, J. (2000) 'Going Missing from Residential and Foster Care: Linking Biographies and Contexts', *British Journal of Social Work* 30(2): 211–225.

Biehal, N., Clayden, J., Stein, M. and Wade, J. (1995) *Moving On: Young People and Leaving Care Schemes*. London: HMSO.

Bilson, A. and White, S. (2005) 'Representing Children's Views and Best Interests in Court: An International Comparison', *Child Abuse Review* 14(4): 220–239.

Birchall, E. and Hallett, C. (1995) *Working Together in Child Protection*. London: HMSO.

Blewett, J., Lewis, J. and Tunstill, J. (2007) *The Changing Roles and Tasks of Social Work: A Literature Informed Discussion Paper*. London: General Social Care Council.

Booth, T. and Booth, W. (1997) *Exceptional Childhoods, Unexceptional Children: Growing Up with Parents Who Have Learning Disabilities*. London: Family Policy Studies Centre.

Booth, T. and Booth, W. (1999) 'Parents Together: Action Research and Advocacy Support for Parents with Learning Difficulties', *Health and Social Care in the Community* 7(6): 464–474.

Booth, T., McConnell, D. and Booth, W. (2006) 'Temporal Discrimination and Parents with Learning Difficulties in the Child Protection System', *British Journal of Social Work* 36(6): 997–1015.

Bowlby, J. (1953) *Child Care and the Growth of Love*. London: Pelican.

Boylan, J. and Braye, S. (2006) 'Paid, Professionalised and Proceduralised: Can Legal and Policy Frameworks for Child Advocacy Give Voice to Children and Young People?', *Journal of Social Welfare and Family Law* 28(3–4): 233–249.

Cleaver, H. (2000) *Fostering Family Contact*. London: The Stationery Office.

Cleaver, H. (2002) 'Assessing Children's Needs and Parents' Responses', in H. Ward and W. Rose (eds), *Approaches to Needs Assessment*. pp. 261–276.

Cleaver, H. and Walker, S. (2004) *Assessing Children's Needs and Circumstances: The Impact of the Assessment Framework*. London: Jessica Kingsley.

Cleaver, H., Unell, I. and Aldgate, J. (1999) *Children's Needs, Parenting Capacity: The Impact of Illness, Problem Alcohol and Drug Use, and Domestic Violence on Children's Development*. London: The Stationery Office.

Cleaver, H., Nicholson, D., Tarr, S. and Cleaver, D. (2007) *Child Protection, Domestic Violence and Parental Substance Misuse: Family Experiences and Effective Practice*. London: Jessica Kingsley.

Clough, R., Bullock, R. and Ward, A. (2006) *What Works in Residential Child Care: A Review of Research Evidence and the Practical Considerations*. London: National Children's Bureau.

Cobley, C. and Sanders, T. (2003) '"Shaken Baby Syndrome": Child Protection Issues when Children Sustain a Subdural Haemorrhage', *Journal of Social Welfare and Family Law* 25(2): 101–119.

Cocks, A. (2000) 'Respite Care for Disabled Children: Micro and Macro Reflections', *Disability and Society* 15(3): 507–519.

Collishaw, S., Maughan, B., Goodman, R. and Pickles, A. (2004) 'Time Trends in Adolescent Mental Health', *Journal of Child Psychology and Psychiatry* 45(8): 1350–1362.

Collishaw, S., Pickles, A., Messer, J., Rutter, M., Shearer, C. and Maughan, B. (2007) 'Resilience to Adult Psychopathology Following Childhood Maltreatment: Evidence from a Community Sample', *Child Abuse and Neglect* 31(3): 211–229.

Colton, M. (1988) *Dimensions of Substitute Child Care*. Aldershot: Avebury.

Colton, M. and Hellinckx, W. (eds) (1993) *Child Care in the EC: A Country-specific Guide to Foster and Residential Care*. Aldershot: Arena.

Colton, M. and Roberts, S. (2007) 'Factors That Contribute to High Turnover among Residential Child Care Staff', *Child and Family Social Work* 12(2): 133–142.

Colton, M., Drury, C. and Williams, M. (1995) *Staying Together: Supporting Families under the Children Act*. Aldershot: Arena.

Colton, M., Sanders, R. and Williams, M. (2001) *An Introduction to Working with Children: A Guide for Social Workers*. Basingstoke: Palgrave.

Colton, M., Vanstone, M. and Walby, C. (2002) 'Victimization, Care and Justice: Reflections on the Experiences of Victims/Survivors Involved in Large-scale Historical Investigations of Child Sexual Abuse in Residential Institutions', *British Journal of Social Work* 32(5): 541–551.

Commission for Families and the Wellbeing of Children (2005) *Families and the State: Two Way Support and Responsibilities*. Bristol: Policy Press.

Commission for Social Care Inspection (2006) *The State of Social Care in England 2006*. London: CSCI.

Commission for Social Care Inspection (2007) *Growing Up Matters: Better Transition Planning for Young People with Complex Needs*. London: CSCI.

Commission for Social Care Inspection et al. (2005) *Safeguarding Children: The Second Joint Chief Inspectors' Report on Arrangements to Safeguard Children*. Newcastle: CSCI.

Connolly, M. (2006) 'Fifteen Years of Family Group Conferencing: Coordinators Talk about Their Experiences in Aotearoa New Zealand', *British Journal of Social Work* 36(4): 523–540.

Connors, C. and Stalker, K. (2002) *The Views of Disabled Children and Their Siblings: A Positive Outlook*. London: Jessica Kingsley.

Connors, C. and Stalker, K. (2007) 'Children's Experiences of Disability: Pointers to a Social Model of Childhood Disability', *Disability and Society* 22(1): 19–33.

Conservative Party Commission on Social Workers (2007) *No More Blame Game – The Future for Children's Social Workers*. London: Conservative Party.

Cooke, P. and Standen, P. (2002) 'Abuse and Disabled Children: Hidden Needs?', *Child Abuse Review* 11(1): 1–18.

Cooper, A. (2005) 'Surface and Depth in the Victoria Climbié Inquiry Report', *Child and Family Social Work* 10(1): 1–9.

Corby, B. (2003) 'Towards a New Means of Inquiry into Child Abuse Cases', *Journal of Social Welfare and Family Law* 25(3): 229–241.

Corby, B. (2005) *Child Abuse: Towards a Knowledge Base*, (3rd edn). Maidenhead: Open University Press.

Corby, B., Doig, A. and Roberts, V. (2001) *Public Inquiries into Residential Abuse of Children*. London: Jessica Kingsley.

Corlyon, J. and McGuire, C. (1999) *Pregnancy and Parenthood: The Views and Experiences of Young People in Public Care*. London: National Children's Bureau.

Cosis Brown, H., Fry, E. and Howard, J. (eds) (2005) *Support Care: How Family Placement Can Keep Children and Families Together*. Lyme Regis: Russell House.

Cotson, D., Friend, J., Hollins, S. and James, H. (2001) 'Implementing the *Framework for the Assessment of Children in Need and Their Families* When the Parent Has a Learning Disability', in J. Horwath (ed.), (2001b) *The Child's World*. pp. 287–302.

Coulton, C., Korbin, J. and Su, M. (1999) 'Neighborhoods and Child Maltreatment: A Multi-Level Study', *Child Abuse and Neglect* 23(11): 1019–1040.

Cousins, J. (2005) 'Disabled Children Who Need Permanence: Barriers to Placement', *Adoption and Fostering* 29(3): 6–20.

Cox, A. and Bentovim, A. (2000) *The Family Pack of Questionnaires and Scales*. London: The Stationery Office.

Cox, P., Kershaw, S. and Trotter, J. (eds) (2000) *Child Sexual Assault: Feminist Perspectives*. Basingstoke: Palgrave.

Coy, M. (2007) 'Young Women, Local Authority Care and Selling Sex: Findings from Research', *British Journal of Social Work*, Advance Access, 20 August,

Craft, A. and Killen, S. (2007) *Palliative Care Services for Children and Young People in England: An Independent Review for the Secretary of State for Health*. London: Department of Health.

Cramer, H. and Carlin, J. (2007) 'Family-Based Short Breaks (Respite) for Disabled Children: Results from the Fourth National Survey', *British Journal of Social Work*, Advance Access, 7 February.

Cree, V. (2003) 'Worries and Problems of Young Carers: Issues for Mental Health', *Child and Family Social Work* 8(4): 301–309.

Croke, R. and Crowley, A. (eds) (2007) *Stop, Look, Listen: The Road to Realising Children's Rights in Wales*. Cardiff: Save the Children Fund.

Cunningham, S. and Tomlinson, J. (2005) '"Starve Them Out": Does Every Child Really Matter? A Commentary on Section 9 of the Asylum and Immigration (Treatment of Claimants, etc.) Act 2004', *Critical Social Policy* 25(2): 253–275.

Cusick, L. (2002) 'Youth Prostitution: A Literature Review', *Child Abuse Review* 11(4): 230–251.

Daguerre, A. and Nativel, C. (eds) (2006) *When Children Become Parents: Welfare State Responses to Teenage Pregnancy*. Bristol: Policy Press.

Dale, P. (2004) 'Like a Fish in a Bowl: Parents' Perceptions of Child Protection Services', *Child Abuse Review* 13(2): 137–157.

Dalrymple, J. (2001) 'Safeguarding Young People through Confidential Advocacy Services', *Child and Family Social Work* 6(2): 149–160.

Dalrymple, J. (2004) 'Developing the Concept of Professional Advocacy: An Examination of the Role of Child and Youth Advocates in England and Wales', *Journal of Social Work* 4(2): 179–197.

Daniel, B. and Taylor, J. (2006) 'Gender and Child Neglect: Theory, Research and Policy', *Critical Social Policy* 26(2): 426–439.

Daniel, B., Wassell, S. and Gilligan, R. (1999) *Child Development for Child Care and Protection Workers*. London: Jessica Kingsley.

Davies, J. (ed.) (1993) *The Family: Is It Just Another Lifestyle Choice?* London: Institute of Economic Affairs.

de Waal, M. and Shergill, S. (2004) 'Recognising and Celebrating Children's Cultural Heritage', in V. White and J. Harris (eds), *Developing Good Practice in Children's Services*. London: Jessica Kingsley. pp. 124–136.

Department for Children, Schools and Families (2007a) *Children Looked After in England (Including Adoption and Care Leavers) Year Ending 31 March 2007*. London: DCSF.

Department for Children, Schools and Families (2007b) *The Children's Plan: Building Brighter Futures, Cm 7280*, Norwich: The Stationery Office.

Department for Children, Schools and Families (2008) *Staying Safe: Action Plan*. London: DCSF.

Department of Communities and Local Government (2006) *Mapping the Local Government Performance Reporting Landscape*. London: DCLG.

Department for Education and Employment/Department of Health (2000) *Education of Young People in Public Care: Guidance*. London: DfEE/DH.

Department for Education and Skills (2004) *Working with Voluntary and Community Organisations to Deliver Change for Children and Young People*. London: DfES.

Department for Education and Skills (2005a) *The Children's Workforce in England: A Review of the Evidence*. London: DfES.

Department for Education and Skills (2005b) *Statutory Guidance on Inter-Agency Cooperation to Improve the Wellbeing of Children: Children's Trust Arrangements*. London: DfES.

Department for Education and Skills (2006a) *Children in Need in England: Results of a Survey of Activity and Expenditure as Reported by Local Authority Social Services' Children and Families Teams for a Survey Week in February 2005* (internet only) www.dfes.gov.uk/rsgateway/DB/VOL/v000647/index.shtml

Department for Education and Skills (2006b) *Care Matters: Transforming the Lives of Children and Young People in Care (Cm 6932)*. London: DfES.

Department for Education and Skills (2007a) *Referrals, Assessments and Children and Young People on Child Protection Registers, England – Year Ending 31 March 2007*. London: DfES.

Department for Education and Skills (2007b) *Local Safeguarding Children Boards: A Review of Progress*. London: DfES.

Department for Education and Skills (2007c) *Children Looked after by Local Authorities, Year Ending 31 March 2006*. London: DfES.

Department for Education and Skills (2007d) *Outcome Indicators for Looked After Children: Twelve Months to 30 September 2006, England*. London: DfES.

Department for Education and Skills (2007e) *Care Matters: Time for Change (Cm 7137)*. London: DfES.

Department for Education and Skills/Department for Constitutional Affairs (2006) *Review of the Child Care Proceedings System in England and Wales*. London: DCA.

Department for Education and Skills, Department of Health, Home Office (2003) *Keeping Children Safe: The Government's Response to the Victoria Climbié Inquiry Report and Joint Chief Inspectors' Report Safeguarding Children, Cm 5861*. London: HMSO.

Department for Education and Skills/Department of Health (2006) *Options for Excellence: Building the Social Care Workforce of the Future*. London: DH.

Department of Health (1988) *Protecting Children: A Guide for Social Workers Undertaking a Comprehensive Assessment*. London: HMSO.

Department of Health (1991) *Patterns and Outcomes in Child Placement*. London: HMSO.

Department of Health (1995) *Child Protection: Messages from Research*. London: HMSO.

Department of Health (1998a) *Quality Protects: Transforming Children's Services (LAC(98)28)*. London: DH.

Department of Health (1998b) *Caring for Children Away from Home: Messages from Research.* Chichester: Wiley.

Department of Health (1999) *Me, Survive, Out There? New Arrangements for Young People Living In and Leaving Care.* London: DH.

Department of Health (2000a) *Assessing Children in Need and Their Families: Practice Guidance.* London: The Stationery Office.

Department of Health (2000b) *Safeguarding Children Involved in Prostitution: Supplementary Guidance to Working Together to Safeguard Children.* London: DH.

Department of Health (2001a) *Valuing People: A New Strategy for Learning Disability for the 21st Century, Cm 5086.* London: DH.

Department of Health (2001b) *Health and Personal Social Services Statistics 2000.* London: DH.

Department of Health (2002) *Promoting the Health of Looked After Children.* London: DH.

Department of Health (2003) *Guidance on Accommodating Children in Need and Their Families, LAC (2003)13.* London: DH.

Department of Health (2004) *Disabled Child Standard, National Service Framework for Children.* London: DH.

Department of Health (2008) *Better Care: Better Lives: Improving Outcomes and Experiences for Children, Young People and Their Families Living with Life-Limiting and Life-Threatening Conditions.* London: DH.

Department of Health, Department for Education and Employment, Home Office (2000) *Framework for the Assessment of Children in Need and Their Families.* London: The Stationery Office.

Department of Health and Department for Education and Skills (2007) *Good Practice Guidance on Working with Parents With Learning Disabilities.* London: DH/DfES.

Department of Health and Social Security (1985a) *Social Work Decisions in Child Care: Recent Research Findings and Their Implications.* London: HMSO.

Department of Health and Social Security (1985b) *Review of Child Care Law: Report to Ministers of an Interdepartmental Working Party.* London: HMSO.

Department of Health, Social Services and Public Safety (2006) *Our Children and Young People: Our Shared Responsibility. Inspection of Child Protection Services in Northern Ireland: Overview Report.* Belfast: DHSSPS.

Department of Health, Social Services and Public Safety (2007a) *Families Matter: Supporting Families in Northern Ireland.* Belfast: DHSSPS.

Department of Health, Social Services and Public Safety (2007b) *Care Matters in Northern Ireland: Building a Bridge to a Better Future.* Belfast: DHSSPS.

Dillon, J. and Statham, J. (1998) 'Placed and Paid For: A National Overview of the Use of Private and Voluntary Day Care Facilities for Children in Need', *Child and Family Social Work* 3(2): 113–123.

Dingwall, R., Eekelaar, J. and Murray, T. (1983) *The Protection of Children: State Intervention and Family Life.* Oxford: Blackwell.

Dixon, J. and Stein, M. (2005) *Leaving Care: Throughcare and Aftercare in Scotland.* London: Jessica Kingsley.

Dobson, B., Middleton, S. and Beardsworth, A. (2001) *The Impact of Childhood Disability on Family Life.* York: Joseph Rowntree Foundation.

Dombrowski, S., Gischlar, K. and Durst, T. (2007) 'Safeguarding Young People from Cyber Pornography and Cyber Sexual Predation: A Major Dilemma of the Internet', *Child Abuse Review* 16(3): 153–170.

Dowling, M. and Dolan, L. (2001) 'Families with Children with Disabilities: Inequalities and the Social Model', *Disability and Society* 16(1): 21–35.

Doyle, C. (2006) *Working with Abused Children.* Basingstoke: Palgrave.

Driver, E. and Droisen, A. (1989) *Child Sexual Abuse: A Feminist Perspective.* London: Macmillan.

Dunnett, K. (ed.) (2006) *Health of Looked After Children and Young People.* Lyme Regis: Russell House.

Durham, A. (2003) *Young Men Surviving Child Sexual Abuse: Research Stories and Lessons for Therapeutic Practice.* Chichester: Wiley.

Durham, A. (2006) *Young Men Who Have Sexually Abused: A Case Study Guide.* Chichester: Wiley.

Dutt, R. and Phillips, M. (2000) 'Assessing Black Children in Need and Their Families', in Department of Health (2000a) *Assessing Children in Need.* pp. 37–72.

Edwards, A., Barnes, M., Plewis, I. and Morris, K. (2006) *Working to Prevent the Social Exclusion of Children and Young People: Final Lessons from the National Evaluation of the Children's Fund.* Nottingham: DfES.

Edwards, R. and Gillies, V. (2004) 'Support in Parenting: Values and Consensus Concerning Who to Turn to', *Journal of Social Policy* 33(4): 627–647.

Emerson, E., Malam, S., Davies, I. and Spencer, K. (2005) *Adults with Learning Difficulties in England 2003/4.* London: Office for National Statistics.

Emerson, E. and Hatton, C. (2007) *The Mental Health of Children and Adolescents with Learning Disabilities in Britain.* London: Foundation for People with Learning Disabilities.

Emond, R. (2003) 'Putting the Care into Residential Care: The Role of Young People', *Journal of Social Work* 3(3): 321–337.

Erooga, M. and Masson, H. (eds) (2006) *Children and Young People Who Sexually Abuse Others: Current Developments and Practice Responses,* (2nd edn). Abingdon: Routledge.

Etzioni, A. (1993) *Parenting Deficit.* London: Demos.

Every Disabled Child Matters (2006a) *Off the Radar: How Local Authority Plans Fail Disabled Children.* London: National Children's Bureau.

Every Disabled Child Matters (2006b) *Between A Rock and a Hard Place.* London: National Children's Bureau.

Fahlberg, V. (1994) *A Child's Journey through Placement.* London: British Agencies for Adoption and Fostering.

Falkov, A. (2002) 'Addressing Family Needs When a Parent is Mentally Ill', in H. Ward and W. Rose (eds), *Approaches to Needs Assessment.* pp. 235–259.

Famularo, R., Kinscherff, R. and Fenton, T. (1992) 'Parental Substance Abuse and the Nature of Child Maltreatment', *Child Abuse and Neglect* 16(4): 475–483.

Farmer, E. (2004) 'Patterns of Placement, Management and Outcome for Sexually Abused and/or Abusing Children in Substitute Care', *British Journal of Social Work* 34(3): 375–393.

Farmer, E. and Owen, M. (1995) *Child Protection: Private Risks and Public Remedies: A Study of Decision Making, Intervention and Outcome in Child Protection Work.* London: HMSO.

Farmer, E. and Parker, R. (1991) *Trials and Tribulations: Returning Children from Local Authority Care to Their Families.* London: HMSO.

Farmer, E. and Moyers, S. (2005) *Children Placed with Family and Friends: Placement Patterns and Outcomes – Briefing.* www.bristol.ac.uk/sps/downloads/Hadley/kinship%20care.doc

Fawcett, B., Featherstone, B. and Goddard, J. (2004) *Contemporary Child Care: Policy and Practice.* Basingstoke: Palgrave.

Featherstone, B. (2004) 'Fathers Matter: A Research Review', *Children and Society* 18(4): 312–319.

Featherstone, B. (2006) 'Rethinking Family Support in the Current Policy Context', *British Journal of Social Work* 36(1): 5–19.

Ferguson, H. (2004) *Protecting Children in Time: Child Abuse, Child Protection and the Consequences of Modernity.* Basingstoke: Palgrave.

Finkelhor, D., Araji, S., Baron, L., Browne, A., Peters, S. and Wyatt, G. (1986) *A Sourcebook on Child Sexual Abuse.* Beverly Hills, CA: Sage.

Flynn, R. (2002) *Short Breaks: Providing Better Access and More Choice for Black Disabled Children and Their Parents.* Bristol: Policy Press.

Fonagy, M., Steele, M., Steele, H., Higgitt, A. and Target, M. (1994) 'The Theory and Practice of Resilience', *Journal of Child Psychology and Child Psychiatry* 35(2): 231–257.

Ford, H. (2006) *Women Who Sexually Abuse Children.* Chichester: Wiley.

Fox Harding, L. (1997) *Perspectives in Child Care Policy*, (2nd edn). Harlow: Longman.

Francis, J., McGhee, J. and Mordaunt, E. (2006) *Protecting Children in Scotland: An Investigation of Risk Assessment and Inter Agency Collaboration in the Use of Child Protection Orders.* Edinburgh: Scottish Executive.

Franklin, A. and Sloper, P. (2006) 'Participation of Disabled Children and Young People in Decision Making within Social Services Departments: A Survey of Current and Recent Activities in England', *British Journal of Social Work* 36(5): 723–741.

Franklin, B. (ed.) (2002) *The New Handbook of Children's Rights: Comparative Policy and Practice.* Routledge: London.

Freeman, P. and Hunt, J. (1998) *Parental Perspectives on Care Proceedings.* London: HMSO.

Freeman, R. (1999) 'Recursive Politics: Prevention, Modernity and Social Systems', *Children and Society* 13(4): 232–241.

Frost, N. (2003) 'Understanding Family Support: Theories, Concepts and Issues', in N. Frost, A. Lloyd, and L. Jeffrey (eds), *The RHP Companion to Family Support.* Lyme Regis: Russell House. pp. 3–12.

Frost, N. and Stein, M. (1989) *The Politics of Child Welfare: Inequality, Power and Change.* Hemel Hempstead: Harvester Wheatsheaf.

Frost, N., Johnson, L., Stein, M. and Wallis, L. (2000) 'Home-start and the Delivery of Family Support', *Children and Society* 14(5): 328–342.

Fry, E. (2005) 'Support Care: The Wider Context', in H. Cosis Brown et al. (eds), *Support Care.* pp. 7–22.

Furedi, F. (2001) *Paranoid Parenting: Abandon Your Anxieties and Be a Good Parent.* London: Allen Lane.

Furlong, A. and Cartmel, F. (2007) *Young People and Social Change: New Perspectives.* Maidenhead: Open University Press.

Fyson, R. (2005) *Young People with Learning Disabilities Who Show Sexually Inappropriate or Abusive Behaviours.* Nottingham: Ann Craft Trust.

Gallagher, B. (2000) 'The Extent and Nature of Known Cases of Institutional Child Sexual Abuse', *British Journal of Social Work* 30(6): 795–817.

Gallagher, B. (2001) 'Assessment and Intervention in Cases of Suspected Ritual Child Sexual Abuse', *Child Abuse Review* 10(4): 227–242.

Gallagher, B., Bradford, M. and Pease, K. (2002) 'The Sexual Abuse of Children by Strangers: Its Extent, Nature and Victims' Characteristics', *Children and Society* 16(5): 346–359.

Gallagher, B., Fraser, C., Christmann, K. and Hodgson, B. (2006) *International and Internet Child Sexual Abuse and Exploitation: Research Report.* Huddersfield: University of Huddersfield.

Garbarino, J., Stocking, H. and Collins, A. (1980) *Protecting Children from Abuse and Neglect: Developing and Maintaining Effective Support Systems for Families.* San Francisco, CA: Jossey-Bass.

Garrett, P. (2003) *Remaking Social Work with Children and Families.* London: Routledge.

Garrett, P. (2004) 'Talking Child Protection: The Police and Social Workers "Working Together"', *Journal of Social Work* 4(1): 77–97.

Garrett, P. (2005) 'Social Work's "Electronic Turn": Notes on the Deployment of Information and Communication Technologies in Social Work with Children and Families', *Critical Social Policy* 25(4): 529–553.

Garrett, P. (2006) 'How to Be Modern: New Labour's Neoliberal Modernity and the *Change for Children* Programme', *British Journal of Social Work,* Advance Access, 18 October.

Ghate, D., Shaw, C. and Hazel, N. (2000) *Fathers and Family Centres: Engaging Fathers in Preventive Services.* York: Joseph Rowntree Foundation.

Ghate, D., Hazel, N., Creighton, S., Finch, S. and Field, J. (2003) *The National Study of Parents, Children and Discipline in Britain.* London: Policy Research Bureau.

Gibbons, J., Conroy, S. and Bell, C. (1995a) *Operating the Child Protection System: A Study of Child Protection Practices in English Local Authorities.* London: HMSO.

Gibbons, J., Gallagher, B., Bell, C. and Gordon, D. (1995b) *Development After Physical Abuse in Early Childhood: A Follow-up Study of Children on Protection Registers.* London: HMSO.

Giddens, A. (1992) *Transformations of Intimacy: Sexuality, Love and Eroticism in Modern Societies.* Cambridge: Polity.

Giddens, A. (1998) *The Third Way: The Renewal of Social Democracy.* Cambridge: Polity.

Gil, D. (1970) *Violence against Children: Physical Child Abuse in the United States.* Cambridge, MA: Harvard University Press.

Gillen, S. (2007) 'NSPCC Study Finds Reluctance to Report Child Abuse among British Asians' *Community Care,* 19 March.

Gillies, V. (2005) 'Meeting Parents' Needs? Discourses of "Support" and "Inclusion" in Family Policy', *Critical Social Policy* 25(1): 70–90.

Gilligan, R. (1999) 'Working with Social Networks: Key Resources in Helping Children at Risk', in M. Hill (ed.), *Effective Ways of Working with Children and Their Families.* London: Jessica Kingsley. pp. 70–91.

Gilligan, R. (2001) 'Promoting Positive Outcomes for Children in Need: The Assessment of Protective Factors', in J. Horwath (ed.), *The Child's World.* pp. 180–193.

Glaser, D. (2002) 'Emotional Abuse and Neglect (Psychological Maltreatment): A Conceptual Framework', *Child Abuse and Neglect* 26(6–7): 697–714.

Glass, N. (1999) 'Sure Start: The Development of an Early Intervention Programme for Young Children in the United Kingdom', *Children and Society* 13(4): 257–264.

Glennie, S. (2007) 'Developing Interprofessional Relationships: Tapping the Potential of Inter-Agency Training', *Child Abuse Review* 16(3): 171–183.

Goddard, J., Feast, J. and Kirton D. (2005) *A Childhood on Paper: Accessing the Child-care Files of Former Looked After Children in the UK.* Bradford: University of Bradford.

Goldstein, J., Freud, A. and Solnit, A. (1979) *Before the Best Interests of the Child.* New York: Free Press.

Golombok, S. (2000) *Parenting: What Really Counts?.* London: Routledge.

Goodinge, S. (1998) *Removing Barriers for Disabled Children: Inspection of Services to Disabled Children and Their Families,* London: DH.

Gordon, D., Parker, R., Loughran, F. and Heslop, P. (2000) *Disabled Children in Britain: A Re-analysis of the OPCS Disability Survey.* London: The Stationery Office.

Gray, B. (2003) 'Social Exclusion, Poverty, Health and Social Care in Tower Hamlets: The Perspectives of Families on the Impact of the Family Support Service', *British Journal of Social Work* 33(3): 361–380.

Gray, J. (2004) 'The Interface between the Child Welfare and Criminal Justice Systems in England', *Child Abuse Review* 13(5): 312–323.

Greco, V., Sloper, P., Webb, R. and Beecham, J. (2005) *An Exploration of Different Models of Multi-Agency Partnerships in Key Worker Services for Disabled Children: Effectiveness and Costs.* London: DfES.

Green, L. (2005) 'Theorizing Sexuality, Sexual Abuse and Residential Children's Homes: Adding Gender to the Equation', *British Journal of Social Work* 35(4): 453–481.

Greenland, C. (1987) *Preventing CAN Death: An International Study of Deaths Due to Child Abuse and Neglect.* London: Tavistock.

Gustafsson, U. and Driver, S. (2005) 'Parents, Power and Public Participation: Sure Start, an Experiment in New Labour Governance', *Social Policy and Administration* 39(5): 528–543.

Hackett, S. (2003) A Framework for Assessing Parenting Capacity, in M. Calder and S. Hackett (eds), *Assessment in Child Care.* pp. 156–171.

Hackett, S., Masson, H. and Phillips, S. (2005) *Services for Young People Who Sexually Abuse: A Report on Mapping and Exploring Services for Young People Who Have Sexually Abused Others.* London: Youth Justice Board.

Hagell, A. (1998) *Dangerous Care: Reviewing the Risks to Children from Their Carers.* London: Policy Studies Institute.

Hagell, A. and Jeyarajah-Dent, R. (eds) (2006) *Children Who Commit Acts of Serious Interpersonal Violence: Messages for Best Practice.* London: Jessica Kingsley.

Halpern, D. (2004) *Social Capital.* Cambridge: Polity Press.

Harbin, F. and Murphy, M. (eds) (2006) *Secret Lives: Growing with Substance: Working with Children and Young People Affected by Familial Substance Misuse.* Lyme Regis: Russell House.

Hardiker, P., Exton, K. and Barker, M. (1991) *Policies and Practices in Preventive Child Care.* Aldershot: Avebury.

Harker, R., Dobel-Ober, D., Berridge, D. and Sinclair, R. (2004) 'More than the Sum of Its Parts? Inter-professional Working in the Education of Looked After Children', *Children and Society* 18(3): 179–193.

Harlow, E. and Shardlow, S. (2006) 'Safeguarding Children: Challenges to the Effective Operation of Groups', *Child and Family Social Work* 11(1): 65–72.

Hart, R. (1997) *Children's Participation: The Theory and Practice of Involving Young Citizens in Community Development and Environmental Care.* London: Earthscan.

Harwin, J., Owen, M., Locke, R. and Forrester, D. (2003) *Making Care Orders Work.* London: The Stationery Office.

Hatton, C., Akram, Y., Shah, R., Robertson, J. and Emerson, E. (2004) *Supporting South Asian Families with a Child with Severe Disabilities.* London: Jessica Kingsley.

Hayden, C. (2005) 'More than a Piece of Paper? Personal Education Plans and "Looked After" Children in England', *Child and Family Social Work* 10(4): 343–352.

Hendrick, H. (2003) *Child Welfare: Historical Dimensions, Contemporary Debate.* Bristol: Policy Press.

Henricson, C. (2003) *Government and Parenting: Is There a Case for a Policy Review and a Parents' Code?* York: Joseph Rowntree Foundation.

Hester, M., Pearson, C. and Harwin, N. (eds) (2006) *Making an Impact: Children and Domestic Violence. A Reader.* London: Jessica Kingsley.

Hicks, S. (2005) 'Lesbian and Gay Foster Care and Adoption: A Brief UK History', *Adoption and Fostering* 29(3): 42–56.

Higgins, K. (2000) 'Understanding and Developing Family Support in Northern Ireland: The Challenge to Policy, Practice and Research', in D. Iwaniec and M. Hill (eds), *Child Welfare Policy.* pp. 97–118.

Hill, A. (2001) '"No-one Else Could Understand": Women's Experiences of a Support Group Run by and for Mothers of Sexually Abused Children', *British Journal of Social Work* 31(3): 385–397.

Hill, A. (2003) 'Issues Facing Brothers of Sexually Abused Children: Implications for Professional Practice', *Child and Family Social Work* 8(4): 281–290.

Hill, M. (Michael) and Laing, P. (1979) *Social Work and Money.* London: Allen and Unwin.

Hill, M. (Malcolm), Lockyer, A., Morton, P., Batchelor, S. and Scott, J. (2003) 'Safeguarding Children's Interests in Welfare Proceedings: The Scottish Experience', *Journal of Social Welfare and Family Law* 25(1): 1–21.

HM Government (2005) *Children's Workforce Strategy: A Strategy to Build a World-Class Workforce for Children and Young People.* Nottingham: DfES.

HM Government (2006a) *Working Together to Safeguard Children: A Guide to Inter-Agency Working to Safeguard and Promote the Welfare of Children.* London: The Stationery Office.

HM Government (2006b) *Making Safeguarding Everyone's Business – Response to the Second Joint Chief Inspectors' Report on Safeguarding Children*. London: DfES.

HM Inspectors of Schools and the Social Work Services Inspectorate (2001) *Learning with Care: The Education of Children Looked After Away from Home by Local Authorities*. Edinburgh: The Stationery Office.

HM Treasury/Department for Education and Skills (2007a) *Policy Review of Children and Young People: A Discussion Paper*. Norwich: HMSO.

HM Treasury/Department for Education and Skills (2007b) *Aiming High for Disabled Children: Better Support for Families*. London: HM Treasury.

Hogan, D. (1998) 'Annotation: The Psychological Development and Welfare of Children of Opiate and Cocaine Users: Review and Research Needs', *Journal of Child Psychology and Psychiatry* 39(5): 609–620.

Hoggarth, L. and Smith, D. (2004) *Understanding the Impact of Connexions on Young People at Risk*. London: DfES.

Holland, S. (2004) *Child and Family Assessment in Social Work Practice*. London: Sage.

Holland, S., Scourfield, J., O'Neill, S. and Pithouse, A. (2005) 'Democratising the Family and the State? The Case of Family Group Conferences in Child Welfare', *Journal of Social Policy* 34(1): 59–77.

Holman, B. (1988) *Putting Families First: Prevention and Child Care*. Basingstoke: Macmillan.

Holman, B. (1998) 'From Children's Departments to Family Departments', *Child and Family Social Work* 3(3): 205–211.

Holman, B. (2002) *The Unknown Fostering: A Study of Private Fostering*. Lyme Regis: Russell House.

Holt, J. (1975) *Escape from Childhood: The Needs and Rights of Children*. Harmondsworth: Penguin.

Home Office (1998) *Supporting Families: A Consultation Document*. London: The Stationery Office.

Home Office (2002) *Achieving Best Evidence: Guidance for Vulnerable or Intimidated Witnesses, Including Children*. London: Home Office.

Home Office (2007) *Drug Use among Vulnerable Young People: Developing a Local Picture*, from www.everychildmatters.gov.uk/resources-and-practice/IG00237/

Horwath, J. (2000) 'Childcare with Gloves On: Protecting Children and Young People in Residential Care', *British Journal of Social Work* 30(2): 179–191.

Horwath, J. (2001a) 'Assessing the World of the Child in Need', in J. Horwath (ed.) (2001b) *The Child's World*. pp. 23–34.

Horwath, J. (ed.) (2001b) *The Child's World: Assessing Children in Need*. London: Jessica Kingsley.

Horwath, J. (2007) *Child Neglect: Identification and Assessment*. Basingstoke: Palgrave.

Horwath, J. and Morrison, T. (2000) 'Identifying and Implementing Pathways for Organizational Change – Using the *Framework for the Assessment of Children in Need and Their Families* as a Case Example', *Child and Family Social Work* 5(3): 245–254.

Horwath, J. and Morrison, T. (2007) 'Collaboration, Integration and Change in Children's Services: Critical Issues and Key Ingredients', *Child Abuse and Neglect* 31(1): 55–69.

Hothersall, S. (2006) *Social Work with Children, Young People and Their Families in Scotland*. Exeter: Learning Matters.

House of Commons (1984) *Children in Care, Volume 1: Second Report of the Social Services Committee, 1983/4*. London: HMSO.

Howard, J. (2005) Partnership with Parents: Making It Happen', in H. Cosis Brown et al. (eds), *Support Care*. pp. 23–38.

Howe, D. (2001) 'Attachment', in J. Horwath (ed.) (2001b) *The Child's World*. pp. 194–206.

Howe, D. (2003) 'Assessments Using an Attachment Perspective', in M. Calder and S. Hackett (eds), *Assessment in Child Care*. pp. 375–387.

Howe, D. (2005) *Child Abuse and Neglect: Attachment, Development and Intervention*. Basingstoke: Palgrave.

Howe, D. (2006a) 'Disabled Children, Maltreatment and Attachment', *British Journal of Social Work* 36(5): 743–760.

Howe, D. (2006b) 'Disabled Children, Parent–Child Interaction and Attachment', *Child and Family Social Work*, 11(2): 95–106.

Howe, D. and Feast, J. (2000) *Adoption, Search and Reunion: The Long Term Experience of Adopted Adults*. London: The Children's Society.

Howe, D., Brandon, M., Hinings, D. and Schofield, G. (1999) *Attachment Theory, Child Maltreatment and Family Support*. Basingstoke: Macmillan.

Hudson, B. (2006) 'Making and Missing Connections: Learning Disability Services and the Transition from Adolescence to Adulthood', *Disability and Society* 21(1): 47–60.

Humphreys, C. (1999) 'Avoidance and Confrontation: Social Work Practice in Relation to Domestic Violence and Child Abuse', *Child and Family Social Work* 4(1): 77–87.

Humphreys, C. (2006) 'Relevant Evidence for Practice', in C. Humphreys and N. Stanley (eds), *Domestic Violence*. pp. 19–35.

Humphreys, C. and Stanley, N. (eds) (2006) *Domestic Violence and Child Protection: Directions for Good Practice*. London: Jessica Kingsley.

Humphreys, C., Atkart, S. and Baldwin, N. (1999) 'Discrimination in Child Protection Work: Recurring Themes in Work with Asian Families', *Child and Family Social Work* 4(4): 283–291.

Hunt, J. (2003) *Family and Friends Carers: Scoping Paper*. London: DH.

Husain, F. (2006) 'Cultural Competence, Cultural Sensitivity and Family Support', in P. Dolan, J. Canavan and J. Pinkerton (eds), *Family Support as Reflective Practice*. London: Jessica Kingsley. pp. 165–180.

Information Centre (2008) *Personal Social Services Expenditure and Unit Costs England, 2006-7*. London: Information Centre.

Iwaniec, D. and Hill, M. (eds) (2000) *Child Welfare Policy and Practice: Issues and Lessons Emerging from Current Research*. London: Jessica Kingsley.

Iwaniec, D., Larkin, E. and Higgins, S. (2006) 'Research Review: Risk and Resilience in Cases of Emotional Abuse', *Child and Family Social Work* 11(1): 73–82.

Jack, G. (2000) 'Ecological Influences on Parenting and Child Development', *British Journal of Social Work* 30(5): 703–720.

Jack, G. (2005) 'Assessing the Impact of Community Programmes Working with Children and Families in Disadvantaged Areas', *Child and Family Social Work* 10(4): 293–304.

Jack, G. (2006) 'The Area and Community Components of Children's Well-being', *Children and Society* 20(5): 334–347.

Jack, G. and Jordan, B. (1999) 'Social Capital and Child Welfare', *Children and Society* 13(4): 242–256.

Jackson, S. (ed.) (2001) *Nobody Ever Told Us School Matters: Raising the Educational Attainments of Children in Care*. London: British Agencies for Adoption and Fostering.

James, A. (Ann) (1998) 'Supporting Families of Origin: An Exploration of the Influence of the Children Act 1948', *Child and Family Social Work* 3(3): 173–181.

James, A. (Alison), Jenks, C. and Prout, A. (1998) *Theorising Childhood*. Cambridge: Polity.

Jenks, C. (1996) *Childhood*. London: Routledge.

Joint Committee on Human Rights (2007*) The Treatment of Asylum Seekers Tenth Report of Session 2006–07, Volume I* . London: The Stationery Office.

Jolowicz, A. (1973) *The Hidden Parent*. New York: Department of Public Affairs.

Jones, A., Jeyasingham, D. and Rajasooriya, S. (2002) *Invisible Families: The Strengths and Needs of Black Families in Which Young People Have Caring Responsibilities*. Bristol: Policy Press.

Jones, D. (2001) 'The Assessment of Parental Capacity', in J. Horwath (ed.) (2001b) *The Child's World*. pp. 255–272.

Jones, G. (2002) *The Youth Divide: Diverging Paths to Adulthood.* York: York Publishing Services.

Jones, L., Atkin, K. and Ahmad, W. (2001) 'Supporting Asian Deaf Young People and Their Families: The Role of Professionals and Services', *Disability and Society* 16(1): 51–70.

Jordan, B. (1997) 'Partnership with Service Users in Child Protection and Family Support', in N. Parton (ed.), *Child Protection.* pp. 212–222.

Jordan, L. and Lindley, B. (eds) (2006) *Special Guardianship: What Does It Offer Children Who Cannot Live with Their Parents?* London: Family Rights Group.

Katz, I. and Hetherington, R. (2006) 'Co-operating and Communicating: A European Perspective on Integrating Services for Children', *Child Abuse Review* 15(6): 429–439.

Kehily, M. (ed.) (2004) *An Introduction to Childhood Studies.* Maidenhead: Open University Press.

Kelly, B. and Sinclair, R. (2005) 'Understanding and Negotiating Identity: Children from Cross-Community Families in Public Care in Northern Ireland', *Child and Family Social Work* 10(4): 331–342.

Kelly, G. and Pinkerton, J. (1996) 'The Children (Northern Ireland) Order 1995: Prospects for Progress?', in M. Hill and J. Aldgate (eds), *Child Welfare Services: Developments in Law, Policy, Practice and Research.* London: Jessica Kingsley. pp. 40–55.

Kelly, L., Regan, L. and Burton, S. (1991) *An Exploratory Study of the Prevalence of Sexual Abuse in a Sample of 16–21 year olds.* London: University of North London.

Kendall, L. and Harker, L. (2002) *From Welfare to Well-Being: The Future of Social Care.* London: Institute for Public Policy Research.

Kennedy, M. and Wonnacott, J. (2003) 'Disabled Children and the Assessment Framework', in M. Calder and S. Hackett (eds), *Assessment in Child Care.* pp. 172–192.

Kent, R. (1997) *Children's Safeguards Review.* Edinburgh: Scottish Office.

Kenway, J. and Bullen, E. (2001) *Consuming Children: Education, Entertainment, Advertising.* Buckingham: Open University Press.

Kilbrandon, Lord (1964) *Children and Young Persons, Scotland: Report by the Committee Appointed by the Secretary of State for Scotland, Cmnd 2306.* Edinburgh: HMSO.

Kilkelly, U. (1999) *The Child and the European Convention on Human Rights.* Aldershot: Ashgate.

Kirby, J. (2006) *The Nationalisation of Childhood.* London: Centre for Policy Studies.

Kirton, D. (2000) *'Race', Ethnicity and Adoption.* Buckingham: Open University Press.

Kirton, D. (2007) '"Step Forward? Step Back?" – The Professionalisation of Fostering', *Social Work and Social Sciences Review* 13(1): 6–24.

Kitzinger, J. (2004) *Framing Abuse: Media Influence and Public Understanding of Sexual Violence against Children.* London: Pluto.

Knight, A. (1998) *Valued or Forgotten? Independent Visitors and Disabled Young People.* London: National Children's Bureau.

Knight, A. and Aggleton, P. (1999) *Social Care Services for Children and Families Affected by HIV in London.* London: Thomas Coram Research Unit.

Kogan, S. (2005) 'The Role of Disclosing Child Sexual Abuse on Adolescent Adjustment and Revictimization', *Journal of Child Sexual Abuse* 14(2): 25–47.

Kohli, R. (2007) *Social Work with Unaccompanied Asylum Seeking Children.* Basingstoke: Palgrave.

Koramoa, J., Lynch, M. and Kinnair, D. (2002) 'A Continuum of Child-Rearing: Responding to Traditional Practices', *Child Abuse Review* 11(6): 415–421.

Korbin, J. (2003) 'Neighborhood and Community Connectedness in Child Maltreatment Research', *Child Abuse and Neglect* 27(2): 137–140.

Kroll, B. and Taylor, A. (2003) *Parental Substance Misuse and Child Welfare.* London: Jessica Kingsley.

La Fontaine, J. (1994) *The Extent and Nature of Organised and Ritual Abuse: Research Findings.* London: HMSO.

Laming, Lord (2003) *The Victoria Climbié Inquiry: Report of an Inquiry by Lord Laming, Cm 5730.* London: The Stationery Office.

Lancaster, E. and Lumb, J. (1999) 'Bridging the Gap: Feminist Theory and Practice Reality in Work with the Perpetrators of Child Sexual Abuse', *Child and Family Social Work* 4(2): 119–129.

Lancaster, P. and Broadbent, V. (2003) *Listening to Young Children.* Maidenhead: Open University Press.

Langerman, C. and Worrall, E. (2005) *Ordinary Lives - Disabled Children and Their Families.* London: New Philanthropy Capital.

Lawton, D. (1998) *Complex Numbers: Families with More than One Disabled Child.* York: University of York.

Layzer, J., Goodson, B., Bernstein, L. and Price, C. (2001) *National Evaluation of Family Support Programs.* Cambridge, MA: Abt Associates.

Lee, N. (2001) *Childhood and Society: Growing Up in an Age of Uncertainty.* Buckingham: Open University Press.

Leece, J. and Bornat, J. (eds) (2006) *Developments in Direct Payments.* Bristol: Policy Press.

Leigh, S. and Miller, C. (2004) 'Is the Third Way the Best Way? Social Work Intervention with Children and Families', *Journal of Social Work*, 4(3): 245–267.

Levy, A. and Kahan, B. (1991) *The Pindown Experience and the Protection of Children.* Stafford: Staffordshire County Council.

Lewis, E. (2001) *Afraid to Say: The Needs and Views of Young People Living with HIV/AIDS.* London: National Children's Bureau.

Liberal Democrats (2006) *Stronger Families, Brighter Futures.* London: Liberal Democrats.

Lillywhite, R. and Skidmore, P. (2006) 'Boys Are Not Sexually Exploited? A Challenge to Practitioners', *Child Abuse Review* 15(5): 351–361.

Lindsay, M. and Morgan, R. (2006) *Young People's Views on Residential Family Centres.* London: Commission for Social Care Inspection.

Lipscombe, J. (2006) *Care or Control? Foster Care for Young People on Remand.* London: British Association for Adoption and Fostering.

Lister, R. (2006) 'Children (But Not Women) First: New Labour, Child Welfare and Gender', *Critical Social Policy* 26(2): 315–335.

Little, M. and Mount, K. (1999) *Prevention and Early Intervention with Children in Need.* Aldershot: Ashgate.

Little, M., Axford, N. and Morpeth, L. (2004) 'Research Review: Risk and Protection in the Context of Services for Children in Need', *Child and Family Social Work* 9(1): 105–117.

Littlechild, B. (2005) 'The Stresses Arising from Violence, Threats and Aggression against Child Protection Social Workers', *Journal of Social Work* 5(1): 61–82.

Lloyd, E. (ed.) (1999) *Parenting Matters: What Works in Parenting Education?* Ilford: Barnardo's.

Lord, P., Wilkin, A., Kinder, K., Murfield, J., Jones, M., Chamberlain, T., Easton, C., Martin, K., Gulliver, C., Paterson, C., Ries, J., Moor, H., Stott, A., Wilkin, C. and Stoney, S. (2006). *Analysis of Children and Young People's Plans 2006.* Slough: National Foundation for Education Research.

Lownsbrough, H. and O'Leary, D. (2005) *The Leadership Imperative: Reforming Children's Services from the Ground Up.* London: Demos.

Luckock, B. and Hart, A. (2005) 'Adoptive Family Life and Adoption Support: Policy Ambivalence and the Development of Effective Services', *Child and Family Social Work* 10(2): 125–134.

Luckock, B., Lefevre, M., Orr, D., Jones, M., Marchant, R. and Tanner, K. (2006) *Teaching, Learning and Assessing Communication Skills with Children and Young People in Social Work Education.* Bristol: Policy Press.

Lupton, C. (1998) 'User Empowerment or Family Self-Reliance? The Family Group Conference Model', *British Journal of Social Work* 28(1): 107–128.

Lyon, C. (2007) 'Interrogating the Concentration on the UNCRC Instead of the ECHR in the Development of Children's Rights in England?', *Children and Society* 21(2): 147–153.

Macaskill, C. (2006) *Beyond Refuge: Supporting Young Runaways*. London: NSPCC.

Macdonald, G. (1999) *What Works in Child Protection*. Ilford: Barnardo's.

Main, M. and Goldwyn, R. (1984) 'Predicting Rejection of Her Infant from Mother's Representation of Her Own Experience: Implications for the Abused–Abusing Intergenerational Cycle', *Child Abuse and Neglect* 8(2): 203–217.

Mallon, G. (1998) *We Don't Exactly Get the Welcome Wagon: The Experiences of Gay and Lesbian Adolescents in Child Welfare Systems*. New York: Columbia University Press.

Maluccio, A., Fein, E. and Olmstead, K. (1986) *Permanency Planning for Children: Concepts and Methods*. London: Tavistock.

Marchant, R. and Jones, M. (2000) 'Assessing the Needs of Disabled Children and their Families', in Department of Health (2000a) *Assessing Children in Need*. pp. 73–112.

Marsh, P. and Crow, G. (1998) *Family Group Conferences in Child Welfare*. Oxford: Blackwell.

Marsh, P. and Peel, M. (1999) *Leaving Care in Partnership: Family Involvement with Care Leavers*. London: HMSO.

Martin, G., Bergen, H., Richardson, A., Roeger, L. and Allison, S. (2004) 'Sexual Abuse and Suicidality: Gender Differences in a Large Community Sample of Adolescents', *Child Abuse and Neglect* 28(5): 491–503.

Martin, P. and Jackson, S. (2002) 'Educational Success for Children in Public Care: Advice from a Group of High Achievers', *Child and Family Social Work* 7(2): 121–130.

Masson, J. and Winn Oakley, M. (1999) *Out of Hearing: Representing Children in Court*. Chichester: Wiley.

Masson, J., McGovern, D., Pick, K. and Winn Oakley, M. (2007) *Protecting Powers: Emergency Intervention for Children's Protection*. Chichester: Wiley.

May, T., Duffy, M., Few, B. and Hough, M. (2005) *Understanding Drug Selling in Communities: Insider or Outsider Trading?* York: Joseph Rowntree Foundation.

May-Chahal, C. and Coleman, S. (2003) *Safeguarding Children and Young People*. London: Routledge.

McAuley, C. and Bunting, L (2006) *The Views, Cares and Aspirations of Care-Experienced Children and Young People*. Belfast: Voice of Young People in Care.

McAuley, C. and Cleaver, D. (2006) *Improving Service Delivery – Introducing Outcomes-Based Accoun-tability*. Southampton: University of Southampton.

McCann, J. (2006) *Working with Parents Whose Children Are Looked After*. London: National Children's Bureau.

McCluskey, U. and Hooper, C.-A. (eds) (2000) *Psychodynamic Perspectives on Abuse*. London: Jessica Kingsley.

McConkey, R., Truesdale, M. and Conliffe, C. (2004) 'The Features of Short-Break Residential Services Valued by Families Who Have Children with Multiple Disabilities', *Journal of Social Work* 4(1): 61–75.

McConnell, D. and Llewellyn, G. (2002) 'Stereotypes, Parents with Intellectual Disability and Child Protection', *Journal of Social Welfare and Family Law* 24(3): 297–317.

McGaw, S. and Newman, T. (2005) *What Works for Parents with Learning Disabilities* (2nd edn). Ilford: Barnardo's.

McGhee, J. and Waterhouse, L. (2002) 'Family Support and the Scottish Children's Hearings System', *Child and Family Social Work* 7(4): 273–283.

McMahon, L. and Ward, A. (eds) (2001) *Helping Families in Family Centres: Working at Therapeutic Practice*. London: Jessica Kingsley.

Melrose, M. and Barrett, D. (eds) (2004) *Anchors in Floating Lives: Interventions with Young People Sexually Abused through Prostitution*. Lyme Regis: Russell House.

Meltzer, H., Gatward, R., Corbin, T., Goodman, R. and Ford, T. (2003) *The Mental Health of Young People Looked After by Local Authorities in England*. London: The Stationery Office.

Mencap (2001) *No Ordinary Lives: The Support Needs of Parents Caring for Children and Adults with Profound and Multiple Learning Disabilities*. London: Mencap.

Mesie, J., Gardner, R. and Radford, L. (2007) *Towards a Public Service Agreement on Safeguarding*. London: DfES.

Middleton, L. (1999) *Disabled Children: Challenging Social Exclusion*. Oxford: Blackwell.

Millar, M. and Corby, B. (2006) 'The *Framework for the Assessment of Children in Need and Their Families* – A Basis for a "Therapeutic" Encounter?', *British Journal of Social Work* 36(6): 887–899.

Milligan, I. and Stevens, I. (2006) *Residential Child Care: Collaborative Practice*. London: Sage.

Ministry of Justice (2007) *Judicial and Court Statistics 2006. Cm 7273*. London: Ministry of Justice.

Mitchell, F. (2003a) 'The Social Services Response to Unaccompanied Children in England', *Child and Family Social Work* 8(3): 179–189.

Mitchell, F. (2003b) '"Can I Come Home?" The Experiences of Young Runaways Contacting the *Message Home* Helpline', *Child and Family Social Work* 8(1): 3–11.

Mitchell, F. (2007) *When Will We Be Heard? – Advocacy Provision for Disabled Children*. London: Children's Society.

Monck, E., Reynolds, J. and Wigfall, V. (2003) *The Role of Concurrent Planning: Making Permanent Placements for Young Children*. London: British Association for Adoption and Fostering.

Moran, P. and Ghate, D. (2005) 'The Effectiveness of Parenting Support', *Children and Society* 19(4): 329–336.

Morgan, P. (1998) *Adoption and the Care of Children*. London: Institute of Economic Affairs.

Morgan, R. (2006) *Being a Young Carer: Views from a Young Carers Workshop*. London: CSCI.

Morgan, R. (2007) *Children's Messages on Care: A Report by the Children's Rights Director for England*. London: OFSTED.

Morgan, R. and Lindsay, M. (2006) *Young People's Views on Leaving Care: What Young People in, and Formerly in, Residential and Foster Care Think about Leaving Care*. London: CSCI.

Morris, J. (1995) *Gone Missing: A Research and Policy Review of Disabled Children Living Away from their Families*. London: Who Cares? Trust.

Morris, J. (2001) 'Social Exclusion and Young Disabled People with High Levels of Support Needs', *Critical Social Policy* 21(1): 161–183.

Morris, J. (2003) *The Right Support: Report of the Task Force on Supporting Disabled Adults in Their Parenting Role*. York: Joseph Rowntree Foundation.

Morris, J. and Wates, M. (2006) *Supporting Disabled Parents and Parents with Additional Support Needs*. Bristol: Policy Press.

Morris, J., Abbott, D. and Ward, L. (2002) 'At Home or Away? An Exploration of Policy and Practice in the Placement of Disabled Children at Residential Schools', *Children and Society* 16(1): 3–16.

Mullender, A. (ed.) (1999) *We Are Family: Sibling Relationships in Placement and Beyond*. London: British Agencies for Adoption and Fostering.

Mullender, A., Hague, G., Imam, U., Kelly, L., Malos, E. and Regan, L. (2002) *Children's Perspectives on Domestic Violence*. London: Sage.

Muncie, J. (2004) *Youth and Crime: A Critical Introduction* (2nd edn). London: Sage.

Munro, E. (2002) *Effective Child Protection*. London: Sage.

Munro, E. (2005) 'A Systems Approach to Investigating Child Abuse Deaths', *British Journal of Social Work* 35(3): 531–546.

Munro, E. (2006) *Child Protection*. London: Sage.

Murphy, M. (2004) *Developing Collaborative Relationships in Interagency Child Protection Work*. Lyme Regis: Russell House.

Murphy, M. and Harbin, F. (2003) 'The Assessment of Parental Substance Misuse and Its Impact on Childcare', in M. Calder and S. Hackett (eds), *Assessment in Child Care*. pp. 353–361.

Murray, C. (Cathy) (2006) 'State Intervention and Vulnerable Children: Implementation Revisited', *Journal of Social Policy* 35(2): 211–227.

Murray, C. and Hallett, C. (2000) 'Young People Who Sexually Abuse: The Scottish Context', *Journal of Social Welfare and Family Law* 22(3): 245–260.

Murray, C. (Charles) (1990) *The Emerging British Underclass*. London: Institute of Economic Affairs.

Myers, S. (2005) 'A Signs of Safety Approach to Assessing Children with Sexually Concerning or Harmful Behaviour', *Child Abuse Review* 14(2): 82–96.

National Children's Homes (2005) *Close the Gap for Children in Care*. London: NCH.

Neil, E. and Howe, D. (eds) (2004) *Contact in Adoption and Permanent Foster Care: Research, Theory and Practice*. London: British Association for Adoption and Fostering.

Newburn, T. and Pearson, G. (2002) *The Place and Meaning of Drug Use in the Lives of Young People in Care*. London: University of London.

Nixon, P., Burford, G. and Quinn, A. (2005) *A Survey of International Practices, Policy and Research on Family Group Conferencing and Related Practices*. London: Family Rights Group.

O'Brien, M., Bachmann, M. and Husbands, C. (2007) *Children's Trust Pathfinders: Innovative Partnerships for Improving the Well-Being of Children and Young People*. University of East Anglia/National Children's Bureau.

Office of the First Minister and Deputy First Minister (2006) *Our Children and Young People – Our Pledge: A Ten Year Strategy for Children and Young People in Northern Ireland 2006–2016*. Belfast: OFMDFM.

O'Hagan, K. (2006) *Identifying Emotional and Psychological Abuse*. Maidenhead: Open University Press.

O'Halloran, K. (2003) *Child Care and Protection: Law and Practice in Northern Ireland*. Dublin: Thomson Round Hall.

Okitikpi, T. (ed.) (2005) *Working with Children of Mixed Parentage*. Lyme Regis: Russell House.

Oliver, C., Knight, A. and Candappa, M. (2006) *Advocacy for Looked After Children and Children in Need: Achievements and Challenges*. London: DfES.

Olsen, R. and Clarke, H. (2003) *Parenting and Disability: Disabled Parents' Experiences of Raising Children*. Bristol: Policy Press.

Olsen, R. and Tyers, H. (2004) *Think Parent: Supporting Disabled Adults as Parents*. London: National Family and Parenting Institute.

O'Neill, T. (2001) *Children in Secure Accommodation: A Gendered Exploration of Locked Institutional Care for Children in Trouble*. London: Jessica Kingsley.

Owen, M. (1999) *Novices, Old Hands and Professionals: A Study of Adoption by Single People*. London: British Agencies for Adoption and Fostering.

Packman, J. and Hall, C. (1998) *From Care to Accommodation: Support, Protection and Control in Child Care Services*. London: The Stationery Office.

Packwood, D. (2007) *Commissioning, Contracting and Service Delivery of Children's Services in the Voluntary and Community Sector*. London: DfES.

Palmer, S. (2006) *Toxic Childhood: How the Modern World Is Damaging Our Children and What We Can Do about It*. London: Orion.

Parker, R., Ward, H., Jackson, S., Aldgate, J., and Wedge, P. (1991) *Looking after Children: Assessing Outcomes in Child Care*. London: HMSO.

Parry, O., Pithouse, A., Anglim, C. and Batchelor, C. (2008) '"The Tip of the Ice Berg": Children's Complaints and Advocacy in Wales – An Insider View from Complaints Officers', *British Journal of Social Work* 38(1): 5–19.

Parton, N. (1985) *The Politics of Child Abuse*. Basingstoke: Macmillan.

Parton, N. (1991) *Governing the Family: Child Care, Child Protection and the State*. Basingstoke: Macmillan.

Parton, N. (1997a) Child Protection and Family Support: Current Debates and Future Prospects', in N. Parton (ed.), *Child Protection*. pp. 1–24.

Parton N. (ed.) (1997b) *Child Protection and Family Support: Tensions, Contradictions and Possibilities*. London: Routledge.

Parton, N. (2006) *Safeguarding Childhood: Early Intervention and Surveillance in a Late Modern Society*. Basingstoke: Palgrave.

Pascall, G. and Hendey, N. (2004) 'Disability and Transition to Adulthood: The Politics of Parenting', *Critical Social Policy* 24(2): 165–186.

Pearce, J. (2006) 'Who Needs to Be Involved in Safeguarding Sexually Exploited Young People?', *Child Abuse Review* 15(5): 326–340.

Pecora, P., Williams, J., Kessler, R., Downs, A., O'Brien, K. and Hiripi, E. (2004) *Assessing the Effects of Foster Care: Early Results from the Casey National Alumni Study*. Seattle, WA: Casey Family Programs.

Penn, H. and Randall, V. (2005) 'Childcare Policy and Local Partnerships under Labour', *Journal of Social Policy* 34(1): 79–97.

Penna, S. (2005) 'The Children Act 2004: Child Protection and Social Surveillance', *Journal of Social Welfare and Family Law* 27(2): 143–157.

Percy-Smith, J. (2006) 'What Works in Strategic Partnerships for Children: a Research Review', *Children and Society* 20(4): 313–323.

Philpot, T. (2001) *A Very Private Practice: An Investigation into Private Fostering*. London: British Agencies for Adoption and Fostering.

Pigot, T. (1989) *Report of the Advisory Group on Video Evidence*. London: Home Office.

Pillai, R., Rankin, J. and Stanley, K. (2007) *Disability 2020: Opportunities for the Full and Equal Citizenship of Disabled People in Britain in 2020*. London: Institute for Public Policy Research.

Pinkerton, J. (2003) 'From Parity to Subsidiarity? Children's Policy in Northern Ireland under New Labour: The Case of Child Welfare', *Children and Society* 17(3): 254–260.

Pinney, A. (2005) *Disabled Children in Residential Placements*. London: DfES.

Pinney, A. (2007) *A Better Start: Children and Families with Special Needs and Disabilities in Sure Start Local Programmes*. Nottingham: DfES.

Piper, H., Powell, J. and Smith, H. (2006) 'Professionals, and Paranoia: The Touching of Children in a Culture of Fear', *Journal of Social Work* 6(2): 151–167.

Pithouse, A. and Holland, S. (1999) 'Open Access Family Centres and Their Users: Positive Results, Some Doubts and New Departures', *Children and Society* 13(3): 167–178.

Pithouse, A., Holland, S. and Davey, D. (2001) 'Assessment in a Specialist Referred Family Centre: Outcomes for Children', *Children and Society* 15(5): 302–314.

Platt, D. (2001) 'Refocusing Children's Services: Evaluation of an Initial Assessment Process', *Child and Family Social Work* 6(2): 139–148.

Plumtree, A. (2005) *Child Care Law: A Summary of the Law in Scotland*. London: British Association for Adoption and Fostering.

Postman, N. (1982) *The Disappearance of Childhood*. London: W. H. Allen.

Powell, M. (ed.) (2002) *Evaluating New Labour's Welfare Reforms*. Bristol: Policy Press.

Precey, G. (2003) 'Children at Risk of Illness Induction or Fabrication (Fabricated or Induced Illness): How Helpful Is the Assessment Framework?, in M. Calder and S. Hackett (eds), *Assessment in Child Care*. pp. 302–315.

PricewaterhouseCoopers (2006) *Overarching Report on Children's Services Markets*. London: DfES.

Priestley, M., Rabiee, P. and Harris, J. (2003) 'Young Disabled People and the New Arrangements for Leaving Care in England and Wales', *Children and Youth Services Review* 25(11): 863–890.

Prime Minister's Strategy Unit (2004) *The Alcohol Harm Reduction Strategy*. London: PMSU.

Prime Minister's Strategy Unit (2005) *Improving the Life Chances of Disabled People*. London: PMSU.

Prior, V. and Glaser, D. (2006) *Understanding Attachment and Attachment Disorders: Theory, Evidence and Practice*. London: Jessica Kingsley.

Pugh, R. (2007) 'Variations in Registration on Child Protection Registers', *British Journal of Social Work* 37(1): 5–21.

Putnam, R. (2000) *Bowling Alone: The Collapse and Revival of American Community*. New York: Simon and Schuster.

Quinton, D. (2004) *Supporting Parents: Messages from Research*. London: Jessica Kingsley.

Quinton, D., Rushton, A., Dance, C., and Mayes, D. (1997) 'Contact between Children Placed Away from Home and Their Birth Parents: Research Issues and Evidence', *Clinical Child Psychology and Psychiatry* 2(3): 393–413.

Quinton, D., Selwyn, J., Rushton, A., and Dance, C. (1999) 'Contact between Children Placed Away from Home and Their Birth Parents: Ryburn's "Reanalysis" Analysed', *Clinical Child Psychology and Psychiatry* 4(4): 519–531.

Rainer (2007) *Home Alone: Housing and Support for Young People Leaving Care*. Brasted: Rainer.

Read, J. and Harrison, C. (2002) 'Disabled Children Living Away from Home in the UK: Recognizing Hazards and Promoting Good Practice', *Journal of Social Work* 2(2): 211–231.

Reder, P. and Duncan, S. (1999) *Lost Innocents*. London: Routledge.

Reder, P. and Duncan, S. (2003) 'Understanding Communication in Child Protection Networks', *Child Abuse Review* 12(2): 82–100.

Rees, G. (2001) *Working with Young Runaways: Lessons from Practice*. London: Children's Society.

Richards, A. and Ince, L. (2000) *Overcoming the Obstacles: Looking after Children: Quality Services for Black and Minority Ethnic Children and Their Families*. London: Family Rights Group.

Riddell, S. and Watson, N. (2003) *Disability, Culture and Identity*. Harlow: Pearson.

Ridge, T. and Millar, J. (2000) 'Excluding Children: Autonomy, Friendship and the Experience of the Care System', *Social Policy and Administration* 34(2): 160–175.

Roberts, K. and Lawton, D. (2001) 'Acknowledging the Extra Care Parents Give Their Disabled Children', *Child: Care, Health and Development* 27(4): 307–319.

Robinson, L. (2007) *Cross-Cultural Child Development for Social Workers: An Introduction*. Basingstoke: Palgrave.

Roche, J. (2002) 'The Children Act 1989 and Children's Rights: A Critical Reappraisal', in B. Franklin (ed.), *The New Handbook*. pp. 60–80.

Rose, R. and Philpot, T. (2004) *The Child's Own Story: Life Story Work with Traumatized Children*. London: Jessica Kingsley.

Rose, W. (2001) 'Assessing Children in Need and Their Families: An Overview of the Framework', in J. Horwath (ed.) (2001b) *The Child's World*. pp. 35–49.

Rowe, J. and Lambert, L. (1973) *Children Who Wait*. London: Association of British Adoption Agencies.

Ruegger, M. (ed.) (2001) *Hearing the Voice of the Child: The Representation of Children's Interests in Civil Law Proceedings*. Lyme Regis: Russell House.

Rushton, A. and Dance, C. (2002) *Adoption Support Services for Families in Difficulty: A Literature Review and UK Survey*. London: British Association for Adoption and Fostering.

Russell, P. (2003) '"Access and Achievement or Social Exclusion?" Are the Government's Policies Working for Disabled Children and Their Families?', *Children and Society* 17(3): 215–225.

Rutter, M. (2007) 'Resilience, Competence, and Coping', *Child Abuse and Neglect* 31(3): 205–209.

Ryan, M. and Butcher, J. (2006) *Talking about Alcohol and Other Drugs: A Guide for Looked After Children's Services.* London: National Children's Bureau.

Ryan, T. and Walker, R. (2007) *Life Story Work: A Practical Guide to Helping Children Understand Their Past* (3rd edn). London: British Association for Adoption and Fostering.

Ryburn, M. (ed.) (1994a) *Contested Adoptions: Research, Law, Policy, and Practice.* Aldershot: Arena.

Ryburn, M. (ed.) (1994b) *Open Adoption: Research, Theory and Practice.* Aldershot: Avebury.

Ryburn, M. (1999) 'Contact between Children Placed Away from Home and Their Birth Parents: A Reanalysis of the Evidence in Relation to Permanent Placements', *Clinical Child Psychology and Psychiatry* 4(4): 505–518.

Samuel, M. (2007) 'Private Equity Accused of Undercutting Long-Term Home Providers', *Community Care*, 11 October.

Sanders, R. (2004) *Sibling Relationships: Theory and Issues for Practice.* Basingstoke: Palgrave.

Sanders, R. and Mace, S. (2006) 'Agency Policy and the Participation of Children and Young People in the Child Protection Process', *Child Abuse Review* 15(2): 89–109.

Schnitzer, P. and Ewigman, B. (2005) 'Child Deaths Resulting from Inflicted Injuries: Household Risk Factors and Perpetrator Characteristics', *Pediatrics* 116(5): 687–693.

Schofield, G. (2003) *Part of the Family: Pathways Through Foster Care.* London: British Association for Adoption and Fostering.

Schofield, G. and Brown, K. (1999) 'Being There: A Family Centre Worker's Role as a Secure Base for Adolescent Girls in Crisis', *Child and Family Social Work* 4(1): 21–31.

Schofield, G., Thoburn, J., Howell, D. and Dickens, J. (2007) 'The Search for Stability and Permanence: Modelling the Pathways of Long-stay Looked After Children', *British Journal of Social Work* 37(4): 619–642.

Scott, S., Knapp, M., Henderson, J. and Maughan, B. (2001). 'Financial Costs of Social Exclusion: Follow up Study of Antisocial Children into Adulthood', *British Medical Journal* 323: 191–194.

Scottish Children's Reporter Administration (2007) *Annual Report 2006/07.* Stirling: SCRA.

Scottish Executive (2002) *It's Everyone's Job to Make Sure I'm Alright.* Edinburgh: Scottish Executive.

Scottish Executive (2005a) *Getting It Right for Every Child: Proposals for Action.* Edinburgh: Scottish Executive.

Scottish Executive (2005b) *Integrated Assessment Framework for Scotland's Children.* www.scotland.gov.uk/Publications/2005/06/20135608/56144

Scottish Executive (2006a) *Draft Children's Services (Scotland) Bill Consultation.* Edinburgh: Scottish Executive.

Scottish Executive (2006b) *Changing Lives: Report of the 21st Century Social Work Review.* Edinburgh: Scottish Executive.

Scottish Government (2007a) *Protecting Children and Young People: Interim Guidance for Child Protection Committees for Conducting a Significant Case Review.* Edinburgh: Scottish Government.

Scottish Government (2007b) *Child Protection Statistics 2006-7.* Edinburgh: Scottish Government.

Scottish Government (2007c) *Children Looked After Statistics 2006–07.* Edinburgh: Scottish Government.

Scourfield, J. (2002) *Gender and Child Protection.* Basingstoke: Palgrave.

Scourfield, J. and Welsh, I. (2003) 'Risk, Reflexivity and Social Control in Child Protection: New Times or Same Old Story?', *Critical Social Policy* 23(3): 398–420.

Scraton, P. (ed.) (1997) *'Childhood' in 'Crisis'.* London: UCL Press.

Seden, J. (2002) 'Underpinning Theories for the Assessment of Children's Needs', in H. Ward and W. Rose (eds), *Approaches to Needs Assessment.* pp. 195–216.

Self, A. and Zealey, L. (2007) *Social Trends No. 37.* Basingstoke: Palgrave.

Sellick, C. (2002) 'The Aims and Principles of Independent Fostering Agencies – A View from the Inside', *Adoption and Fostering* 26(1): 56–63.

Sellick, C. (2006) 'Relational Contracting between Local Authorities and Independent Fostering Providers: Lessons in Conducting Business for Child Welfare Managers', *Journal of Social Welfare and Family Law* 28(2): 107–120.

Sellick, C., Thoburn, J. and Philpott, T. (2004) *What Works in Adoption and Foster Care.* Ilford: Barnardo's.

Selman, P. (ed.) (2000) *Intercountry Adoption: Developments, Trends and Perspectives.* London: British Agencies for Adoption and Fostering.

Sergeant, H. (2006) *Handle with Care: An Investigation into the Care System.* London: Centre for Young Policy Studies.

Sharland, E. (1999) 'Justice for Children? Child Protection and the Crimino-Legal Process', *Child and Family Social Work* 4(4): 303–313.

Shaw, M. and Hipgrave, T. (1983) *Specialist Fostering.* London: Batsford.

Shemmings, Y. and Shemmings, D. (2001) 'Empowering Children and Family Members to Participate in the Assessment Process', in J. Horwath (ed.) (2001b) *The Child's World.* pp. 114–128.

Sheppard, M. (2001) *Social Work Practice with Depressed Mothers in Child and Family Care.* London: The Stationery Office.

Sheppard, M. (2004) 'An Evaluation of Social Support Intervention with Depressed Mothers in Child and Family Care', *British Journal of Social Work* 34(7): 939–960.

Sheridan, M. (2003) 'The Deceit Continues: An Updated Literature Review of Munchausen Syndrome by Proxy', *Child Abuse and Neglect* 27(4): 431–451.

Sidebotham, P. and Heron, J. (2006) 'Child Maltreatment in the "Children of the Nineties": A Cohort Study of Risk Factors', *Child Abuse and Neglect* 30(5): 497–522.

Sinclair, I. (2005*) Fostering Now: Messages from Research.* London: Jessica Kingsley.

Sinclair, I. and Gibbs, I. (1998) *Children's Homes: A Study in Diversity.* Chichester: Wiley .

Sinclair, I., Wilson, K. and Gibbs, I. (2005) *Foster Placements: Why They Succeed and Why They Fail.* London: Jessica Kingsley.

Smale, G. and Tuson, G. (1993) *Empowerment, Assessment, Care Management and the Skilled Worker.* London: HMSO.

Smith, C. (2005) 'Trust v Law: Promoting and Safeguarding Post-Adoption Contact', *Journal of Social Welfare and Family Law* 27(3–4): 315–332.

Smith, K. and Leon, L. (2002) *Turned Upside Down.* London: Mental Health Foundation.

Smith, M., Bee, P., Heverin, A. and Nobes, G. (1995) *Parental Control within the Family: The Nature and Extent of Parental Violence to Children.* London: Thomas Coram Research Unit.

Smith, M. and Grocke, M. (1995). *Normal Family Sexuality and Knowledge in Children.* London: Royal College of Psychiatrists/Gorkill Press.

Smith, S. (2005) 'Keeping It Local', in H. Cosis Brown et al. (eds), *Support Care.* pp. 65–80.

Smith, T. (1996) *Family Centres and Bringing Up Young Children.* London: HMSO.

Smith, T. (1999) 'Neighbourhood and Preventive Strategies with Children and Families: What Works?', *Children and Society* 13(4): 265–277.

Social Care Institute for Excellence (2004a) *Preventing Teenage Pregnancy in Looked After Children.* London: SCIE.

Social Care Institute for Excellence (2004b) *Short Breaks (Respite Care) for Children with Learning Disabilities.* London: SCIE.

Social Exclusion Unit (1999) *Teenage Pregnancy, Cm 4342.* London: The Stationery Office.

Social Exclusion Unit (2002*) Young Runaways.* London: SEU.

Social Exclusion Unit (2003) *A Better Education for Children in Care.* London: SEU.

Social Justice Policy Group (2006) *The State of the Nation Report: Educational Failure.* London: Centre for Social Justice.

Social Services Inspectorate of Wales (2006) *The Report of the Chief Inspector: Social Services in Wales, 2004–2005*. Cardiff: SSIW.

Sorkhabi, N. (2005) 'Applicability of Baumrind's Parent Typology to Collective Cultures: Analysis of Cultural Explanations of Parent Socialization Effects', *International Journal of Behavioral Development* 29(6): 552–563.

Spratt, T. and Callan, J. (2004) 'Parents' Views on Social Work Interventions in Child Welfare Cases', *British Journal of Social Work* 34(2): 199–224.

Stanley, J. and Goddard, C. (2002) *In the Firing Line: Violence and Power in Child Protection Work*. Chichester: Wiley.

Stanley, N., Penhale, B., Riordan, D., Barbour, R. and Holden, S. (2003) *Child Protection and Mental Health Services: Interprofessional Responses to the Needs of Mothers*. Bristol: Policy Press.

Stanley, N., Riordan, D. and Alaszewski, H. (2005) 'The Mental Health of Looked After Children: Matching Response to Need', *Health and Social Care in the Community* 13(3): 239–248.

Statham, J. and Biehal, N. (2005) *Supporting Families. Every Child Matters Change for Children Research and Practice Briefing*. Dartington: Research in Practice.

Statham, J. and Greenfield, M. (2005) 'Investing to Save?', in H. Cosis Brown et al. (eds), *Support Care*. pp. 123–137.

Statham, J. and Holtermann, S. (2004) 'Families on the Brink: The Effectiveness of Family Support Services', *Child and Family Social Work* 9(2): 153–166.

Steele, L. (2000) 'The Day Fostering Scheme: A Service for Children in Need and Their Parents', *Child and Family Social Work* 5(4): 317–325.

Stein, M. (2004) *What Works for Young People Leaving Care,* (2nd edn). Ilford: Barnardo's.

Stein, M. (2006) 'Missing Years of Abuse in Children's Homes', *Child and Family Social Work* 11(1): 11–21.

Stein, M. and Carey, K. (1986) *Leaving Care*. Oxford: Blackwell.

Stevenson, O. (ed.) (1999) *Child Welfare in the United Kingdom 1948–1998*. Oxford: Blackwell.

Stobart, E. (2006) *Child Abuse Linked to Accusations of 'Possession' and 'Witchcraft'*. London: DfES.

Straus, M., Gelles, R. and Steinmetz, S. (1980) *Behind Closed Doors: Violence in the American Family*. New York: Anchor Books.

Stuart, M. and Baines, C. (2004) *Safeguards for Vulnerable Children: Three Studies on Abusers, Disabled Children and Children in Prison*. York: Joseph Rowntree Foundation.

Sullivan, P. and Knutson, J. (2000) 'Maltreatment and Disabilities: A Population-Based Epidemiological Study', *Child Abuse and Neglect* 24(10): 1257–1273.

Tanner, K. and Turney, D. (2003) 'What Do We Know about Child Neglect? A Critical Review of the Literature and Its Application to Social Work Practice', *Child and Family Social Work* 8(1): 25–34.

Tarleton, B., Ward, L. and Howarth, J. (2006) *Finding the Right Support? A Review of Issues and Positive Practice in Supporting Parents with Learning Difficulties and Their Children*. London: Baring Foundation.

Taylor, A. and Kroll, B. (2004) 'Working with Parental Substance Misuse: Dilemmas for Practice', *British Journal of Social Work* 34(8): 1115–1132 .

Taylor, C. (Carolyn) (2004) 'Underpinning Knowledge for Child Care Practice: Reconsidering Child Development Theory', *Child and Family Social Work* 9(3): 225–235.

Taylor, C. (Claire) (2006) *Young People in Care and Criminal Behaviour*. London: Jessica Kingsley.

Thoburn, J. (1999) 'Trends in Foster Care and Adoption', in O. Stevenson (ed.), *Child Welfare*. pp. 121–155.

Thoburn, J., Wilding, J. and Watson, J. (2000a) *Family Support in Cases of Emotional Maltreatment and Neglect.* London: The Stationery Office.

Thoburn, J., Norford, L. and Rashid, S. (2000b) *Permanent Family Placement for Children of Minority Ethnic Origin.* London: Jessica Kingsley.

Thoburn, J., Chand A. and Procter, J. (2004) *Child Welfare Services for Minority Ethnic Families.* London: Jessica Kingsley.

Thomas, C. and Beckford, V. (1999) *Adopted Children Speaking.* London: British Agencies for Adoption and Fostering.

Thomas, N. and O'Kane, C. (2000) 'Discovering What Children Think: Connections between Research and Practice', *British Journal of Social Work* 30(6): 819–835.

Thomas, N., Stainton, T., Jackson, S., Wai, Yee Cheung, Doubtfire, S. and Webb, A. (2003) '"Your Friends Don't Understand": Invisibility and Unmet Need in the Lives of Young Carers', *Child and Family Social Work* 8(1): 35–46.

Thomas, T. (2003) 'Child Protection and Covert Video Surveillance: A New Regulatory Framework', *Journal of Social Welfare and Family Law* 25(1): 57–68.

Thorpe, D. and Bilson, A. (1998) 'From Protection to Concern: Child Protection Careers without Apologies', *Children and Society* 12(5): 373–386.

Tilbury, C. (2004) 'The Influence of Performance Measurement on Child Welfare Policy and Practice', *British Journal of Social Work* 34(2): 225–241.

Tilbury, C. (2005) 'Counting Family Support', *Child and Family Social Work* 10(2): 149–157.

Tisdall, E. Kay (2006) 'Antisocial Behaviour Legislation Meets Children's Services: Challenging Perspectives on Children, Parents and the State', *Critical Social Policy* 26(1): 101–120.

Tisdall E. Kay, Marshall, K., Cleland, A. and Plumtree, A. (2002) 'Listening to the Views of Children? Principles and Mechanisms within the Children (Scotland) Act 1995', *Journal of Social Welfare and Family Law* 24(4): 385–399.

Tracy, E. and Whittaker, J. (1990). 'The Social Network Map: Assessing Social Support in Clinical Social Work Practice', *Families in Society,* 71(8): 461–470.

Triseliotis, J. (2002) 'Long-Term Foster Care or Adoption? The Evidence Examined', *Child and Family Social Work* 7(1): 23–33.

Triseliotis, J., Sellick, C. and Short, R. (1995) *Foster Care: Theory and Practice.* London: Batsford.

Triseliotis, J., Shireman, J. and Hundleby, M. (1997) *Adoption: Theory, Policy and Practice.* London: Cassell.

Tunstill, J. (1997) 'Implementing the Family Support Clauses of the 1989 Children Act', in N. Parton (ed.), *Child Protection.* pp. 39–58.

Tunstill, J. and Aldgate, J. (2000) *Services for Children in Need.* London: The Stationery Office.

Tunstill, J., Aldgate, J. and Hughes, M. (2006) *Improving Children's Services Network: Lessons from Family Centres.* London: Jessica Kingsley.

Turnell, A. and Essex, S. (2006) *Working with 'Denied' Child Abuse: The Resolutions Approach.* Maidenhead: Open University Press.

Turney, D. (2000) 'The Feminising of Neglect', *Child and Family Social Work* 5(1): 47–56.

Turning Point (2006) *Bottling It Up: The Effects of Alcohol Misuse on Children, Parents and Families.* London: Turning Point.

Tyler, S., Allison, K. and Winsler, A. (2006) 'Child Neglect: Developmental Consequences, Intervention, and Policy Implications', *Child and Youth Care Forum* 35(1): 1–20.

United Nations Children's Fund (2007) *Child Poverty in Perspective: An Overview of Child Well-Being in Rich Countries.* Florence: UNICEF.

Utting, W. (1997) *People Like Us: The Review of the Safeguards for Children Living Away from Home.* London: HMSO.

Vallender, I. (2006) 'Every Child Matters and the Voluntary and Community Sector', *Children and Society* 20(3): 235–238.

Wade, J., Mitchell, F. and Baylis, G. (2005) *Unaccompanied Asylum Seeking Children: The Response of Social Work Services*. London: British Association for Adoption and Fostering.

Wade, J. and Dixon, J. (2006) 'Making a Home, Finding a Job: Investigating Early Housing and Employment Outcomes for Young People Leaving Care', *Child and Family Social Work* 11(3): 199–208.

Walker, A., Barclay, A., Hunter, L., Kendrick, A., Malloch, M., Hill, M. and McIvor, G. (2005) *Secure Accommodation in Scotland: Its Role and Relationship with 'Alternative' Services*. Edinburgh: Scottish Executive.

Wall, N. (2006) *A Report to the President of the Family Division on the Publication by the Women's Aid Federation of England Entitled Twenty-Nine Child Homicides: Lessons Still to Be Learnt on Domestic Violence and Child Protection*. London: Royal Courts of Justice.

Ward, A., Kasinski, K., Pooley, J. and Worthington, A. (2003) *Therapeutic Communities for Children and Young People*. London: Jessica Kingsley.

Ward, H. (1995) *Looked After Children: Research into Practice*. London: HMSO.

Ward, H. (2001) 'The Developmental Needs of Children: Implications for Assessment', in J. Horwath (ed.) (2001b) *The Child's World*. pp. 167–179.

Ward, H. and Rose, W. (eds) (2002) *Approaches to Needs Assessment in Childrens' Services*. London: Jessica Kingsley.

Ward, H., Munro, E. and Dearden, C. (2006) *Babies and Young Children in Care: Life Pathways, Decision-Making and Practice*. London: Jessica Kingsley.

Ward., H., Skuse, T. and Munro, E. (2005), "The Best of Times, the Worst of Times": Young People's Views of Care and Accommodation', *Adoption and Fostering* 29(1): 8–17.

Ward, J., Henderson, Z. and Pearson, (2003) *One Problem Among Many: Drug Use Among Care Learners in Transition to Independent Living*. London: Home Office.

Ward, H., Jones, H., Lynch, M. and Skuse, T. (2002) 'Issues Concerning the Health of Looked After Children', *Adoption and Fostering* 26(4): 8–18.

Warren-Adamson, C. (2006) 'Family Centres: A Review of the Literature', *Child and Family Social Work* 11(2): 171–182.

Waterhouse, L. and McGhee, J. (2002) 'Children's Hearings in Scotland: Compulsion and Disadvantage', *Journal of Social Welfare and Family Law* 24(3): 279–296.

Waterhouse, S. and Brocklesby, E. (2001) 'Placement Choice in Temporary Foster Care: A Research Study', *Adoption and Fostering* 25(3): 39–46.

Wates, M. (2002a) *Supporting Disabled Adults in Their Parenting Role*. York: Joseph Rowntree Foundation.

Wates, M. (2002b) 'Disability and Adoption: How Unexamined Attitudes Discriminate against Disabled People as Parents', *Adoption and Fostering* 26(2): 49–56.

Wattam, C. (1999) 'Prevention of Child Abuse', *Children and Society* 13(4): 317–329.

Webster, R. (2005) *The Secret of Bryn Estyn: The Making of a Modern Witch Hunt*. Oxford: Orwell Press.

Weir, A. (2003) 'A Framework for Assessing Parents with Mental Health Problems', in M. Calder and S. Hackett (eds), *Assessment in Child Care*. pp. 316–332.

Welbourne, P. (2002) 'Videotaped Evidence of Children: Application and Implications of the Memorandum of Good Practice', *British Journal of Social Work* 32(5): 553–571.

Welsh Assembly Government (2004) *Children and Young People: Rights to Action*. Cardiff: Welsh Assembly.

Westcott, H. and Jones, D. (1999) 'Annotation: The Abuse of Disabled Children', *Journal of Child Psychology and Child Psychiatry* 40(4): 497–506.

Wheeler, P. (2003) 'Shaken Baby Syndrome – An Introduction to the Literature', *Child Abuse Review* 12(6): 401–415.

Williams, B. (2004) *Review of Projects and Initiatives That Support Children and Families Affected by Alcohol Misuse*. London: Alcohol Concern.

Williams, F. (1989) *Social Policy: A Critical Introduction, Issues of Race, Gender and Class.* Cambridge: Polity Press.

Williams, F. (2004) 'What Matters Is Who Works: Why Every Child Matters to New Labour. Commentary on the DfES Green Paper *Every Child Matters*', *Critical Social Policy* 24(3): 406–427.

Williams, K. (2004) 'Child Pornography Law: Does It Protect Children?', *Journal of Social Welfare and Family Law* 26(3): 245–261.

Wilson, K., Sinclair, I., Taylor, C., Pithouse, A. and Sellick, C. (2004) *Fostering Success: An Exploration of the Research Literature in Foster Care.* Bristol: Policy Press.

Woodcock, J. (2003) 'The Social Work Assessment of Parenting', *British Journal of Social Work* 33(1): 87–106.

Worsley, R. (2007) *Young People in Custody 2004–2006: An Analysis of Children's Experiences of Prison.* London: HM Inspectorate of Prisons/Youth Justice Board.

Wright, C., Parkinson, K. and Drewett, R. (2006) 'How Does Maternal and Child Feeding Behavior Relate to Weight Gain and Failure to Thrive? Data from a Prospective Birth Cohort', *Pediatrics* 117: 1262–1269.

Wyness, M., Harrison, L. and Buchanan, I. (2004) 'Childhood, Politics and Ambiguity: Towards an Agenda for Children's Political Inclusion', *Sociology* 38(1): 81–99.

INDEX

Lord, P. 182
Lownsborough, H. 181
Lupton, C. 56
Lyon, C. 9

Mace, S. 70
McGhee, J. 46
maltreatment *see* child maltreatment
managerialism 16, 177, 178, 185
Marchant, R. 162
marriage 5
Marsh, P. 152
matching 127–8, 129
    ethnic 135
May-Chahal, C. 70, 73
May, T. 150
Meadow, Sir Roy 84
media reporting 79–80
'Megan's Law' 66
'Memorandum of GoodPractice' 77
men
    as abusers 91–2, 97
    see also fathers
mental health problems
    care leavers 150, 152
    disabled children 168
    looked after children 118–19, 144
    parental 32, 33, 49, 50, 78, 93
    in the secure estate 121
Millar, M. 25
Mills, C. Wright 99
mixed economy of provision 141, 179
mobile phones 67
'modern defence of the birth family' perspective
    7, 10, 11, 40, 56, 133
Morgan, R. 154
Morris, J. 33, 49, 172, 173, 175
Morrison, T. 181
mothers 6, 28–9, 31, 97
    lone 5
    young 119–20
multi-agency public protection panels 66
Munchausen's Syndrome by Proxy *see* fabricated
    or induced illness 84
Munro, E. 96
Murphy, M. 34

National Child Care Strategy 16
National Family and Parenting Institute 6
National Indicator Set 178
National Leaving Care Advisory Service
    (NLCAS) 147
national minimum standards (NMS) 178
Neave, Ricky 65
neglect 84–5, 87, 89, 91, 92, 95, 100
New Labour government 5, 6, 9, 15–17, 18,
    37, 41, 66, 147, 156, 159–60, 178, 183–4

'no order' principle 11
Northern Ireland 13, 46, 76, 115, 129, 130, 147, 181
NSPCC 64, 76, 88

offending 13
    care leavers 151, 152
    and looked after children 119, 120–1, 128
    see also crime
O'Leary, D. 181
Options for Excellence 182–3
'Orange Book' 22, 25
Owen, M. 72–3

paedophiles 66, 67, 94
palliative care 167
Palmer, G. 2
parallel planning 112, 128–9
parental responsibility orders (PROs)
    (Scotland) 105
parental rights and responsibilities 1, 6, 7, 11, 41
parental risk factors, for child maltreatment 93,
    94, 95
parenthood, young 93, 119–20, 147
parenting 6, 45
    capacity 6, 24, 30–5, 36, 85, 162
    'corporate' 109–10, 117, 123
    deficit 6
    education 6, 45
    styles 31
Parentline Plus 6
parents
    with additional support needs 32–3, 49, 50, 85
    and child care services partnership 10, 14,
        43, 109
    with learning disabilities 32, 34–5, 50, 93
    mental health problems 32, 33, 49, 50, 78, 93
    physically disabled 50, 60
    substance misuse 32, 33–4, 50, 78, 93
Parker, R. 15, 42–3, 114
participation, children's 4, 30, 70, 113,
    121–2, 161–2
participation rights 8, 9, 12
partnership
    inter-agency *see* inter-professional/agency
        working; 'joined up' working
    parent-child care services 10, 14, 43, 109
Parton, N. 64, 66, 70, 80, 186
Pascall, G. 172, 174
paternalism 7, 8, 133
Pathfinder trusts 181
patriarchal family 7
Peake, A. 34
Peel, M. 152
peer relationships 100, 142, 173
Percy-Smith, J. 181
Performance Assessment Framework (PAF) 178
performance management 178